THE CRITICAL DOUBLE

THE
CRITICAL DOUBLE
Figurative Meaning
in Aesthetic Discourse

Paul Gordon

With a Foreword by
J. Hillis Miller

The University of Alabama Press
Tuscaloosa and London

Copyright © 1995
The University of Alabama Press
Tuscaloosa, Alabama 35487-0380
All rights reserved
Manufactured in the United States of America

Recipient in 1992 of the Eugene N. Kayden University of Colorado
at Boulder Faculty Manuscript Award
∞
The paper on which this book is printed meets the minimum
requirements of American National Standard for Information
Science-Permanence of Paper for Printed Library Materials,
ANSI Z39.48-1984.

Library of Congress Cataloging-in-Publication Data

Gordon, Paul, 1951–
    The critical double : figurative meaning in aesthetic discourse /
    Paul Gordon.
        p.   cm.
    Includes bibliographical references (p.) and index.
    ISBN 0-8173-0710-9 (alk. paper)
        1. Literature—Philosophy.   2. Opposition, Theory of.   3. Polarity
    (Philosophy)   4. Polarity in literature.   5. Rhetoric.   6. Metaphor.
    I. Title.
    PN45.G62   1995
    801'.95—dc20   93-47085

British Library Cataloguing-in-Publication Data available

So Jacob was left alone, and a man wrestled with him there till daybreak. When the man saw that he could not throw Jacob, he struck him in the hollow of his thigh, so that Jacob's hip was dislocated as they wrestled. The man said, "Let me go, for day is breaking," but Jacob replied, "I will not let you go unless you bless me. . . . Tell me, I pray, your name." He replied, "Why do you ask my name?," but he gave him his blessing there. Jacob called the place Peniel, "because," he said, "I have seen God face to face and my life is spared."
—Genesis 32:22

Contents

Foreword by J. Hillis Miller ix

Acknowledgments xix

Righting an Introduction 1

1 The Metaphoric Double 19

2 The Rhetorical Double: Protagoras and the *Dissoi Logoi* 38

3 The Parabolic Double: Christ's and Kafka's Parables of Parable 51

4 The Tragic Double: A Dionysian Theory of Greek Tragedy 62

5 The Psychoanalytic Double: Psychoanalysis, Art, and "The Antithetical Sense of Primary Words" 74

6 The Critical Double: Figuring Out Henry James's "The Figure in the Carpet" 93

7 The Deconstructive Double: Sign and Symbol in the Aesthetics of Paul de Man 112

8 The Comparative Double: Romanticism, Figuration, and Comparative Literature 128

Notes 145

Bibliography 167

Index 175

J. Hillis Miller

THE CRITICAL DOUBLE shows that many different kinds of texts in the Western tradition exemplify Protagoras's *dissoi logoi*. This is the proposition that "on every question there are two opposing statements, including this one." This defiance of the law of noncontradiction, in various forms, is shown to be of crucial importance in contemporary critical theory, in theories of metaphor from Aristotle to the present day, in Greek rhetorical theory as exemplified by Protagoras, in biblical parables, in Greek tragedy, in psychoanalysis, in modern fiction (the example is Henry James's "The Figure in the Carpet"), and in concepts of comparative literature as a discipline. Admirably original and perceptive readings of a wide variety of works are made in the course of investigating "the critical double."

What good is such a book now? What good is rhetorical criticism at the present time? Is it not already, as Hegel said art was, a thing of the past? Have not the accomplishments of such criticism either been assimilated so that they can be taken for granted or, alternatively, shown to be no longer relevant, perhaps even harmful, to present projects? Rhetorical criticism, it is often argued, is an aestheticism, detached from the material and historical worlds. These are the realms of class struggles, gender wars, struggles for ethnic survival, all that belongs to the body and to the solid realities of material production, distribution, and consumption. Rhetorical criticism is elitist, likely to be politically neutral or even reactionary. It is concerned only to perpetuate canonical works of the hegemonic culture, works written exclusively by dead white European males. Paul Gordon's brilliant book provides an opportunity to try to think these issues through. It also admirably exemplifies the current relevance of rhetorical criticism.

The charge of political neutrality or conservatism is easy enough to answer. So-called deconstruction is routinely lumped by reactionaries of the right with feminism, multiculturalism, and reader response criticism as one of the new developments that are "destroying literary studies" or even destroying Western civilization as a whole. Where there is smoke there is fire. There can be no doubt that rhetorical criticism has contributed fundamentally to the rapid transformation of curricula and teaching practice in the humanities over the past twenty years. The radical shift during the 1980s in the humanities to a primary concern with history, politics, society, feminism, to multicultural, ethnic, and minority discourse study, was no doubt overdetermined, but so-called deconstruction contributed much to this change, even when the changes were in supposed reaction to rhetorical criticism. One motive for the changes was a laudable desire to make the humanities count for something in the real world, to make that real world better. Rhetorical criticism now needs to justify itself in those terms. It always did need to justify itself in those terms, like any other approach in the humanities. So—what good is rhetorical criticism at the present time? More specifically, what good is Paul Gordon's *The Critical Double*?

Two quite different answers to these questions must be given. First answer: cultural studies, multiculturalism, feminism, and studies of minority discourses provide one perhaps unintentional benefit, a perspective by incongruity on the so-called hegemonic culture. That culture will never be quite the same. We see it differently now. We see it in the context of all the other things that are being studied and taught in the humanities. The strangeness and heterogeneity of that dominant culture's monuments can now be seen better. The rereadings by so-called deconstructive critics of major canonical texts is an indispensable precondition for multicultural work. Those rereadings, however, cannot be taken for granted and forgotten. They must be continuously repeated and extended, for example in books like Paul Gordon's *The Critical Double*. Moreover, the mystified misreadings of canonical texts that have been so influential must also be continuously reread and diagnosed. If these two kinds of reading are not done, the danger is that we might fall back into the traditional assumptions that are being put in question, for example assumptions about referentiality, or about the "I" (whether feminine or masculine) as preordained essence, or about the organic unity of all good texts, or about the continuity and reasonableness of history, or about the sovereign power of a single principle of reason.

The humanities are unlike the sciences in not being able to take previous work for granted as a stable foundation on which newer work may be built. It all has to be done over again in a different way in different social and political circumstances by each generation, or rather by each individual. You cannot trust anyone else to do the work of reading for you. It does not go without saying in the humanities, as it more or less does in the sciences, that each new generation is an advance on the previous ones. History shows rather a series of advances and retreats, as ground once gained is lost and then found again by crossing a different boundary. An example is the loss during the later nineteenth century, with some important exceptions, of insights into the relation of allegory to symbolism that had been achieved by the German romantics. These were then recovered in the twentieth century by thinkers such as Walter Benjamin and Paul de Man.

The power of the dominant culture to impose its ideologies even on those who think they are most liberated from them should never be underestimated. A perhaps debased form of "Western civilization" is embodied everywhere around us in what Althusser called "ideological state apparatuses": schools, media, law, government. That dominant culture can be contested only if it is studied and understood. Otherwise the danger is that it will inadvertently be reaffirmed in symmetrical mirror images that reflect its errors and injustices. Those who do not study history are condemned to repeat it. *The Critical Double*, with its rereadings of canonical texts from Aristotle and the Sophists to the present day, has therefore an indispensable function in relation to current projects in the humanities.

But Paul Gordon's book has another quite different role. If the dominant tradition is as strange and heterogeneous as rhetorical criticism finds it to be, there may be within it ideas that have been crossing against the grain the apparent monolithic unity of that tradition all along. These may be of immense help in current projects, for example in thinking out and helping to materialize new forms of democracy. Such democracies would be nonhierarchical and differentiated. They would not be based on a single reigning principle of reason. *The Critical Double* identifies a major example of such a counter-thought within major works in the canonical tradition.

But what good is a thought, even a thought that goes counter to the reigning concepts that make up what is normally thought? What is needed, it might be said, is praxis. We most need a political intervention that will change society and its institutions, for example the university. Political praxis, however, always happens in the name of conceptual formulations. That is conspicuously true of projects to change the university. Those formulations are not only conceptual. They are also performative. Thinking is inextricably embodied in material conditions. It has a kind of stubborn materiality. It tends to get itself incarnated in institutions, such as university departments and curricula. The difficulty with attempts to change such materializations, as is well known, is that the language we have tends to replicate what is being contested. The terms *pluralism* and *cultural diversity*, for example, are contaminated by the hierarchical and single-centered assumptions about culture that they are meant to challenge. *Pluralism* suggests "e pluribus unum," some single order governing a hierarchically arranged plurality. *Cultural diversity* suggests some single concept of culture that defines the minority cultures as deviating from it. Minority cultures are, precisely, "minority"—subaltern and not quite complete versions of the main culture. Changes attempted in the name of such terms may leave the dominant culture still imperturbably in charge. The idea or figure, the constative or performative assertion (it is all these at once), of the critical double cannot easily be recuperated in this way. It might form a continuously self-recreating ground for that better democracy many teachers in the humanities these days desire.

Just what does Paul Gordon mean by "the critical double"? Without wanting to be evasive, I must begin by saying that answers to those questions cannot be adequately given in a purely general and conceptual form. In order to find out what Gordon means you must read his book. His formulations arise in the course of rigorous readings leading to insights about what he calls the critical double. These are different in the case of each text he reads, whatever he says in his introduction about seeking in them "a certain common denominator . . . which could then be tested against the far greater number of theories and artworks not discussed here." If the critical double is always the same, it is at the same time always different in each of its specifications, as *The Critical Double* persuasively shows. It is not a denominator as an identifiable digit of which you can say, "I've got its number."

What is meant in this case (or in general) by "rigorous reading"? As practiced by Paul Gordon, or by any good reader, it means two apparently different things, each difficult to attain or to combine after attaining them. One is an ability to let what happens in reading happen, not to blind oneself to a text by imposing prejudices or preconceptions about what the text in question is going to mean. Only in this way can the true strangeness of literature, philosophy, or critical theory be encountered. It is extremely difficult to do this, in part because so many learned and authoritative voices have already told us what these canonical texts mean. An example, rightly scorned by Gordon, is Gerald F. Else's strange assertion that the chapters of the *Poetics* including the analysis of metaphor "have very little—astonishingly little—connection with any other part of Aristotle's theory of poetry." But another example, more challenging for Gordon, is Jacques Derrida's influential discussion of Aristotle's theory of metaphor in "La mythologie blanche." Gordon is nevertheless able to go back to the *Poetics*, suspend what both Else and Derrida say, and let the *Poetics* say what it says afresh.

The other requisite of rigorous reading is also exemplified in *The Critical Double*. This is the need of an active, interested, interrogative intervention by the reader. Rigorous reading is by no means a passive reception of what the work says. To read passively is merely to slip words through your

mind and so not read at all. The active intervention required by good reading takes several forms. One of them is a habit of asking the text questions,
such as "Why is this here?" "Why is it formulated in just this way?" or
"If that is so, then what follows?" For example: What follows from the
fact that the word Aristotle uses to define metaphor, *allotrios* ("belonging
to something else"), is also the word Aeschylus uses in the *Agamemnon* to
name adulterous courtship? What follows from that (metaphorical) connection? How is a metaphor adulterous, perhaps even incestuous, like the
relation of Oedipus to Jocasta, so important as an example of tragedy for
Aristotle? Another form of interventionist reading is the habit of comparison, primarily for the sake of identifying what is distinctive about the text
in question. A third, and perhaps the most important, form is the attempt,
for example in teaching or in commentary, to say again what the text says,
to add more words to its words. These new words must be, in the strict
sense Gordon gives the term, the critical double of the text in question.
Nothing teaches you more about your limited understanding of a text in a
foreign language than the attempt to translate it into your own tongue.
This is another form of the critical double. Trying to explain in your own
words what a given text means is another form of translation. This critical
doubling too may facilitate, even in its inadequacy, an encounter with what
is alien or "other" in the text in question. Paul Gordon excels in both these
forms of rigorous reading. He can let what happens in reading happen, and
he can actively translate that happening into the critical doubling of his
own text.

   Just what is the "critical double"? Can I not double Paul Gordon's
doubling in a brief reading of his readings?

   The word *critical* is as important as the word *double* in Gordon's title.
Critical is used with the full force of its several meanings. A *critical* double
is one that can be used by a reader or that has been used by the author as
an instrument of criticism or critique. Moreover, the derivation of *critical*
from Greek *krinein*, "to divide or sift," as in separating the wheat from
the chaff, implies a division of the critical double within its own unity, an
originary difference or differentiation. No original unity that is not yet divided exists. Division, difference, goes all the way down, so to speak. This
means that the doubles are not versions of some single archetype. A "critical double" must therefore be sharply distinguished (another division there)
from our ordinary notion of doubles as matching pairs, symmetrical mirror
images, like Tweedledum and Tweedledee, or like the encounter with one's
own double, as in the "Doppelgänger" motif: "The Magus Zoroaster, my
dead child, / Met his own image walking in the garden." [1] The inevitable
resonances of the word *double* with that traditional concept of a duplica-

tion governed by a presiding model are an example of those difficulties I mentioned earlier. This is the difficulty of twisting traditional terms (which are all the terms we have) "anasemically," against their normal semantic usage, to express a different insight.

If *critical* is a double word in Gordon's usage, *double* is also a double word. Gordon stresses the etymological connection of *double* with *doubt*. The word suggests not only a mirroring duplication but also a putting in doubt. A critical double, as opposed to a more benign doubling (if there is such a thing), puts in question, and at the same time reestablishes in a new form, what it doubles. That image of myself I meet in the garden is no exact copy, while at the same time it is an exact copy. That image is an uncanny ghost or guest in my garden that is both like and unlike me. This ghostly double undermines both my identity and the grounds for that identity, while at the same time reaffirming them.

Gordon's book is made up of identifications of the way the critical double works in examples drawn from Heidegger, Gadamer, Derrida, Aristotle, Protagoras, New Testament parable, Kafka, Euripides, Sophocles, Freud, Henry James, de Man, Wellek, and Friedrich Schlegel. All belong to that dominant culture I began by discussing. All are white males. Almost all are dead white European males. But they can hardly, even at the most abstract level, be accused of saying the same thing. The diversity and even heterogeneity of the list is an important aspect of Gordon's book. His book is a conclusive demonstration, if there had been any doubt about it, that the so-called dominant culture can in no way be reduced to any monolithic unity of the "e pluribus unum" sort. One of the features of what might be called intellectual generosity in Gordon's book is the way he does not set Gadamer against Derrida, Wellek against Schlegel, Aristotle against Protagoras or Nietzsche, Christ against Kafka, as one might expect. He finds rather different versions of the critical double in both of the apparent antagonists. Each is doubled within himself as well as being the critical double of the other. This means, on the one hand, that Gordon wants to show, for example, that Derrida in "Restitutions" inevitably enacts a form of the grounding restititution he challenges in Heidegger and Meyer Schapiro and, on the other hand, that Gordon unexpectedly finds in Wellek, for example, or in Gadamer, versions of Protagoras's *dissoi logoi*.

Four different dimensions or features of the critical double may be identified in Gordon's readings. One is the relation of unlikeness in likeness between two doubled elements. Another is the doubling within each of the doubled elements. A third is the putting in question of the assumption of a unitary origin for the doubled and doubling elements. The fourth is the necessity of using an alogical language to describe the critical double and its effects. Let me say a further word about each of these.

In normal usage doubles make a pair. One says of twins, "They are as alike as two eggs." They are alike because they are both modeled on the same archetype. This similarity allows logical statements to be made about the relation between the two. But in the case of critical doubling no such negotiation is possible. The two eggs are both like and at the same time so unlike that they cannot be brought together within ordinary logical discourse. Gordon puts this aspect of the critical double under the aegis of Derrida by citing as an epigraph a passage from "Restitutions," the essay in *La verité en peinture* that makes so much of the question of whether the shoes painted by Van Gogh are or are not a pair: "S'il y a paire, il y a contrat possible, on peut chercher le sujet, l'espoir reste permis. Le colloque—et la collocation—pourra avoir lieu, la dispute [s']engager. . . . Pas de contrat symbolique dans le cas d'un *double* qui ne ferait pas la paire. Qui ne serait pas une [même] chose en deux, mais un deux dans l'identité. [If there is a pair, there is a possible contract; one can look for the subject, and hope is permitted. The colloquium—the collocation—can take place, and the dispute can be engaged. . . . There is no symbolic contract in the case of a double which does not constitute a pair. The double is not one (selfsame) thing in two, but a 'two' within identity.]"[2]

If the relation between the two elements doubled in a critical doubling defies the law of noncontradiction, the same thing may be said of each half taken separately. It is as if we were compelled to say of each egg that it is not what it is. This applies especially, in Gordon's readings, to the impossibility of reducing any of the texts he discusses to a single logocentric meaning. Metaphor for Aristotle, for example, is governed by nature and returns the same to the same, as Derrida says in "La mythologie blanche." At the same time, in Aristotle's own formulations, metaphor is said to import the strange, foreign, or alien into the economy or homemaking of the same. Aristotle's fascination with metaphor indicates a recognition that metaphors defy logic and the law of noncontradiction, the sovereign principle he had himself established. Or metaphors are a higher logic within logic. To give another quite different example, the literature of each country, in Wellek's characterizations, is both the critical double of the literature of other countries and at the same time differentiated within itself, partly by borrowings from other countries, so that there cannot be said to be a pure unity of French literature or German literature. Each national literature is at once the critical double of other literatures and at the same time doubled within itself.

This means that for each of the cases of critical doubling Gordon analysizes, and in all those he does not analyze, there is not one single transcendent concept that governs the play of doubling. No unequivocal concept of literal language exists for Aristotle against which the illicit transfers of metaphor may be measured; no universal concept of literature exists for Wellek against which the literature of each country may be measured and the literature of different countries compared; no ascertainable "figure in the carpet" exists either in James's story or for the characters of James's story. The originary matrix is rather already differentiated within itself, critically doubled. One might say that it is "others" rather than merely "other" to the play of doubling over which it "presides." Rather than being a solid ground, it is a kind of swarming or pullulation. The origin is, in Wallace Stevens's phrase, "an insolid billowing of the solid."[3] It does not provide a stable basis for the truth value of any unequivocal assertion. It is the infirm beneath each affirmation. As Stevens, himself a great master of the critical double (though it is not of course masterable), says in another place: "It is not in the premise that reality / Is a solid."[4] This differentiated logos is the ground not only of a given statement but also an equally solid (or insolid) ground for the opposing statement, including the opposite of this one here.

As will have been evident from my own formulations, the fourth element in this complex of features making up the critical double is the impossibility of speaking of it in strictly logical language. This necessity must not be misunderstood. It does not mean some blind irrationalism that allows the critic to say anything he or she likes about the text in question because it is "indeterminate" in meaning anyway. No, the nature of the critical double rigorously determines the language that must be used to speak of it. Gordon's book abounds in scrupulously formulated phrases and sentences that defy the law of noncontradiction because they must do so if they are to account for what is going on in the text in question. Metaphor for Aristotle, for example, is "a transgression of logic which is more fundamental, or logical, than logic itself." For Nietzsche, "myths, metaphors, and dreams all have the double status of masks whose revelation is their own disguise." The text of James's "The Figure in the Carpet" is "its own hidden meaning which conceals or denies itself at the very moment of its revelation." René Wellek insists that comparative literature is "the study of literature as one totality while at the same time claiming that the study of parallels, of comparisons as such, can only be marginal concerns." For Paul de Man, whose own formulations exemplify Gordon's theme, "autobiography veils a defacement of the mind of which it is itself the cause."[5]

In each chapter Gordon encounters the critical double in a different way in a different context, but all these encounters are put under the sign of Protagoras's *dissoi logoi*. The characteristic twist in the critical double is not in the statement that there are two opposing statements on every question, but in the phrase at the end that pulls the rug out from the clear logic of the first statement by applying it to the statement itself. The critical double demands to be spoken of in language of this sort, even though such language, if the compelling forces of the multiple logoi are not felt, is always open to being seen as mere wordplay. But such locutions are implacably demanded by what is being spoken of. Jacques Derrida, in a footnote to "Fors," speaking of the strange alogic of the crypt in the work of Nicolas Abraham and Maria Torok, gives eloquent expression to the constraints on language imposed by the demand to speak of something that defies the ordinary decorums of clear, logical language, language in which figures stay in their places and are firmly controlled by literal, referential meaning: "Point de jeu, ici, sur les mots ou sur la syntaxe, point de contamination gratuite, seulement les contraintes de cette topique singulière. Celle-ci produit la nécessité de ce langage avant d'être écrite en ses tournures bizarres, ses équivoques syntaxiques, ses dehors ressemblants. [This is not mere wordplay, or syntax twisting, not a gratuitous contamination of meanings; only the constraints of this topography. This topography has already produced the *necessity* of this kind of language, even before being described through its bizarre turns of phrase, its syntactical ambiguities, its outward resemblances ('resembling outsides' might be a better translation).]"[6]

I leave it to the reader to follow the intricacies of Gordon's readings of the critical double in the texts he discusses. He encounters the critical double not so much as a common denominator of those texts as rather the critical double of a common denominator. This strange doubled double is a simultaneous zero and infinity that produces alogical results when it is divided into a given text. *The Critical Double* must be read with the same double procedures of reading Gordon himself uses, a passive/aggressive letting the text speak accompanied by an active intervention that challenges it to speak. If you do not already know how to read in this way (and which of us can say we do?), you need to read *The Critical Double* to find out how to read it. I hope that Paul Gordon's book will be read and reread in the coming years by those who want to know what Aristotle or Nietzsche, Sophocles, James, Freud, de Man, and the others really said. I hope it will also be read by those who want to find effective conceptual grounds for new curricular and disciplinary projects as well as for the concomitant social changes that are the horizons of our hope.

Notes

1. Percy Bysshe Shelley, *Prometheus Unbound*, 1.192–93.
2. Jacques Derrida, *La verité en peinture* (Paris: Flammarion, 1978), 322–23; Gordon's translation slightly altered.
3. Wallace Stevens, "Reality Is an Activity of the Most August Imagination," in *Opus Posthumous* (New York: Knopf, 1957), 111.
4. Wallace Stevens, "An Ordinary Evening in New Haven," in *The Collected Poems* (New York: Knopf, 1954), 489.
5. Paul de Man, "Autobiography as De-Facement," in *The Rhetoric of Romanticism* (New York: Columbia University Press, 1984), 81.
6. Jacques Derrida, "Fors," note reference to *Cryptonymie: Le Verbier de l'homme aux loups*, by Nicolas Abraham et Maria Torok (Paris: Aubier Flammarion, 1976), 21; "Fors: The Anglish Words of Nicolas Abraham and Maria Torok," trans. Barbara Johnson, *Georgia Review* 31, no. 1 (Spring 1977): 75.

Acknowledgments

THE DISCUSSION of Aristotle's theory of metaphor in chapter 1 was published in *Metaphor and Symbolic Activity* 5, no. 2 (1990) as "The Enigma of Aristotelian Metaphor: A Deconstructive Analysis"; the section of chapter 3 on Kafka's parable "On Parables" was published in *Cithara* 27, no. 2 (1988). Part of chapter 4 was published in *Women's Studies* 17, no. 3 (1989) as "Misogyny, Dionysianism, and a New Model of Greek Tragedy." Chapter 5 appeared recently in *Style* (24, no. 2) under the title "Freud's *'Uber den Gegensinn der Urworte'*: Psychoanalysis, Art, and the Antithetical Senses"; chapter 7 has also been published in its entirety, in *Neohelicon* 15, no. 2 (1988), as "Romanticism, Figuration, and Comparative Literature." Finally, the essay on Paul de Man (chapter 6) is forthcoming in *Language and Style*. Thanks to all these journals for permission to reprint those articles here.

To the Mauritshuis Museum, I am very grateful for permission to reproduce Vermeer's *Head of a Girl*.

For permission to quote from published works, acknowledgments are as follows:

From *The Truth in Painting*, by Jacques Derrida, translated by Geoff Bennington and Ian McLeod, copyright © 1987 The University of Chicago Press. By permission of the publisher.

From "The Origin of the Work of Art," from *Poetry, Language, Thought*, by Martin Heidegger. Copyright © 1971 by Martin Heidegger. Reprinted by permission of HarperCollins Publishers, Inc.

From *Parables and Paradoxes* by Franz Kafka. Copyright 1946, 1947, 1948, 1953, 1954, © 1958 and renewed 1975 by Schocken Books, Inc. Reprinted by permission of Schocken Books, published by Pantheon Books, a division of Random House, Inc.

From *The Poems of W. B. Yeats: A New Edition*, edited by Richard J. Finneran. Copyright 1919 by Macmillan Publishing Company, renewed 1947 by Bertha Georgie Yeats. Reprinted with permission of Macmillan Publishing Company.

From *Dialogue on Poetry and Literary Aphorisms*, by Friedrich von Schlegel, © 1962 by The Pennsylvania State University Press. By permission of the publisher.

Thanks also to Robert Pois and the other members of the Kayden Committee for supporting this work, and to the readers and editors of The University of Alabama Press for their efforts in bringing this book to completion. I especially want to thank Nicole Mitchell and Ellen Harris for their careful attention to this chimerical volume, and to J. Hillis Miller for his illuminating Foreword. Finally, I wish to acknowledge the extraordinary intellectual gifts and constant inspiration of my students in the Humanities Department at the University of Colorado.

THE CRITICAL DOUBLE

Righting an Introduction

Van Gogh's Shoes *and* the Critical Double

S'il y a paire, il y a contrat possible, on peut chercher le sujet, l'espoir reste permis. Le colloque—et la collocation—pourra avoir lieu, la dispute [s']engager. On pourra s'approprier, exproprier, prendre, donner, reprendre, offrir, s'acquitter, faire hommage ou injure. . . . Pas de contrat symbolique dans le cas d'un *double* qui ne ferait pas la paire. Qui ne serait pas une [même] chose en deux, mais un deux dans l'identité.

—Jacques Derrida, *La vérité en peinture*

Left foot right foot left foot right
Feet in the morning and feet at night.
—Dr. Seuss, *The Foot Book*

A PROPER INTRODUCTION, as Hegel maintains in his *Phenomenology*,[1] is a contradiction in terms, for such would not be an introduction but the book itself. Still, there is a rhetorical, or even ritual,[2] compulsion to start a book "off on the right foot" that preexists any logical certainty whether this or any introduction is right and necessary and which also defies any certainty we might have about *not* writing/righting an introduction. And, if writing an introduction is a "contradiction in terms," the same may be true of all writing, or at least of all writing that demands an introduction: We must start off on the right foot because we cannot start off on the right foot and because we cannot *not* start off on the right foot. Hence the epigraph from Dr. Seuss (the citation from Derrida is more obvious).[3]

It is particularly difficult to start off "on the right foot" a book that bases itself on Protagoras's dictum that "on every question there are two opposing answers, *including this one*."[4] For it is just as likely that the left foot may turn out to be, as it is for many, the right foot (and vice versa) as it is that the "answer" to any aesthetic question may or may not be the right one. The right foot is and is not the right one, the right answer is and is not the right answer, but in either case one must move forward and try to be right, for not to do so would demonstrate an arrogant degree of certitude that Protagoras's doctrine of "double meanings" certainly precludes.

If one starts an introduction "off on the right foot" (Can one be "off" and "on" at the same time? One would have to be, if Protagoras is right), does that mean one has started the *book* off correctly? Or, has one already stumbled? Such reservations notwithstanding, one way to start *The Critical Double* "off on the right foot" would be to analyze the recent discussion of Van Gogh's *Shoes* in which the initial critical doubling is itself repeatedly doubled as Derrida discusses Meyer Schapiro, who discusses Heidegger's discussion of the two shoes depicted in Van Gogh's painting.[5] Moreover, the doubling of the shoes themselves is made a critical part of Derrida's essay, which repeatedly raises the question of whether the shoes are really a pair. The latter may seem like a trivial concern, especially when one recalls that the shoes depicted in Van Gogh's painting were probably not made with a right versus a left.[6] But the weighty implications of Derrida's concerns are not much affected by this historical detail. What really concerns Derrida is the presumption that there must be a "right way" to interpret a work of art just as there must be a right shoe. Is the "truth in painting" any more or less determinable than deciding whether one of the shoes is the right one, or whether one has started a book "off on the right foot"? And what is the right way to evaluate Derrida's own concerns about "logocentric" rightness? What is the right way to avoid being right?

*

It is possible to extend the textbook definition of the rhetorical trope autonomasis[7] from a substitution of epithets for proper names to a far-reaching deconstruction of the rhetorical self. It would not be difficult, that is, to demonstrate that any attempt to define the self relies on tropes and figures. We are all like the clothesless Emperor of the fairy tale, ever deluded and ever deluded about our delusions. One of Derrida's main goals in "Restitutions" is to show that Heidegger, who interprets Van Gogh's *Shoes* as those of a peasant, and Schapiro, who insists that the shoes are those of an artist (Van Gogh himself), are both naive in positing identities that are supposed to be the "truth in painting." Moreover, Heidegger and Schapiro are also donning their own sorts of autonomastic masks, for each is acquiring his own false identity as the one responsible for the proper attributes of the Van Gogh painting:

> It is only just beginning but already one has the impression that the pair in question, if it is a pair, might well not come back to anyone. The *two things* might then exasperate . . . the desire for retribution. . . . Let us posit as an axiom that the desire for attribution is a desire for appropriation, in matters of art as it is everywhere else. To say: this (this painting or these shoes) is due to [*revient à*] X, comes down to [*revient à*] saying:

it is due to me, via the detour of the "it is due to [*à*] me." Not only: it is properly due to such-and-such, man or woman, to the male or female wearer ("Die Bäuerin auf dem Acker dagegen *trägt* die Schuhe," says the one in 1935, "They are clearly pictures of the artist's *own* shoes, not the shoes of a peasant," replies the other in 1968 [Derrida's emphasis]), but it is properly due to *me* via a short detour: the identification, among many other identifications, of Heidegger with the peasant and Schapiro with the city dweller.[8]

It is this moment of "restitution," when Heidegger and Schapiro attribute meaning to the painting and, indirectly, to themselves, that is critical for Derrida's analysis of all three works. This is also the moment which involves us in *doubt* and *doubling* (the etymological relationship between these two words shall be a frequent concern throughout this work) insofar as any doubt about the critical doublings involved is supposedly eschewed by Heidegger and Schapiro. This is also the moment when, in our own analysis of all these works, we must allow for a certain doubt about Derrida's own identification of Heidegger with the peasant and Schapiro with the artist.

One could argue that Derrida is himself guilty of the very same "restitutional fallacy" he decries in Heidegger and Schapiro. For if Derrida insists that Heidegger and Schapiro are guilty of imposing their own appropriations on the *Shoes*, hasn't he imposed on the two critics his own identities, which are part of his own attempt to restitute meaning in the painting? Lumping Heidegger's monumental essay "On the Origin of the Work of Art" (*Der Ursprung des Kunstwerkes*) with Schapiro's far shorter and less significant work lends credence to the notion that a "restitution" is taking place which is at least as suspect as Schapiro's certainty that "these are clearly pictures of the artist's own shoes."[9] Keeping in mind Derrida's own criticism of Heidegger and Schapiro, one must also wonder how much of Derrida's own identity is restituted by identifying the two critics' similar restitutions (also restituted to each other) with the artist and the peasant. Is Derrida's claim to avoid such blatantly logocentric thinking itself too right thinking? One need not go back over every word of Heidegger's famous essay to show that the two critics—Heidegger and Schapiro—are definitely not a pair, and that the restitution of Heidegger's restitution of the shoes with the peasant to Schapiro's much more blatant identification with the shoes of an artist is itself as fallacious as any other restitution.

From the outset, Heidegger's essay seems to deny anything like the facile restitutions of which Schapiro is certainly guilty:

> What art is should be inferable from the work. What the work of art is we can come to know only from the nature of art. Anyone can easily see

> that we are moving in a circle. Ordinary understanding demands that this circle be avoided because it violates logic. [One believes] what art is can be gathered from a comparative examination of actual art works. But how are we to be certain that we are indeed [*in der Tat*] basing such an examination on art works if we do not know beforehand what art is? ("Origin," 18; English translation slightly modified)

Where does art come from? Is it a posteriori, coming from the art object itself, or a priori, coming from an aesthetic sensibility that predetermines what art shall be? These two opposing possibilities, which are genuinely *double* in maintaining a considerable degree of *doubt*, are welcomed by Heidegger as a circular "feast" and "strength of thought" ("Stärke und Fest des Denkens," 9). Although it is readily understandable why Heidegger's titular reference to an "origin" would have set Derrida off in search of restitutions, thus far it seems that such a search is more restitution-ridden than Heidegger's text. Discussing origins the way Heidegger does may be considerably less logocentric than denying them the way Derrida does.

Related to the "hermeneutic circle" of art's simultaneously subjective and objective essence is its figurative, allegorical status as symbolically "something else":

> The art work is something else over and above the thingly element [*das Dinghafte*]. This something else in the work constitutes its artistic nature. [*Dies Andere, was daran ist, macht das Künstlerische aus.*] The art work is, to be sure, a thing that is made, but it says something other than the mere thing itself is, *allo agoreuei*. The work makes public something other than itself; it manifests something other; it is an allegory. In the work of art something other is brought together with the thing that is made. To bring together is, in Greek, *sumballein*. The work is symbol. (20)

Heidegger's use of the terms *allegory* and *symbol* implies the double, figurative meaning of all aesthetic objects. Art, the art object, is "something else" because it is never one thing, never either a priori or a posteriori. But neither is art not these things, for to insist on that would be to deny its inherent status as "something else." Art is double, "neither one nor two,"[10] but both. In this respect the controversy surrounding Van Gogh's *Shoes*— whether they are his, whether they are a pair, et cetera—might be recast as a sort of "category mistake" whereby the everyday term *pair* is confused with its aesthetic counterpart, that of the *double*.

It stands to reason, then, that Heidegger's sense of "origin" has nothing to do with mere causality, but, rather, with the idea of art as originality. Artistic originality is a revelation of truth as unconcealedness (*alētheia*) that is not at all impaired by the confusion one has in assigning a place of origin to the aesthetic experience, or by the lack of truth as what Heidegger calls "propositional correctness." Although the latter are things we do not know about the artwork, that is because we experience something more, the unconcealed Being of beings which suddenly appears—"springs forth" (compare *Ur-sprung*)—in the artwork as originality. In this aesthetic experience

> there is much in being [*am Seienden*] that man cannot master [*bewältigen*]. There is but little that comes to be known. What is known remains inexact, what is mastered [*das Gemeisterte*] insecure. What is, is never of our making or even merely the product of our minds as it might all too easily seem. When we contemplate this whole as one, then we apprehend, so it appears, all that is—though we grasp it crudely enough. (53)

It is because the aesthetic experience brings us into contact with more than what is known, the Being of beings, that we must always experience the doubling of art as "something else," as a figurative, allegorical encounter. We experience the Being of art the way Jacob encountered the angel with whom he wrestled, for only in being "overmastered"[11] can we experience the "something else" that is unconcealed in the work of art:

> Beyond what is, not away from it but before it, there is still something else [*ein Anderes*] that happens. In the midst of beings as a whole an open place occurs. There is a clearing, a lighting [*Eine Lichtung ist*]. Thought of in reference to what is, to beings, this clearing is in a greater degree than are beings (*seiender als das Seiende*). This open center (*Mitte*) is therefore not surrounded by what is (*vom Seienden*); rather, like the Nothing which we scarcely know, the lighting center itself encircles all that is. (53)

No better description of the work of art, of the origin/originality of the work of art, can possibly exist. No artwork is an object, the being, it contains. Vermeer's painting *Head of a Girl* (see frontispiece) is as much of a pearl as of a girl, as much of both as it is of neither. The artwork is the space which is opened, unconcealed, around the object as much as it is the object itself—the artwork is double.

*

Leopards break into the temple. This happens over and over until it becomes part of the ceremony.[12]

Heidegger chooses the Greek temple as the perfect embodiment of this notion of the artwork as a "clearing, a lighting." Yet the grounded temple is actually no more perfect than the grounded *Shoes* of Van Gogh, to which the Greek temple is curiously conjoined in Heidegger's essay on the "springing forth" (*der Ursprung*) of the work of art. It is an indication of Heidegger's real sense of "restitution" that however different the two artworks may seem, they belong together—they are a pair. Both the description of Van Gogh's *Shoes* and Heidegger's description of the Greek temple exemplify the "origin of the artwork." The fact that Derrida does not talk at all about Heidegger's description of the Greek temple in his "Restitutions" strengthens the view that the goal of searching out "restitutional fallacies" is itself logocentric, for the restitution in Heidegger's essay of the *Shoes* with the temple is entirely missing from Derrida's analysis. Curiously, something essential needs to be restituted to Derrida's essay concerning the fallacy of restitutions.

The Greek temple, Heidegger begins, reveals the god whose effigy is contained within by concealing it. The Greeks, one must remember, did not usually worship within their temples. By virtue of this concealment of the god within itself, the temple discloses, unconceals, the god through the clearing that is opened up, thus revealing the god. This double, figuratively metonymical relationship is further clarified by Heidegger's description of the temple itself:

> Standing there, the building rests on the rocky ground. This resting of the work draws up out of the rock the mystery [*das Dunkle*] of that rock's clumsy yet spontaneous support. Standing there, the building holds its ground against the storm raging above it and so first makes the storm itself manifest in its violence [*Gewalt*]. The luster and gleam of the stone, though itself apparently glowing only by the grace of the sun, yet first brings to light the light of the day, the breadth of the sky, the darkness of the night. The temple's firm towering makes visible the invisible space of air. The steadfastness of the work contrasts with the surge of the surf, and its own repose brings out the raging of the sea. Tree and grass, eagle and bull, snake and cricket first enter into their distinctive shapes and thus come to appear as what they are. (42)

Heidegger's point, to begin with, is not that an artwork which is taken out of its native context—its world—has completely lost its claim to truth. Although "the Aegina sculptures in the Munich collection, Sophocles' *Antigone* in the best critical edition, are, as the works they are, torn out of their own native sphere" (40), the modern "museum" is not lacking its own aesthetic context, one with clear links to the temples of the past. Heidegger's point is that the aesthetic essence of the artwork, its origin/originality, lies not in what it represents but in the process of originating that happens in the work of art. Because of this original process of originating that is the origin of the artwork, the rocky hillside out of which the temple emerges, unconcealing itself, is part of the temple's aesthetic essence. Likewise, the surrounding sea is necessarily part of that out of which the temple emerges, just as the earth acquires its meaning as more than a mere "mass of matter deposited somewhere" (42) by virtue of the very disjunctions that bring forth the aesthetic splendor of the light-ridden temple. Heidegger's project is indeed one of restituting the temple to the world—the earth, the air, the sky—to which it belongs. But neither logocentric nor naive, Heidegger's restitution is radically illogical—metaleptically figural, to be precise—in reversing the natural sequence of events that produce the temple:

> But men and animals, plants and things, are never present and familiar as unchangeable objects, only to represent incidentally also a fitting environment for the temple, which one fine day is added to what is already there. We shall get closer to what *is*, rather, if we think of all this in reverse order, assuming of course that we have, to begin with, an eye for how differently everything then faces us [*zukehrt*]. Mere reversing [*Umkehren*], done for its own sake, reveals nothing. (43)

"Mere reversing, done for its own sake, reveals nothing." To say that the earth emerges from the temple reveals nothing because what is really at stake here is a double "reversal of reversal" that restitutes the temple and the ground at the same time as it denies that restitution. The reversal of reversal of any logocentric, natural order of things is not simply the negation of such a relationship, any more than the reversal of writing a proper introduction would be simply denying the process, as if that were not the most logocentric gesture of all. It is as important to get a book "off on the right foot" as it is for the Greek temple to emerge from the ground and for Van Gogh to paint his *Shoes*. One can challenge, as Derrida does so brilliantly, the literal, logocentric notion of a ground, but not the fact that all such challenges, unless they are ungrounded, must themselves be grounded. That the notion of a ground is itself a figurative one—indeed, it is *the* figure underlying all figuration—simply means that all thought, all truth, must be placed on its properly figural basis.

*

Derrida's choice of the *Shoes* of Van Gogh as a locus for analyzing the problematics of restitution is indeed brilliant. For the two shoes of Van Gogh's painting can be interpreted, "on the one foot," as a fundamental depiction of grounding, and/or the grounded. The *Shoes* would thus represent the most basic, fundamental, humble aspect of our humanity's humility. The fact that the *Shoes* may be Van Gogh's own allows this humanistic reading to include the painter's love for his fellow man and woman, his well-known identification with the peasant folk he worshiped, and so on. *On the other foot,* one might also see in Van Gogh's painting a representation of modernism's troubled lack of grounding. The *Shoes* would then be seen as evidence of the loss of our humanity in modern times: the Freudian undermining of all higher thought, the Marxist undermining of ideals that only serve to alienate us from our material world, the Nietzschean preference for the anti-Platonic body, the surrealist's iconoclastic disregard for the good and the beautiful, and so on. In the case of both hands, or feet, the painting can be seen as a comment on restitutionalization or (which is largely the same thing) its lack.

But, as Derrida admits in the final pages of his essay, one cannot restitute Heidegger's discussion of the *Shoes* quite so quickly.[13] Heidegger's discussion of Van Gogh in his essay "On the Origin of the Work of Art" is very plainly embedded in a lengthy analysis of "the thing," a discussion that is itself embedded in the essay's overriding concern with the work of art. Our ability to fathom "the thing" has been severely crippled by our habit of defining it negatively, as that which (a) underlies predication, (b) precedes form, or (c) preexists the usefulness of equipmental tools as objects. Moreover, if we don't properly understand the underlying thing, we do not, Heidegger insists, really understand predication, form, or the equipmental nature of beings:

> These three modes of defining thingness conceive of the thing as a bearer of traits, as the unity of a manifold of sensations, as formed matter. In the course of the history of truth about beings, the interpretations mentioned have also entered into combinations . . . In such combination they have further strengthened their innate tendency to expand so as to apply in similar way to thing, to equipment, and to work. . . . *Thus it comes about that prevailing thing-concepts obstruct the way toward the thingly character of the thing as well as toward the equipmental character of equipment, and all the more toward the workly character of the work.* (30–31; italics mine)

Heidegger begins his way out of the impasse created by all these "thing-concepts" by suggesting that the resistance of the thing to the "assaults" brought upon it by definitions that purport to understand the thing in terms of what it is not (namely, predication, form, equipment) might itself be a way to begin understanding the thing: "Must not this strange and uncommunicative [*verschlossene*] feature of the nature of the thing become intimately familiar to thought that tries to think the thing? If so, then we should not force our way to its thingly character [*zum Dinghaften des Dinges*]" (32). The thing must be understood as that which overcomes our assaults of thinking, not by mastering us, but by our mastering it. Again, this pattern of "overmastering" can be usefully compared to Jacob's belief that he is successfully wrestling with the angel of God—a belief that gradually turns into the recognition that Jacob's defeat is itself mastery.

With this warning in mind, Heidegger adopts a new strategy: to reconsider the "equipmental nature of equipment" so as to allow one to begin to grasp, or grapple with, the thing: "How shall we discover what a piece of equipment truly is? The procedure necessary at present must plainly avoid any attempts that again immediately entail the encroachments of the usual interpretations. We are most easily insured against this if we simply describe some equipment without any philosophical theory" (32).

It is at this juncture, not even midway along the course of his analysis "On the Origin of the Work of Art," that Heidegger begins his discussion of Van Gogh's depiction of an old pair of shoes. Heidegger's point in using Van Gogh's painting, an artistic representation rather than a "real" piece of equipment, is that it is precisely the question of using, of usefulness, which is at stake. The three definitions of the thing that Heidegger is anxious to avoid are all based on the mastery of scientific definitions and notions of usefulness to which Van Gogh's artwork is immune. Heidegger wants to apprehend the thing itself by looking "simply" at the "equipmental nature of equipment" without relying on the usual definitions and ideas of equipment, definitions and ideas that would "lose by winning" in stifling the very nature of the thing itself. If there is something to be said here about the question of "restitution," it is that the passage itself in which Heidegger discusses Van Gogh's *Shoes* needs to be restituted, resituated, in the context of Heidegger's argument about the thing. That kind of restitution is very different from the restitution that Schapiro and Derrida criticize, Heidegger's supposedly fallacious restitution of the *Shoes* with those of a peasant.

If Heidegger had begun with the painting itself and then claimed to identify the shoes as those of a peasant woman the way Schapiro claimed the *Shoes* are Van Gogh's own "artist's shoes," one would be justified in attacking Heidegger's restitutional fallacy. But nothing like that occurs in Heidegger's text. Heidegger is plainly justified in looking at the painting to see the artistic, versus conceptual, depiction of equipment. Those suffering from "restitutionalitis," one might contend, would be those eager to identify Heidegger with the peasant because of a supposedly fallacious identification of the *Shoes* with the shoes of a peasant. Anyone who simply looks at the painting would say exactly the same thing as Heidegger does, namely, that the old shoes look like the shoes of a peasant; Heidegger never says that they must be that. Finally, Heidegger's reference to the shoes of a "peasant woman," when the gender of the shoes is indeterminate, is clearly not meant to be taken literally, and so exceeds no hermeneutical bounds.

Having explained why he chose to look at Van Gogh's painting, Heidegger begins his discussion of the *Shoes* by confessing that the very simplicity he is after—the observation of the "mere" thing, a pair of old shoes—is likely to cause us to see nothing but the mostly obvious and banal representation there before us: "But what is there to see here?" Yet, "for those who have eyes to see and ears to hear,"[14] there is indeed much to see in the simple painting, as there is also much to hear in Heidegger's simple disclaimer. For Heidegger has already said that a first step toward recognizing "the thing" would be to avoid "forcing our way into its thingly character" (32) by acknowledging that our typical preconceptions about subject/predicate, form/content, and so forth make such disappointment regarding the mere "thingness of the thing" inevitable, even desirable.

Looking at the painting, we realize that the "equipmental nature of equipment" (*das Zeughafte des Zeuges*) has been lost. The shoes are not meant to be merely looked at if we wish to understand them as equipment. But it is at the very moment when we see nothing in the painting but a mere pair of old shoes that something happens, for we are in just the right position to grasp the mereness of the equipment and of the thing itself. Just as in the case of the Greek temple, where the god within reveals itself outside the temple, it is the very moment when we see nothing in the painting but mere equipment that we find ourselves in just the right position to see something more, the "something else" which we do not see when we do not look at what is merely there, but only at what is significant: "A pair of peasant shoes and nothing more. And yet— [*Und dennoch*]."

And yet. Schapiro and Derrida are quick to ridicule the description which follows this "and yet" of the "toilsome tread of the worker which stares forth from the dark opening of the worn insides of the shoes," the "silent call of the earth."[15]

And yet—
From the dark opening [*dunklen Öffnung*] of the worn insides of the shoes the toilsome tread of the worker stares forth. In the stiffly rugged heaviness of the shoes there is the accumulated tenacity of her slow trudge through the far-spreading and ever-uniform furrows of the field swept by a raw wind. On the leather lie the dampness and richness of the soil. Under the soles slides the loneliness of the field-path as evening falls. In the shoes vibrates the silent call [*verschwiegene Zuruf*] of the earth, its quiet gift [*stille Verschenken*] of the ripening grain and its unexplained self-refusal [*unerklärtes Sichversagen*] in the fallow desolation of the wintry fields. This equipment is pervaded by uncomplaining anxiety as to the certainty of bread, the wordless joy of having once more withstood want, the trembling before the impending childbed and shiv-

ering at the surrounding menace of death. This equipment belongs to the *earth*, and it is protected in [*behütet*] the *world* of the peasant woman. From out of this protected belonging the equipment itself rises to its rest-ing-within-itself [*Insichruhen*]. (33–34)

As the "and yet" indicates, Heidegger is anything but quick to restitute the shoes with their world. In looking at the painting as such, Heidegger has indeed discerned in it what is not there: the soil, toil, the earth, and so on. But who would ever claim that the purpose of painting, not to mention interpretation, is to show us just what is there? True, Heidegger restitutes the peasant with the shoes, but at least his interpretation, unlike Schapiro's, is based on his view of the painting itself. Heidegger's interpretation is not only hermeneutically valid, but it follows from his stated goal of simply looking at Van Gogh's painting of old shoes in order to fathom more than the mere "equipmental nature of equipment." Heidegger wants to fathom the double "something else" which our customary, everyday way of think-ing does not see in a mere pair of old shoes.

Although Heidegger's discussion of the *Shoes* seems to ignore the ar-tistic status of the painting in favor of questions concerning ontology (that of the "thing itself") and technology (the "equipmental nature of equip-ment"), nothing could be further from the truth. The essay is, first and last, an essay "On the Origin of the Work of Art." By looking at the paint-ing of the actual pair of old peasant shoes and thus eschewing the usual "barriers of our preconceptions" and of our "current pseudo-concepts," Heidegger was able to grasp what equipment actually is (the "silent call of the earth," et cetera) as well as the mere "thingness" to which it is related. These revelations of the "equipmental nature of equipment" and the mere "thingness of the thing" are only made possible by the painting because the artwork, in its double, allegorical essence, says "something else" (*allo ti*) and thereby reveals what Heidegger calls the "Being of being" (*Sein des Seienden*). It is art which, according to Heidegger, reveals the truth of the thing itself and the Being of beings by virtue of a double, deconstructive "de-con-cealing" of the space which the artwork, by definition, mysteri-ously occupies:

> *Leopards break into the temple. This happens over and over until it becomes part of the ceremony.*

*

Almost twenty-five centuries ago, the sophist-rhetor Protagoras equated his famous man-as-measure notion with a surprising corollary which declared that "on every question there are two opposing answers, *including this one*."[16] The purpose of *The Critical Double* is to demonstrate that this Protagorean notion (together with the final, self-undermining phrase included in the Senecan attribution) constitutes a fundamental principle of aesthetic/rhetorical discourse. From the opening chapters on metaphor, rhetoric, parable, and tragedy to the concluding chapters on Freud, Paul de Man, and comparative literature, the "critical double" is identified with the way all literary and rhetorical texts utilize structures of meaning to deny the very structures of meaning on which they are based. By calling attention to this fundamental principle of aesthetic discourse, I hope that a certain common denominator might be recognized that could then be tested against the far greater number of theories and artworks not discussed here.

"The double" is frequently used to refer to that curious species of uncanny literature discussed by Freud and others which presents the self confronting itself—the so-called *Doppelgänger* motif. Although "On the Uncanny" is discussed in this work as part of my analysis of Freud's "On the Antithetical Sense of Primary Words" (chapter 5), I am here interested in a more general, language-based notion than that of the personal double. Critical phrases like "the metaphor of metaphor,"[17] "the reversal of reversal," "the death of death," and "the criticism of criticism" are commonly found in philosophy and literary criticism, but they are seldom addressed as such. Such notions are much more than witty phrases, for they point the way toward an understanding of how all art and literature is neither thematic nor antithematic, but both. All are keys to the way aesthetic, figurative doublings can at once assert and deny their own meaning, asserting their denials as well as denying their assertions. This is the first work to use the double as a model of the way all rhetorical and poetical works construct and destruct—de-con-struct—their own meaning.

Much has been written of late informing us that "deconstruction is dead," having yielded its place to the current popularity of cultural and multicultural, historical and new historical methodologies.[18] While it is interesting to speculate whether the so-called revelations about the "bad politics" of Paul de Man, Heidegger, and others were the cause, or the effect, of such a death, it seems highly likely that the frequent declarations of deconstruction's "death" are more wish than fact, and that the unwillingness of its practitioners to contest such a view is wrongly perceived as a *nolo contendere*. The compelling force of political correctness notwithstanding, deconstruction's relative silence in the face of these challenges is more likely the result of its inherent resistance to polemics and the positing of all boundary lines, including that of "deconstruction" itself. Indeed, the method's "founders" at Yale and elsewhere made a point of eschewing the term themselves and only reluctantly allowed it to be mouthed by others, the assumption being that no one in literary studies could fail to notice the neologism's singular paradoxicality and self-destructiveness. This, it seems, was a mistake.

The occlusion of deconstruction's attack on referentiality by historical and cultural studies need not have more than momentarily drowned out the more hushed tones of deconstructive complexity. (Such studies are not precluded from such a process except insofar as they pretend to establish a "cultural hegemony" within the persistent underminings of the text itself.) Meanwhile, the reputations of all the major deconstructive writers, Gadamer, Heidegger, Adorno, de Man, and Miller have remained surprisingly intact for such a moribund discipline. For this reason, I close this introduction by briefly indicating the compatibility of my model of doubling with the work of two of these influential critics: the German hermeneutic critic Hans-Georg Gadamer and the French deconstructive critic Jacques Derrida.[19]

*

Gadamer's sensitivity to the doubleness inherent in all the languages of the humanistic, versus methodological, sciences is already apparent in the opening excursus of *Wahrheit und Methode* (*Truth and Method*) on the term *Bildung* ("culture," "education"), where Gadamer carefully sets up terms for his key notion of the hermeneutic "question of truth as it emerges in the work of art."[20] What interests Gadamer in his survey of the term's history are its two distinct strands of meaning, the one having to do with "developing one's natural talents and abilities"—cultural education—the other having to do with the realization of the "form" or "formation" (*Bild*) of our indwelling spirit. Hegel's dialectical process of self-realization through the alienating abstraction of the world and history is obviously closer to the latter, for it "seeks one's own in the alien, to become at home in it, [which is] the basic movement of spirit, whose being is only a return to itself from what is other" (*Truth and Method*, 15). Hegel's self/other dialectic as just described is too similar to the famous "hermeneutic circle" to be criticized sharply, but Gadamer does point out that this self/other relationship is less stable and progressive than Hegel would like it to be: "A particular is not determined by a universal, nothing is proved conclusively. The universal viewpoints to which the cultivated man [*gebildet*] keeps himself open are not a fixed applicable yardstick, but are present to him only as the viewpoints of possible others" (17–18).

In Gadamer's notion of *Bildung* the self does not appropriate the other to itself but, rather, realizes the false separation between the self and other and hence the unbreachable "distance" that exists between the self and itself: "*Bildung* embraces a general sense of proportion and distance in relation to itself, and hence is capable of being raised above itself to universality" (19). Gadamer pauses over the distinction between *Bildung* as the educative process of "leading one outside" oneself and *Bildung* as the realization of our in-dwelling "form" (the English "formation" captures both senses) because what is found within one is always in the process of formation, and what is being formulated is always the preexistent form within. In other words, the *doubling* inherent in the humanistic *Bildung* distinguishes it from the "artificial narrowness in which nineteenth-century methodology was caught": the indwelling form of the *gebildete Seele* ("cultivated soul") is profoundly universal and particular at one and the same time.

Gadamer is equally concerned with the universal/particular status of aesthetic truth in the discussion of *taste* (*Geschmack*) which forms the bridge from the earlier discussion of *Bildung* to the explicit discussion of the "retrieval of the question of artistic truth." Since it was Kant who established the category of aesthetic judgment as a realm of "subjective universality," Gadamer devotes most of this section to a constructive critique of what he sees as the real contribution, as well as the devastating impact, of Kant's third Critique for our understanding of art and the human sciences in general. For, in correctly removing aesthetic judgment from the realm of objective understanding (*taste* realizes the universal principle inherent in a nonuniversal particular), Kant unfortunately left the door open for the "methodologies of the natural sciences" to be reapplied to a realm that had otherwise lost its claim to truth.

Gadamer is understandably concerned with Kant's valorization of natural over artistic, "disinterested" over "interested," and "free" over "dependent" beauty ("dependent" because it is governed by an idea or purpose). Notwithstanding the questionableness of basing an aesthetic ideal on the objectless arabesque, the Kantian ideal of human beauty, where a moral element is at work "without which the object could not be pleasing," belies this supposed preference: "In Kantian terms, the intellectualised and interested pleasure in this represented ideal of beauty does not distract us from the aesthetic pleasure, but is rather one with it. Only in the representation of the human form does the whole meaning of the work speak to us simultaneously as the expression of its object" (45).

This is the critical moment in Gadamer's thought, which also corresponds to the model of "critical doubling" offered here. For Gadamer's goal is to reverse Kant's privileging of the natural over the artistic and the "disinterested" over the "interested" while, at the same time, sustaining the reversed polarities of each. That is to say, "interested art" is more representative of aesthetic judgment than "disinterested nature" because the former includes an element of "productive finality" *which is nonetheless* not *contained within the work of art itself.* Taste realizes the universal principle inherent in a nonuniversal particular, for the latter is not subordinated to the general principle it exemplifies, "but itself co-determines it." This "subjectivization of art" is not to be confused with a view of art as subjective, for it is a real doubling that corresponds, in Kantian terms which Gadamer approves, to "the new beauty of teleological finality" of the natural world realized within us after the (Copernican) "dissolution of ancient cosmological thought" (47).

The third and final example of doubling in Gadamer's notion of the "retrieval of artistic truth" moves from the Kantian notion of taste to the romantic notion of "experience" (*Erlebnis*). The nineteenth-century concept of *Erlebnis* devolves upon a process at once radically individual—one might even say Heraclitean—and yet expressly teleological insofar as an experience (*Erlebnis*) is framed by definite borders as a lasting experience. "Experience" is defined as that which embodies the essence of life (*Leben*) itself precisely because it exists outside the process of life itself. Gadamer follows Georg Simmel in his view of *Erlebnis* as a "reaching out of life beyond itself," as an "adventure" that teaches us the meaning of our lives by taking us outside of the parameters of our particular existences. Just as the notion of "adventure" is an artistic—more specifically, narrative—term, Gadamer identifies "experience" as specifically aesthetic: "The aesthetic experience represents the essence of experience itself" (63).

In this notion of *Erlebnis* as specifically aesthetic the process of artistic doubling comes clearly to light. As is the case with experience, we experience the artwork as simultaneously inside and outside us, as paradoxically representing us to ourselves, as having teleological implications that extend far beyond us while, at the same time, necessitating our own subjective involvement before those implications can be tested. Another literary term we might apply to this relation is *synecdoche*, provided one appreciates the true doubling that occurs when a part becomes a whole yet remains but a part. Artistic truth is the essence of experience, and vice versa, because it is in the individual work of art that one also experiences "the meaningful whole of life" (63). If the "whole of life is present" in the art experience without ever being present, then the essence of art is necessarily double, both present in its absence and absent in its presence. We will have ample occasion to recall what is here seen as the critical etymological link between *doubling* and *doubt* (from Latin *dubitare*, "to be of two minds"): the art-work is always something doubtful, but as Gadamer has shown through his analysis of *Erlebnis*, such doubt is of a higher type than mere certainty, which is doubtful in a much less meaningful way.

*

In "Comment ne pas parler: Dénégations" ("How to Avoid Speaking: Denials"),[21] Derrida turns to the question of "negative theology," which he had long since felt the need to address but which is conditioned by just such an impossible need to return. Derrida's interest in negative theology is not to be seen as a departure from the deconstructor's usual stance of hyperbolic doubt, any more than it is to be seen as a confirmation of Habermas's too-flippant dismissal of Derrida as a Jewish mystic.[22] Derrida's essay on negative theology is in fact a continuation of his interest in *différance*, *la trace*, and the like, and it is for this reason that "How to Avoid Speaking" can be taken as exemplary both for its insight into Derrida's own thought as well as for the purpose of demonstrating that such thought is conditioned by a pattern of "critical doubling."

In approaching the question of negative theology Derrida quickly dismisses the patent absurdities of either speaking or not speaking about God in order to fasten onto the more intriguing idea that to speak of God is not to speak of God, and vice versa. "Ordinary language" is inadequate to deal with the notion, which Derrida examines in the writings of Pseudo-Dionysius and Meister Eckhart, that the goodness of God both asserts and denies itself as it "deconstructs grammatical anthropomorphism" ("How to Avoid Speaking," 9). While this denial of goodness is itself denied when the negativity of God is referred to some hyperessential Being, Derrida is not interested in such a reappropriation of the negative. Rather, Derrida's interest in negative theology concerns a reappropriation that is at once inevitable and a failure. Derrida is drawn to theology insofar as the name of God which is crossed out, or deliberately left incomplete, refers not to any other being under erasure or beyond the name, but to a Being which necessarily presents itself incompletely or under erasure. Benjamin's identification of sacred writings and poetry[23] can be defined by this necessary occlusion, for both present meaning figuratively, even when no apparent figure is present.

Derrida has something of a field day with Wittgenstein's famous notion that "one must not speak about that which one cannot speak." This translates to mean, for Derrida, that "there must be a trace" which is past and future but never present, for the status of the necessary contained in Wittgenstein's statement can only be understood as an acknowledgment of the omnipresent silence one needs to avoid. We speak, Derrida maintains, not because we have something to say, but because there always exists the possibility of not saying what we want to say. There is always a secret underlying speech that is never there insofar as it is secret, and always there insofar as its absence conditions the presence of language: "The secret is that there is no secret, *but there are at least* two *ways of thinking or proving this proposition*" (19; my italics). With this statement of the necessary doubling of all "extra-ordinary language," of all sacred/artistic texts, Derrida enunciates the fundamental thesis of this book in its readings of metaphor, Protagorean rhetoric, biblical parable, Henry James's "The Figure in the Carpet," and so on: the "secret" of art is always contained within the art object yet, at the same time, is never to be found there at all.

Derrida takes up the same question raised in Kafka's parable "On Parables" (see chapter 3 of this book) when he considers the paradox of a Being that is beyond beyond and so beyond itself, beyond Being. Much to Derrida's credit, he is always concretizing this abstraction and relating negative theology to the "real world," as, for example, when he opens up the question of the divine *place* occupied—and not occupied—by Jehovah to the Heideggerian question of a similarly paradoxical place occupied by language and thought. For the negative description of God is part of the "double inscription of knowledge" that lies at the critical dividing point where the secret and the nonsecret merge:

> There is a secret of denial and a denial of the secret. The secret as such, *as secret*, separates and already institutes a negativity; it is a negation that denies itself. It de-negates itself. . . . The enigma of which I am speaking here—in a manner that is too elliptical, too "concise," Dionysius would say, and also too verbose—is the *sharing of the secret*. Not only the sharing of the secret with the other, my partner in a sect or in a secret society . . . [but] the essence of a secret that cannot even appear to one alone except in starting to be lost, to divulge itself, hence to dissimulate itself, a secret, in showing itself: dissimulating its dissimulation. (25)

Because of this "double inscription" of God, or Being, the sharing of its secret becomes essential for the secret to be. Such sharing (which I would also identify with the reader or audience of art, although Derrida does not do so here) involves not only communication with another, but within the self as well. For a secret to be it must always already have been divulged, and so might not be a secret, except for the fact that we, or I, do not necessarily know any longer what that secret might be. The secret—of art, of God—is always a figurative "dissimulation of a dissimulation" because it must, like the no-place of Jehovah, appear to be what it can never be. To dismiss this double dissimulation as a mere witticism or sophistry is easy, and it is not surprising that a "positivistic" school of criticism has attached itself in almost every case where such a notion has appeared.

It is not, *pace* Wittgenstein, simply a matter of not speaking about not speaking. The impossibility of language's ever being purely referential *in stricto sensu* always leaves open the possibility of a gap in discourse (Derrida's *écriture*) that in turn leaves ever present the possibility of an absent God, a presence that can satisfy the referential promise of language. Conversely, any attempt to talk about such an ever-*absent* God must revert to all the deflections, misdirections and tropes of language itself. This ties directly into Derrida's often quoted—and misquoted—notion of the "always already":

> This call of the other, having always already preceded the speech to which it has never been present a first time, announces itself in advance as a *recall*. Such a reference to the other will always have taken place. Prior to every proposition and even before all discourse in general— whether a promise, prayer, praise, celebration. The most negative discourse, even beyond all nihilism and negative dialectics, preserves a trace of the other. A trace of an even older than it or of a "taking-place" to come, both of them: here there is neither an alternative nor a contradiction. (28)

Language is always referring back to an original meaning that it can never recapture because it is always posited *après-coup*, after the fact (or, in Freud's term, *nachträglich*). To be sure, "ordinary language" finds such a notion abhorrent precisely because it is not capable of referring back to an original meaning. But the language of God, and the interpretation of art, are two modes of discourse that are defined by such an absent cause, or meaning, which in turn conditions the very possibility of understanding. "The Cause is a kind of absolute reference for it . . . that same to which or rather to whom the responsibility for who speaks and 'speaks well' responds" (28). "Apophatic discourse," the discourse of God and of art, is necessarily double because it must seek to return to a cause or meaning that is not outside the realm of art but nonetheless always beyond it—that is to say, "always already" in being simultaneously present and absent in referring back to something contained *within* the artwork. If this is meant to imply a certain inherent link between literary hermeneutics and "negative theology," it is nonetheless the case that we cannot understand the "higher meaning" outside the work of art without first following out its "traces" within the work of art.

1 | The Metaphoric Double

Il n'y a pas de lieu non métaphorique d'où
l'on pourrait considérer la métaphore. . . .
La suite de cette étude sera à bien des
égards une longue bataille avec ce paradoxe.

—Paul Ricoeur, *La métaphore vive*

ONE OF THE most obvious facts about metaphor, so obvious that it is seldom given much attention, is that metaphor involves a quantitatively dual or doubling aspect:

> When we use a metaphor *we have two thoughts of different things active together and supported by a single word*, or phrase, whose meaning is a resultant of their interaction. "As to metaphorical expression," said Dr. Johnson, "that is a great excellence in style, when it is used with propriety, *for it gives you two ideas for one.*" He is keeping, you see, to the limited traditional view of metaphor.[1]

Yet an essential difference occurs between these two different terms for the notion of two. *Dual* refers merely to two related objects, while *double* refers to an uncanny repetition of the same.[2] The latter thus contains an important paradox which the former does not: to be dual is to be *both* the same and different, while to be double is to be different *and* the same. The paradox lies in the fact that the double is, in the words of Paul de Man, "neither one nor two"; it would also be correct to say that the double is therefore *both* one and two.[3] If metaphor is double in the sense just described, then any attempt to define a specific metaphor or metaphor in general must contend with the notion that doubling asserts an impossible (because unqualified) unity between two distinct things.

Metaphoric doubling, versus "dueling," involves two distinct units that are one. The A and B of metaphor become, respectively, B and A; that is, each becomes the other without suppressing its individual difference. The effect is comparable to that produced by a mirage in a desert which, for the thirsty traveler, is there anyway, despite the traveler's realization of its nonexistence; or to the feeling an ingenious counterfeiter might have when realizing, however momentarily, that his or her false money is real. Because metaphor is double, "neither one nor two," a gap in meaning, synonymous with the *espacement* of Derrida's *écriture*, results which always separates metaphor from itself.[4] Consequently, any definition of metaphor will, in describing it as something, elide this gap and so, by offering a partial truth or resemblance, yield metaphors of metaphorization. For how can we define metaphor when, in logical terms, it is nothing?—when, in other words, it asserts an identity which is not an identity and so is not even a self-contradiction?

The present work attests to the difficulty of escaping the horns of a dilemma that forces us to choose between recognizing our failure to understand metaphor and the inevitable failure of our every recognition—"including that one" (Protagoras).[5] Either in their "definitions" of metaphor or in their acknowledgment that metaphor is that which, by definition, cannot be defined, Aristotle, Richards, Nietzsche, and other theoreticians of this most critical of literary terms demonstrate the moment of doubt or doubling in metaphor that is neither a positive assertion of meaning nor its negation. The purpose of this "return to metaphor," then, is not to argue for yet another theory of metaphor but to show that because doubling—the metaphor of metaphor—is essential to metaphor our understanding, definitions and theories of what metaphor means must all fail—not because they fail to succeed, but because failure is essential to any metaphorical success. Because metaphor is by definition, in either Aristotle's or Freud's view, "strangely familiar and familiarly strange," all we can do, all one can ever do, is "return to metaphor," for there is certainly no place, here or elsewhere, where metaphor "is." Finally, since any theory of metaphor is tantamount to a general aesthetic theory,[6] this analysis of metaphoric doubling is also offered as a succinct formula for the aesthetic doubling of the "other as the same" (*hetero kath' hauto*) which is analyzed in different ways throughout this book.

The Double of Aristotelian Metaphor

If Whitehead's well-known remark that "all philosophy is a footnote to Plato" is valid, how much more so would be the statement that all theories of metaphor are a footnote to Aristotle. The reason for this longevity is not only that Aristotle gave us the fundamental terms and notions with which or against which all succeeding discussions must contend, but because much remains highly suggestive, even enigmatic, in Aristotle's treatment of metaphor. By *enigma* I am referring, first, to a saying, question, picture, or the like containing a hidden meaning and, second, to a puzzling or inexplicable situation that resists understanding. These two definitions are not mutually exclusive. Aristotelian metaphor is enigmatically double when any underlying unity that characterizes the solution of its "hidden meaning" is felt to be inadequate, resulting in the double "enigmatically enigma" of metaphor as both meaningful and meaningless.

Aristotle himself frequently refers to the connection between metaphor and enigma,[7] as when he states in the *Poetics* that if a poet makes exclusive use of metaphors the result is an *ainigma*, or riddle:

> But if a poet writes entirely in such unfamiliar [*xenika*] words the result will be either a riddle or jargon [*barbarismos*]; if made up of metaphors, a riddle and if of rare words, jargon. The essence of a riddle consists in describing a fact by an impossible combination of words. By merely combining the ordinary names of things this cannot be done, but it is made possible by combining metaphors.[8]

Although Aristotle intends this passage, taken in context, to differentiate the "wild" metaphors of enigmas from metaphors per se, this distinction breaks down when one realizes that metaphors are often wild in their own "impossible combination of words" ("Metaphor is the application of a word which does not belong," *Poetics* 21.7) and enigmas are often tame in admitting of some underlying solution.

Within the *Poetics'* pyramid of tragedy's six primary elements, the privileged base of the figure being "plot" (*muthos*) and the least significant apex being "spectacle" (*opsis*), metaphor holds a pivotally double position:

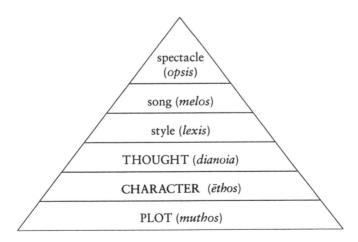

Metaphor is part of "style" (*lexis*) which is almost exactly in the middle of the pyramid, the most important of the three lesser elements of tragedy (style, song, and spectacle). Metaphor is itself the most important of the various elements subdivided within the lesser category of style ("By far the most important thing is a command of metaphor," *Poetics* 22.16); this distinctly echoes what Aristotle says about plot, also called "most important" (*to megiston*). The position of metaphor within Aristotle's system suggests it is at once the most and least important element in the *Poetics*, an enigmatic doubling that shall be shown to characterize other of Aristotle's statements about metaphor as well.

Metaphor is distinguished in the *Poetics* from words which are "rare" (*glottai*, which are "confined to a dialect or borrowed from a foreign language") and "ordinary" (*kuria*), for it can be said to combine these two categories by yielding new ways of using "ordinary" words. This uncanny "native foreignness" (Freud's related notion of *das Unheimliche* will be discussed shortly) is also contained in the famous definition of metaphor from the same section of the *Poetics*: "Metaphora de estin onomatos allotriou epiphora [Metaphor is the introduction (*epiphora*) of a word which belongs to something else (*onomatos allotriou*)]" (*Poetics* 21.7).

Epiphora, judging from its other appearances in Greek, means something more than just "giving," "application," or "transference," as it is usually translated. *Epiphora* also means "a bringing to *or* besides: a donative, addition made to one's pay," that is, "a supplement." Although never discussed by the leading writers on the *Poetics*, the difference between *epiphora* as "supplement" and other translations of the term touches on the very essence of Aristotle's thoughts about metaphor. Epiphoric supplementarity allows metaphor its double significance as standing both *above* the realm of semantic referentiality ("but by far the greatest thing is the use of metaphor. That alone cannot be learnt; it is the token of genius [*euphuias*]"; *Poetics* 22.16–17) as well as *beneath* it because of its merely supplemental nature. The supplemental status of metaphor underscores the enigmatic doubling of a process that adds something new to what is already complete. When, for example, Homer fashions the stunning simile of Apollo as descending on the Greeks "like the night" (*Iliad* 1.47), we can well imagine Aristotle recognizing both the novelty as well as the familiarity of such a trope.

Although the leading deconstructive critic, Jacques Derrida, does not comment specifically on the translation of *epiphora* as "supplement" in either of his essays on metaphor ("La mythologie blanche" and "Le retrait de la métaphore"), he has pioneered discussions of the concept of supplementarity in Plato, Rousseau, Husserl and others.[9] My only disagreement with Derrida regarding his notion of the supplement in Aristotle is that, while commenting in "La mythologie blanche" on the way metaphor "risks interrupting the semantic plenitude to which it *ought* to belong" (287, italics mine), Derrida makes it seem as though Aristotle is trying to avoid metaphor ("elle *devrait* appartenir") rather than describing a metaphoric doubling that deviates from the same semantic process to which it belongs. For example, in his analysis of Aristotle's discussion of the metaphorical catachresis whereby the action of the sun's rays is referred to as "sowing" (*Poetics* 22.11–14), Derrida translates the term *similar* (*homoios*), which refers to the relation of the metaphor of sowing to its literal counterpart, as "the same" (*le même*). Derrida does this in order to support his insistence on Aristotle's centering of meaning within itself, or "logocentricism": "Where has one ever *seen* that there is the same relationship between the sun and its rays as between sowing and seeds?" ("La mythologie blanche," 290). But to say that the scattering of seeds and the sun's rays are *similar* is not to say that they are "the same." Aristotle was expressing his admiration for the fact that this identity is only similar and so a paradoxical "misuse" (catachresis) of what is not for what is. The metaphor of the sun's sowing demonstrates Aristotle's fascination with the uncanny doubling of metaphor which discovers identity where there is none, and so paradoxically defies logic by logic itself.

The significant repetition of the metaphor of motion contained in *epiphora* as well as *metaphora* has been noted by Paul Ricoeur and others: "In order to explain metaphor Aristotle fashions a metaphor borrowed from the order of movement, that of changing place . . . the very word 'metaphor' is thus metaphoric because it is borrowed from another order than that of language." [10] True; but in the *Rhetoric* (3.11) Aristotle says that one purpose of metaphor is to show something in action (*energounta sēmainei*) or in motion (*kinounta*), so that while Aristotle's definition of metaphor is indeed metaphoric, it is no accident that it should be so, but a "true falsehood" which best conveys what Aristotle says is the purpose of metaphor. Another reason *epiphora* is a double "metaphor of metaphoricity"—that is, appropriately inappropriate—is that it gives the impression that in using a metaphor like "the light of reason" I am "conferring in addition" light upon reason rather than its having been there all along, both of which are necessarily true. Like the illicit union of an adulterous couple, the tryst is assumed not to have occurred because it has not yet been discovered. This comparison of metaphor to adultery is not as strange as it might seem, for the strongly proprietary adjective *allotrios* ("belonging to something else"), which also occurs in Aristotle's famous definition of metaphor, is used by Aeschylus to describe courting another man's wife (Aeschylus, *Agamemnon*, 448).

As this use of *allotrios* shows, Aristotle's definition of metaphor requires the distinction between a literal word that "belongs to" its referent and the metaphorical supplement that deviates from yet reestablishes the primacy of identity. In other words, metaphor at once violates and reca-pitulates the law of noncontradiction. It is impossible to conceive of meta-phor, either in general terms or with regard to specific metaphors, except in this double "unified opposition" to the literal, and it is surely no accident that the first analysis of metaphoricity is carried out by the philosopher who also established the so-called "law of noncontradiction."

Aristotle does not, then, view metaphor as simply a deviation from the more fundamental law of noncontradiction, or as an unnecessary redun-dancy.[11] For a proper use of metaphor is a "gift of nature" (*euphuias*), and so there is nothing preventing us from reading Aristotle's famous definition (metaphor as "the addition of a word that belongs to something else") as referring to a transgression of logic that is more fundamental, or logical, than logic itself: "Whence the paradox: how can the literal meaning be 'natural' and the figurative sense 'original'?"[12] Derrida explains this para-doxical "gift" of metaphor as Aristotle's way of controlling its indetermi-nacy through a kind of natural meaning: "Metaphor *returns to* the truth and presence of nature. In metaphor nature rediscovers its proper analogy, its proper resemblance to itself, and can only benefit from itself. In meta-phor nature is presented. That is why, moreover, the power of metaphor is described as a gift of nature."[13] Yet, as Barthes's statement indicates, the relation of this "gift of nature" to the properly literal is double, producing meta-phorical trans-gressions (the two words, which refer to "crossing over," are in a sense synonymous) which are more salutary than the law they violate. Perhaps metaphor's "gift of metaphor" reveals the same dou-bling as that suggested by the English and German "gifts," at once beneficent and poisonous.[14] At any rate, to see Aristotle's reference to the "gift of metaphor" as merely a logocentric strategy of returning meaning to itself is to deny the equally irrational and intuitive nature of metaphor as Aristotle describes it.

Another example of Aristotle's double theory of metaphor is the nec-essary relation between metaphorical clarity and obscurity in both the *Po-etics* and the *Rhetoric*: "The excellence of diction is to be clear but not commonplace . . . we need a mixture of the two" (*Poetics* 22). A rhetorico-poetical style, unlike a philosophic one, must be clearly obscure and ob-scurely clear; Aristotle explicitly relates metaphor to enigma in the *Rheto-ric* (3.10–11) as a way to make language mysterious without being obtuse. However, metaphor can also be seen as more enigmatical than enigma proper by providing "easier learning" than enigma (3.10) *and* by maintain-ing its original obscurity—devoid, that is, of any unequivocal solution.

Although metaphor is singly opposed to *hoi kurioi kai hoi oikeioi*—common, literal words—in the *Rhetoric* (versus the ternary division of the *Poetics* discussed above), it is also its own opposite, for "it is metaphor that gives perspicuity" as well as "pleasure, and a foreign air" (3.2.7–8). Metaphor is thus "uncanny" in the strict Freudian sense ("On the Uncanny") because it is foreign and so "not of the house" (*unheimlich*), as well as being familiar and "of the house" (*heimlich*): "Thus it is clear that if the speaker is good, his speech will be foreign, unnoticeable and clear, and this is the chief merit of rhetorical language. . . . It is metaphor above all that gives perspicuity, pleasure, and a foreign air" (*Rhetoric* 3.2.4–10; translation slightly modified).

If metaphor "cannot be learnt from another" it is because one cannot learn to produce this "foreign air." To teach someone how to be different is a contradiction in terms. The unteachability of metaphor (*pace* Richards) also explains why, as Aristotle elsewhere insists, metaphor "teaches us" (*Rhetoric* 3.10.2). But, again, we must admit that this "unteachability" is elsewhere contradicted by Aristotle's more schematic approach to the genus-species structure underlying metaphor. Contrary to those who focus on one or the other of these two sides of Aristotle's approach to metaphor, I would like to suggest that the metaphoric double requires this unteachable teachability.

A curious shift in the terminology used to describe metaphor occurs between the *Rhetoric* and *Poetics* which further demonstrates this doubling. At *Rhetoric* 3.10.6 Aristotle says, "As to words, they are popular if they contain metaphor, provided it be neither strange [*allotrian*], for then it is difficult to take in at a glance, nor superficial, for then it does not impress the hearer." Aristotle uses the same adjective, *allotrios* ("belonging to another"), which we saw was a crucial word in the definition of metaphor given in the *Poetics*, to mean exactly the opposite here. In the *Poetics* a metaphor was said to be *allotrios* because it "belonged to another" word than that to which it figuratively referred. In the *Rhetoric* Aristotle says that "a metaphor should not belong to something else" because it would therefore be too inappropriate and obscure. Metaphor is truly uncanny and double, for it must be something other than itself in order to be itself.

Aristotle's well-known preference for metaphor over simile is also clarified by the more enigmatical nature of metaphor. Metaphor is a patent absurdity which requires that we provide the solution to its enigma, but simile is "less pleasant because it is longer; it does not say that this is that, so that the mind does not even examine this" (*Rhetoric* 3.10.3); in other words, simile explains itself, whereas metaphor leaves logic in abeyance. Judging from Aristotle's preference for the surprise of metaphorical recognition over the explanation of similes, the cognitive element shared by both is not the decisive one. What is decisive is what metaphor shares with jokes, paradoxes, parables, and other species of wit (*ta asteia*); namely, a physiological release of pleasure that accompanies any sudden recognition:

> Easy learning is naturally pleasant to all, and words mean something, so that all words which make us learn something are most pleasant. Now we do not know the meaning of strange words [*glottai*], and proper terms we know already. It is metaphor, therefore, that above all produces this effect. . . . For the simile, as we have said, is a metaphor differing only by the addition of a word, wherefore it is less pleasant because it is longer; it does not say that this is that, so that the mind does not even examine this. Of necessity, therefore, all style and enthymemes that give us rapid information [*mathêsin taxeian*] are smart. . . . Most smart sayings [*ta asteia*] are derived from metaphor, and also from misleading the hearer beforehand. For it becomes more evident to him that he has learnt something, when the conclusion turns out contrary to his expectation, and the mind seems to say, "How true it is! but I missed it." And smart apothegms arise from not meaning what one says . . . and clever riddles are agreeable for the same reason; for something is learnt, and the expression is also metaphorical. (*Rhetoric* 3.10–11)

There is an important similarity between this sudden recognition of metaphor and the tragic catharsis resulting from *anagnorisis* and *peripeteia* described in the *Poetics*.[15] Simile, enigmas, and the other varieties of wit are all subordinated to metaphor ("It is metaphor *above all* that produces this effect") if they do not move quickly enough to provide the feeling of delight accompanying surprise. Despite the fact that Aristotle is himself being more witty than precise in his denunciation of similes for being too labored, the rationale behind his preference has justification. The sudden recognition that is the essence of metaphor for Aristotle would not be possible if two unrelated terms (for example, sowing, the sun) were not enigmatically related. So Derrida is not entirely correct when he attacks Aristotelian metaphor as "a tool of knowledge" ("La mythologie blanche," 283), although it is certainly that too. Metaphor manifests its enigmatic, double structure by denying the very logic that informs it, by revealing not what it reveals (that is, its secondary cognitive factor) but what is not revealed, what is lost as soon as it is recognized as being "of the house," proper and literal, all along. If Aristotle chooses, at other times, to emphasize the classificatory schemas underlying metaphor, that should not blind us to the fact that it is the simultaneous construction and destruction, *de-con-struction*, required by all true doublings that prompted Aristotle's persistent fascination with the enigma of metaphor.

Richards, Black, Beardsley, and the Interaction Theory of Metaphor

One distressing feature of writing about metaphor is that a certain error seems inherent to the project. More particularly, a pattern emerges when one examines the numerous attempts to define metaphor since Aristotle's that begin by claiming some new insight into the understanding of how metaphor works and then proceed to buttress their claims by opposing them to any of a number of other theories that all made similar discoveries.[16] The spectacle of critics who have successively emerged to resolve the enigma of metaphoric doubling only seems to add to the certainty of finally explaining it; like Oedipus, critics realize too late that the more fiercely they distinguish their own pursuit, the more certainly they are bound to catch themselves—if such a thing were possible.

Although I. A. Richards begins his celebrated treatment of metaphor with an attack on "the evil presence of three of the assumptions" contained in Aristotle's theory, his own theory of the "interaction" between metaphor's two "antithetical" components—"tenor" and "vehicle"—is not fundamentally opposed to Aristotle's theory.[17] Indeed, the fault which Richards lays at Aristotle's door (the "three assumptions" are really one) never touches directly on Aristotle's notion of metaphoric transference from a literal to a figurative *onoma*. Richards instead attacks Aristotle's well-known idea that a good metaphor is "something special and exceptional in the use of language" and that, correspondingly, its practitioner is someone exceptional, not someone who has learned how to make good metaphors in school. In defense of Aristotle, his comments are explicitly and specifically directed toward a "command" of metaphor in a poetic context, and the philosopher himself points out, early in the *Poetics*, that this context is closely related to our general epistemological development. And, as we have just seen, Aristotle's notion of metaphor as enigmatic and its use as ingenious is an extraordinary admission from one whose analytic acumen usually blinds him to metaphor's less rational workings.

Nonetheless, Richards's doctrine of metaphoric "interaction" seems to offer a more democratic view than Aristotle's more condescending notion of the metaphoric substitution of a "foreign" name: "When we use a metaphor we have two thoughts of different things active together and supported by a single word, or phrase, whose meaning is a result of their interaction" (*The Philosophy of Rhetoric*, 93).

These "two thoughts," as Richards explains, are the metaphor's tenor and vehicle. The vehicle is the metaphorical word itself, the tenor "the underlying idea or principal subject," "what is really being said or thought" (*The Philosophy of Rhetoric*, 96–97). The tenor, "what is really being said," seems at first view to mark the resurgence of the Aristotelian ground, the native word infested by its metaphorical parasite. But, despite Richards's allusion to a ground and some "underlying principle," he is in fact referring to some mysterious, oscillating entity that has the features of Aristotle's native referent while maintaining its figurative status. For, later, this notion of a ground which characterized the tenor is applied to the entire metaphorical unit, tenor and vehicle included:

> The co-presence of the vehicle and tenor results in a meaning (to be clearly distinguished from the tenor) which is not attainable without their interaction. . . . At one extreme the vehicle may become almost a mere decoration or coloring of the tenor, at the other extreme, the tenor may become almost a mere excuse for the introduction of the vehicle, and so no longer be "the principle subject." (*The Philosophy of Rhetoric*, 100)

The essence of Richards's definition of metaphor is contained in this notion of a ground which is at once the ground of metaphor and the metaphor of the ground. The "underlying idea" which constitutes the tenor of Richards's metaphor is in fact inseparable from its "antithetical" vehicle. Likewise, the referential sense or meaning of the metaphor is found in the tenor itself and also in the relationship between tenor and vehicle: "We can extract the tenor and believe that as a statement; or extract the vehicle; or, taking tenor and vehicle together, contemplate . . . their relations" (*The Philosophy of Rhetoric*, 135). In his appraisal of this "problem" with Richards's theory, Paul Ricoeur also notes that the distinction between the figurative and literal components of metaphor is both suspended and maintained:

> One has seen that the pairing of "tenor" and "vehicle" entirely ignores this distinction [between the literal and the metaphoric meaning]. . . . the distinction between the literal and the metaphoric is not irrecuperable, but it no longer results from the words' so-called proper meaning; it results from the manner in which the interaction functions on the basis of the theory of contextual meaning. . . . moreover, literal language becomes something quite rare outside of the technical languages of the sciences. (*La métaphore vive*, 107)

The intriguing possibility accounted for in Richards's theory and in Ricoeur's critique of it is that, while we cannot dispense with the idea of the literal in talking about metaphor, or in using metaphor, any literalization of either of these two components cannot be taken literally, and cannot in fact be grounded. The play of difference ascribed by Richards to the doubling of tenor and vehicle is also ascribed to the larger relationship between *signifier* and *signified*, and hence to language itself. Since "*thought is metaphoric, and proceeds by comparisons, and the metaphors of language derive therefrom*" (94), we are therefore justified in inferring that the constant interplay between tenor and vehicle, which produces meaning even as it is taken away, is ultimately derived from the similar doubling of signifier—which, according to Saussure and others, is without meaning—and signified, which is only meaning.

Max Black's contribution to the interaction theory of metaphor offers a philosopher's critical awareness of the metaphoricity of theoretical attempts to "pin down" metaphor.[18] For example, discussing the classical view that metaphor, considered an elided simile, provides fruitful comparisons, Black decries a "vagueness that borders upon vacuity" (*Models and Metaphors*, 37). What troubles Black, and leads him to offer his own version of the interaction theory, is that a metaphor doesn't really—literally—compare things. The strength of figures (even, I might add, of Homeric similes) seems to increase proportionally as any middle ground vanishes. We do, of course, always feel a middle ground to be there, but we can thereby only compare the figure to a comparison, versus its literally being one. Black's point is a good one and will have to be kept in mind as we analyze his own theory of metaphoric interaction. A successful metaphor will always leave out of the comparison something which lends the metaphor its power. Even a much-abused trope like Burns's "red, red rose" regains its beauty immediately when we reflect how strange and unexplained the "comparison" to his beloved really is.

All three critics we have discussed thus far would agree that metaphor has a dual aspect that is the result of the metaphor's relation to its literal context. Richards and Black argue that there is "interaction" between the two, but Black criticizes Richards's "fiction" that this interaction occurs between "ideas": "This picture of two *ideas* working upon each other is an inconvenient fiction" (*Models and Metaphors*, 47; Black's italics). The interaction of ideas or, we might say, names is a fiction because, like the "vague" notion of comparison, the two separate ideas do not themselves really interact. Something happens between the two ideas, but it is that something, and not the ideas, which is responsible for the metaphorical interaction. Put differently, if the ideas—Richards's tenor and vehicle—are really separate, they cannot be united in the metaphor.

In order to resolve this difficulty Black posits his intermediary "associated commonplaces." These *topoi* (the original rhetorical term for "commonplaces") are designed to fill the gap between the two ideas, which is the "common place" where the interaction is thought to occur. While similar to Aristotle's proportional metaphor, which also posits analogous middle terms (the darkness of ignorance would thus be understood by Aristotle to mediate between "light" and "reason"), the interplay of Black's *topoi* is more fluid than Aristotle's rigid schematization allows: "The associated commonplaces themselves suffer metaphorical change of meaning in the process of transfer" (*Models and Metaphors*, 42).

To describe the metaphorical process Black nonetheless relies on terms that are unabashedly rhetorical and metaphoric. Since light (to remain with the example just mentioned) cannot be directly related to reason, a common ground of intermediary ideas is posited which, although it doubtless contains analogous terms like Aristotle's, makes no pretense of filling in this space and eliding the gap that separates the metaphorical term from the literal one. But the very notion of such a common ground existing between metaphor and its referent is just as "fictional" as the notion that metaphor compares one thing to another. Because every metaphor involves a doubling that gives us "two ideas for one" (note that Johnson does not say that metaphor gives us one idea for two), those eager to discover the logic of metaphor are tempted to posit a *tertium quid* that would help ease the contradiction by assuming that somewhere in between the metaphor and its context there are related terms—"associated commonplaces"—that resolve this contradiction. Indeed, the metaphor of an intelligence at work in the metaphorical process is not merely implicit in Black's description: "The metaphor selects, emphasizes, suppresses and organizes features of the principal subject" (*Models and Metaphors*, 44). And so, despite Black's praiseworthy efforts to avoid a fictional, rhetorical, and metaphorical description of metaphor, he, too, falls into the same trap of defining metaphor metaphorically in order to understand—and that means to unify—its inherent doubling.

Caution should be urged, however, with regard to what may be viewed as the equally dogmatic notion that we cannot literalize the metaphorical process. Since none of the three theoreticians implies that their analyses are consciously present in the mind of the one creating or the one appreciating metaphor, it could be objected that a borderline between two very different kinds of questions is ignored here, and that attempts to explain how metaphor works cannot be challenged by demonstrating how metaphor is not reducible to an analysis of the origin of its unity. To explain metaphoric unity is not to unify metaphor.

This criticism would be valid if metaphor involved a basic structural unity to which differences, like so many ornaments or spices, are added.

But, for every living metaphor (dead metaphors are those which have been in some sense reduced to one term), the so-called basis of unity posited by Aristotle, Richards, and Black must itself remain merely analogical, since the essential effect of metaphor is to deny any unity it affirms—*including this*, to add a qualification which I show in the following chapter to be essential to Protagoras's metaphorical view of rhetorical thought. Indeed, because of this "even that" we cannot literalize the metaphoric process; metaphor neither posits a meaning nor fails to posit one. Metaphor, like a rhetorical statement, remains fully meaningful despite the fact that it never means what it says. It is only thus that statements made here like "There is no such thing as metaphor" can have any meaning in a theory of metaphor.

Monroe Beardsley's "controversion theory" of metaphor is formulated in deliberate contrast to three other theories ("emotive," "supervenience," "literalist") which "have all been held at one time or another."[19] Beardsley does not, however, reject these three types, which continue to play an important, if subordinate, role in his own theory. Indeed, the meaning of Beardsley's "controversion theory" becomes clear only when placed alongside the other three, for its function is to emphasize the largely negative aspect of metaphor which the other theories tend to ignore. The cognition-related literalist and "supervenience" theories stress, respectively, the elided middle term which explains the metaphor and any new or additional meanings that metaphor provides. Beardsley, echoing Black, insists that both these theories (the first, "emotive" type being criticized as insufficient in explaining what metaphor does) ignore the crucial fact about metaphor, that it never actually provides the analogical or novel meaning it supposedly supplies ("A metaphor is not an implied comparison"; *Aesthetics*, 138).

The great value of Beardsley's theory is its bold insistence ˯˯ ʳhe logical absurdity of metaphor:

> The fourth theory of metaphor I shall call the *Controversion Theory.*
> This odd name is the best I have been able to discover for either the theory of metaphor or the general rhetorical strategy of which it is a species. Consider first a certain kind of discourse, to be called *Self-Controverting Discourse.* Its essential principle is that the speaker or writer utters a statement explicitly but in such a way as to show that he does not believe what he states, or is not primarily interested in what he states, and thereby call attention to something else that he has not explicitly stated—"If he wins, I'll eat my hat." It is discourse that says more than it states, by canceling out the primary meaning to make room for secondary meaning. . . . the reader can see that you are not asserting the statement you make (to assert is to evince and to invite belief), but since the statement is made, and something is presumably being asserted, he

looks about for a second level of meaning on which something *is* being said. And in poetry the chief tactic for obtaining this result is that of *logical absurdity*. In other words, it is the logical absurdity of statements in poems that gives them meaning on the second level. (*Aesthetics*, 138)

In laying stress on the "rhetorical strategy" of metaphor Beardsley's theory is strongly reminiscent of Protagoras's *dissoi logoi*—the notion that every truth can be contested—as the metaphorical, versus metaphysical, ground of rhetorical meaning. A metaphor, Beardsley insists, is neither what it says nor what it means because, as a "logical absurdity," it says nothing. However else metaphor may function *secondarily* in conjuring up new or additional meanings, Beardsley emphasizes the disparity, or difference, between the two elements involved in every metaphor: "Stern's emphasis [Gustaf Stern, *Meaning and Change of Meaning*] on the "fusion of disparate elements" in a metaphor, and on the "tension between the actual context and the primary meaning" of the modifier are in line with the controversion theory" (*Aesthetics*, 161).

Most theories of metaphor since and including Aristotle's have placed metaphor squarely in the service of meaning. Indeed, one could even argue, as was done in the previous discussion of Aristotle's definition, that the logic that supposedly governs metaphor is a direct result of its literal significance: if a metaphor refers to something objective, then it must do so by virtue of something objective. For Beardsley, on the other hand, the "meaning" of metaphor is the self-negating controversion of its two terms: "In other words, it is the logical absurdity of statements in poems that gives them meaning on the second level" (*Aesthetics*, 138). And if the meaning of metaphor is absurd, what causes us to look for secondary meanings is the belief that, because the author is at least as aware of this absurdity as we are, there must be some reason behind the manifest lack of one.

The only flaw in Beardsley's controversion theory is that, while rightly laying stress on the negative aspect of metaphor—its irreducibility to some common term—this contradictory aspect is not primary, nor are the more positive aspects of metaphor relegated to the first three theories "secondary." Although a metaphor can be shown to contain some formal contradiction, the metaphor itself is neither logical nor, which is almost the same thing, illogical. That there is something else at work in a metaphor is readily apparent from the fact that, while many metaphors are in some sense contradictory, the converse of this relationship is rarely true.

There is, to be sure, profound insight into the workings of metaphor displayed by Beardsley's account; note, for example, the way it explains the uncanniness of a literary interpretation which, although concocted by the critic, seems vouchsafed by the authority of the text. But when we observe our response to a genuine metaphor the contradiction that is doubtless present is never explicit, and a logical contradiction that is not explicit is not really a contradiction. Consider, for example, Yeats's brief poem "The Balloon of the Mind":

> Hands, do what you're bid:
> Bring the balloon of the mind
> That bellies and drags in the wind
> Into its narrow shed.

We do not, as Beardsley would have it, begin with the absurdity of calling the mind a balloon and then search for secondary meanings to justify its usage—not even unconsciously. Beardsley fails to consider another possibility, that, just as every successful metaphor is in a sense a true catachresis in suspending the contradiction which exists between the two different things involved, that same contradiction continues to exist before, during, and after the unity essential to metaphor is realized. The double "contradiction of contradiction" is and is not a contradiction.

Nietzsche and the Metaphoric Double

The importance of Nietzsche's early essay "Über Wahrheit und Lüge im aussermoralischen Sinne" ("On Truth and Lies in an Extra-Moral Sense," 1873) for discussions of metaphoricity or Nietzsche's thought in general can hardly be overestimated. For example, while ostensibly discussing Nietzsche's attitude to metaphor throughout his works, Sarah Kofman returns repeatedly to this essay to establish or develop her analysis of Nietzsche and metaphor.[20] Derrida, de Man, and J. Hillis Miller are but three of the other prominent literary philosophers to single out "Truth and Lies" in recent years,[21] thus supporting Paul de Man's contention that "the general drift" of Nietzsche's thought on rhetorical and linguistic matters "can be better understood by taking into account texts that precede the 1873 Course on Rhetoric, especially the never-completed *Philosophenbuch*."[22] Although the present discussion will focus on a passage from the concluding pages of Nietzsche's essay not previously discussed by the writers just mentioned, I too use Nietzsche's essay to approach the all-important question of the epistemological status of truth in a system governed by the law of metaphoric doubling.

Two key terms in Nietzsche's essay are *Verstellung* ("dissimulation") and *Vergesslichkeit* ("forgetfulness"). *Verstellung* is closely related to the notion of metaphoricity under discussion. The word itself is synonymous with *meta-pherein*, "to put one thing in place of another."[23] Moreover, the sense of impropriety attached to metaphor since Aristotle first defined the term also accrues to *Verstellung*. For just as Aristotle defined metaphor as "the addition [*epiphora*] of a word which belongs to something else [*onomatos allotriou*],"[24] *Ver-stellung* does not only mean putting one thing in place of another but putting something that does not properly belong there in place of something that does; in short, a "deception" (Nietzsche uses *Verstellung* and *Taüschung* interchangeably).[25]

As the deceptive metaphoric process of putting something that does not belong there in place of something that does, *Verstellung* is at work from the very outset of Nietzsche's essay:

> Once upon a time, *in some out of the way corner of that universe which is dispersed into numberless twinkling solar systems*, there was a star upon which clever beasts invented knowing. That was the most arrogant and mendacious minute of "world history," but nevertheless, it was only a minute . . . and only its possessor and begetter takes it so solemnly—*as though the world's axis turned with it*. But if we could communicate with the gnat, we would learn that he likewise flies through the air with the same solemnity, *that he feels the flying center of the universe within himself*. There is nothing so reprehensible and unimportant in nature that it would not immediately swell up like a balloon at the slightest puff of the power of knowing. ("Truth and Lies," 79; italics mine)

Contained within Nietzsche's famous critique of that form of humanism which interprets Protagoras's *homo-mensura* statement as placing mankind at the center of all things is the idea of metaphoric *Verstellung* as essential to the act of knowing.[26] This occurs because knowledge (*Er-kennen* versus *Wissen*, *Vernünft*, *Verstehen*, and so on) is an act of appropriation ("only its possessor and begetter takes it so solemnly") that converts whatever belongs to it into what is. Humans occupy the center of the universe solely through their presumptuous assumption (*Hochmut*) that what is known is what *is* whereas what is unknown is decentered, banished to that corner of the universe where humanity actually resides. In arrogating the center to ourselves we tell time to be our time, place to be our place, and so displace the multiplicity of nature with a human reality that, as Nietzsche later explains, cannot have even the slightest connection with the decentered chaos of "nature."

Unlike the traditional derivation of literal from figurative language found in Rousseau and others,[27] Nietzsche's original metaphoricity immediately turns into literal knowledge (*Erkennen*) because the attraction of replacing originary chaos with a metaphor, image, or *Bild* that can claim to be real is irresistible: "There is nothing so reprehensible and unimportant in nature that it would not immediately swell up like a balloon at the slightest puff of the power of knowing. . . . even the proudest of men, the philosopher, supposes that he sees on all sides the eyes of the universe telescopically focused upon his action and thought." The "power of knowing," "die Kraft des Erkennens," is irresistible because the feeling of power of appropriating the unknown, of becoming the center of experience, is irresistible. Knowledge may well be later described as the antithesis of metaphoricity, but at the beginning of Nietzsche's essay we can see already that the dissimulations of knowledge and metaphor cannot really be opposed.

The second key term for Nietzsche's understanding of metaphoricity in "Truth and Lies" is *Vergesslichkeit*, "forgetfulness." If knowledge is not objective, neither is the apparently impartial medium of language that conveys that knowledge. The tautological structure of literal, logical language is not knowledge of what something really is, but just the opposite: the elimination of individual reality and the resultant forgetfulness (*Vergesslichkeit*) that constitutes consciousness: "It is only by means of forgetfulness that man can ever reach the point of fancying himself to possess a 'truth'" ("Truth and Lies," 81). A = A not because it is reality "according to itself," but because "man" has taken the individual structure A = A and left out the bar; indeed, the figure Nietzsche uses for the tautological structure of knowledge is that of empty husks (*Hülsen*). Knowledge as A = A is an empty husk because, like the coin whose *Bild*—emblem, picture—is eventually effaced, like the pyramids and columbaria also described in Nietzsche's essay, something vital has perished or been forgotten in order that knowledge may become known.

However strange Nietzsche's notion that by remembering we forget and so by forgetting we remember, it is in fact a rather common reversal, at least within the romantic tradition.[28] One might also note the similarity between Nietzsche's notion that by remembering we forget a greater, more primitive reality and Freud's notion of consciousness as forgetting. Yet this distinction between intuitive forgetfulness and conceptual remembering is, in accordance with Nietzsche's fundamental notions, not "hard and fast," particularly with respect to metaphor. If "[conceptual] truths are illusions we have forgotten are illusions" ("Truth and Lies," 84), then metaphors must be illusions we remember are illusions. But what are we to make of metaphors whose epistemological status compels us to remember as well as to forget? Such would surely be the status of "living metaphors" which are neither hardened concepts nor animal intuitions. This middle term of figurative doubling unsettles the comfortable opposition between remembering and forgetting by the curious condition of illusions we remember to forget and forget to remember. We can now turn to Nietzsche's remarkable passage concerning the appearance of the Greek gods to exemplify this anomalous, doubling condition of metaphoricity.

Nietzsche has more in common with such romantics as Friedrich Schlegel, whose notion of "a perpetual parabasis"[29] is close to Nietzsche's forgotten remembering, than with Pascal, whose *pensée* about the workman dreaming he is king Nietzsche has to distort in order to make it fit his notion that reality is a dream which we have forgotten is a dream.[30] This forgotten dream is inferior to more "mobile" (*bewegliche*) dreams of which forgetting is constituent, and not forgotten. Like a coin that is passed from hand to hand until its image is lost, and like the metaphoric word which, through the same plebeian usage, acquires its meaning only by losing it and "dying," reality is merely one dream among an infinite number of others that is drained—"disembossed"—of its significance. However Nietzsche is not, as some lesser romantic might, naively reinscribing reality within the realm of dream. Far from being either remembered or forgotten, myths, metaphors, and dreams all have the double status of masks whose revelation is their own disguise.

> Because of the way that myth takes it for granted that miracles are always happening, the waking life of a mythically inspired people—the ancient Greeks, for instance—more closely resembles a dream than it does the waking world of a scientifically disenchanted thinker . . . when even the goddess Athena herself is suddenly seen in the company of Peisistratus driving through the market place of Athens with a beautiful team of horses—and this is what the honest Athenian believed—*then, as in a dream, anything is possible at each moment, and all of nature swarms around man as if it were nothing but a masquerade of the gods, who were merely amusing themselves by deceiving men in all these shapes.* ("Truth and Lies," 89; italics mine)

I would like to focus on the final lines of this remarkable passage, beginning with Nietzsche's important reference to the "moment" (*Augenblick*).[31] The situation as Nietzsche describes it is, again, not unlike Schlegel's *permanente Parekbase*, where every gesture of "direct address" (*parabasis* is synonymous with the rhetorical figure of *apostrophe*) is a simultaneous assertion of reality and its fiction. Similarly, here *every* appearance of the gods is a deception, a *Verstellung*, so that, far from being drained of their significance, the gods' appearance cannot be said to be a deception. If the gods are deceiving us "in all their shapes," then they exist in a state of deception that is their reality, a state where remembering is always already forgotten.

The metaphoric process is synonymous for Nietzsche with just such a masquerade. Every metaphor wears a mask that, according to Richards's classic terminology, corresponds to the metaphor's "vehicle."[32] Just as Nietzsche's gods reveal themselves only in disguises, metaphors reveal their truth in masks that also veil their hidden truth. The truth of metaphor is an illusion, but, unlike the lesser "illusion of an illusion" involved in assuming knowledge of what the metaphor means, metaphor is a "true illusion" because its "vehicle" (like Athena's chariot) is never what metaphor is or means. Nietzsche's metaphoric "forgetfulness" (*Vergesslichkeit*) thus returns us to the notion of doubling with which we began this chapter, that of a process whereby the truth is the same as and other than itself (*hetero kath' hauto*).

2 | The Rhetorical Double
Protagoras and the Dissoi Logoi

ANY DISCUSSION OF Protagoras's *dissoi logoi*, the notion that "On every question there are two opposing statements—including this one," [1] must begin with the theory of perception (*aisthēsis*) upon which the sophist-rhetor's entire system of thought is based: "elege te mēden einai psuchēn para tas aisthēseis, katha kai Platōn phēsin en Theaitētōi [He said too that soul was nothing apart from its sensations, according to Plato's *Theaetetus*]." [2]

In the part of the *Theaetetus* where this fragment is quoted (152ff.), Protagoras's union of the soul with "perception" (*aisthēsis*) is equated with a relativistic position that would deny humans' relation to reality in itself in lieu of the relative relation (*einai pros ti*) of things to man. [3] If, Plato argues, Protagoras meant to equate thought with the sensory realm, this would be tantamount to a reduction of truth to the experience of every individual. Nor would there be any reason to prefer one mind over another, since everyone's individual thought or sense-perception is created equal. Plato's jibe, that Protagoras would have made a better impression with his theories if he had made a pig the measure of all things, [4] is a reaction against this same notion, for not only would every individual's perception be equal to any other's, but it would also be equal to that of a pig.

In Sextus's account as well as in the *Theaetetus*, this relativism is joined with a materialism that might at first seem contradictory:

> phēsin oun ho anēr tēn hulēn rheustēn einai, rheousēs de autēs sun-echōs prostheseis anti tōn aprophorēseōn gignesthai kai tas aisthēseis metakosmeithai te kai alloiousthai para te [tas] hēlikias kai para tas allas kataskeuas tōn sōmatōn. Legei de kai tous logous pantōn tōn phai-nomenōn hupokeisthai en tēi eph' heautēi panta einai hosa pasi phain-etai.
>
> [Now what he says is that matter is in a state of flux, and that as it changes there is a continuous replacement of the effluvia which it gives off; that, moreover, one's sensations undergo change and alteration in accordance with one's age and other aspects of one's bodily condition. He says too that the reasons [*logoi*] of all the appearances are present in

the matter, so that the matter is capable, as far as lies in its own power, of being everything that appears to everybody.][5]

The material to which Protagoras joins perception is thus not outside, but the same as the thought itself. Although some scholars, scandalized by the apparent absurdity of joining thought to matter, have censured these accounts, there is no good reason for rejecting such a notion out of hand.[6] If Protagoras based his system of thought on the notion that "thought is nothing but perception," he likely viewed thought as a kind of sixth sense, with the same material basis as the others.[7] Language (*logos*)[8] would undoubtedly have to share with thought its material and relativistic status as *aisthēsis*; every *logos*, like every sensory percept, would thus be true by itself, not in referring to any reality outside it. This helps to explain Protagoras's emergence as sophist, rhetor, and epistemologist, for, since every speech-act becomes ipso facto meaningful, the sophist will naturally turn his attention to language as itself productive of meaning.

If Protagoras identified *logos* with mankind as the perceptor and with speech as the sense faculty of knowing, is knowledge as perception no longer knowledge, since everything that is spoken is inherently true? Such, at least, is Plato's understanding of Protagoras's doctrine. In the *Theaetetus* Socrates argues that to equate knowledge with perception as Protagoras does (152c) is to make any *logos* a *muthos*, and he bases his critique, as Protagoras based his system, on the ephemeral nature of sensory perception. We might even take Plato's criticism even further. Since *aisthēsis* is in constant flux as a result of its contingency upon a constantly changing present moment, "as being all of them of whatever kind generated by motion in their intercourse with one another," one might even say that sensation does not even exist for the individual. Socrates concludes:

And this is true of all sensible objects, hard, warm, and the like, which are similarly to be regarded, as I was saying before, not as having any absolute existence, but as being all of them of whatever kind generated by motion in their intercourse with one another; for of the agent and patient, as existing in separation, no trustworthy conception, as they say, can be formed, for the agent has no existence until united with the patient, and the patient has no existence until united with the agent; and that which by uniting with something becomes an agent, by meeting with some other thing is converted into a patient. And from all these considerations, as I said at first, there arises a general reflection, that there is no one self-existent thing, but everything is becoming and in relation; and being must be altogether abolished, although from habit and ignorance we are compelled even in this discussion to retain the use of the term. (*Theaetetus* 157)[9]

Nothing is hard, nothing is soft; nothing is hot, nothing is cold, "but thinking makes it so." Language, as a matter of convenience, misrepresents the flux of sensory percepts and perceptions by calling them names that are not properly ascribed to either (Nietzsche says much the same thing in "On Truth and Lies in an Extra-Moral Sense").[10] Sensation proper is always other: this paper's color is different from whiteness, and the pure sensation is different from this paper's color, since sensation is never any object as such. Any theory of knowledge built upon sensory perception is a myth, because based upon objects that are always other for individuals who are also always other.[11]

Having disposed of the knowability of sensory perception, Socrates also attacks what he perceives to be Protagoras's intention to make the individual the criterion of what is true.[12] Since no individual can make a false statement out of what is merely an individual perception, knowledge that is obviously not merely the individual's truth but a proper way of doing something in accordance with the laws of its own *technē* would seem to be controverted. But with this mention of *technē*, a common term for the rhetorician's "technique," the reader is reminded that Plato has gone too far in depicting Protagoras as a kind of antiepistemologist. Indeed, it is possible to argue that Protagoras's notion of the *logos* does not even imply subjectivism, let alone solipsism.

As has already been shown, language or thought in the Protagorean system has the status of perception (*aisthēsis*); whatever *logos*, word or thought is, is true, not in referring to any reality outside itself, but in its own appearance as speech. Like perception, language is viewed as inherently correct, and truth is not defined in the currency of unchanging ideas "in accordance with themselves" (*kath' hautos*) but as the very act of speaking. The difference between these two modes—between meaning "according to itself" and "according to me"—is not as great as Plato would have it. It is because Plato mistakenly assumes that the problems inherent in sensory perception would automatically reappear in a *logos* which is based on *aisthēsis* that he is able to forge a wedge between his own philosophy and that of Sophists like Protagoras. As far as sense perception goes, Plato (and Protagoras) was correct: no one would try to teach, or persuade, anyone else that a color or taste is other than its individual manifestation (they might, of course, suggest the possibility of adopting another such perception). But a *logos*, or thought, that appears as inherently correct neither has the evanescence of pure perception nor is it the special provenance of the individual. Any *logos* that is true according to me is also, unlike perceptions, meant to be true for all other me's and hence true for everyone.

When I make a statement or *logos* referring, say, to this color as blue

I am saying this color is at least potentially blue for everyone, for the notion of blue is not my own but belongs to the system of language and so to others as well. And if I say to someone, "I am warm," though the feeling itself cannot be communicated outside the individual, I am referring, not to the feeling itself, but to what I have learned is the reaction of everyone to such a feeling. Anything "I" say or hold to be true is meant to be true for everyone (it may not be, and, as we shall find postulated by Protagoras in other statements like that of the *dissoi logoi*, it cannot be). So Socrates' statement to Theaetetus (152a) that "things which appear true to me are true for me, and things which appear true to you are true for you" ignores the important fact that, unlike sensation, a *logos* is meant to be true for others. The problem, then, with Plato's attribution of subjectivism to Protagoras[13] is that the *logos* is not really relative to the individual strictly speaking, but to the individual's perception of the truth for him- or herself as well as for others.

This refutation of Plato's critique is similar to the "defense" that Socrates generously provides Protagoras as a way of defending himself against this challenge to knowledge:

> For I declare that the truth is as I have written, and that each of us is a measure of existence and of non-existence. Yet one man may be a thousand times better than another in proportion as different things are and appear to him. And I am far from saying that wisdom and the wise man have no existence; but I say that the wise man is he who makes the evils which appear and are to a man into goods which are and appear to him. And I would beg you not to press my words in the letter, but to take the meaning of them as I will explain them. Remember what has been already said, that to the sick man his food appears to be and is bitter, and to the man in health the opposite of bitter. Now I cannot conceive that one of these men can be or ought to be made wiser than the other: nor can you assert that the sick man because he has one impression is foolish, and the healthy man because he has another is wise; but the one state requires to be changed into the other, the worse into the better. As in education, a change of state has to be effected, and the sophist accomplishes by words the change which the physician works by the aid of drugs. (*Theaetetus* 167)

To the *aisthēsis* of sensation, which is strictly relative to the individual, are added other, nonsensual perceptions that are true, not only for me, but also for others. Once the notion of *aisthēsis* is broadened to include nonsensual perception as well, it is possible for some to have perceptions others do not and then to communicate them, even to persuade another to change his or her mind. Still others may come along to replace these, but this does not mean that the latter perceptions are false, since the same is true of the former, ad infinitum. Knowledge is thereby salvaged from the danger that every perception is true by the fact that not all perceptions are determined by each individual, as is the case for sensory perception.

Protagoras's defense clearly shows that the *logos* as perception is not only true for each individual, but can be directed toward others as well. The physician's drug, to which the sophist's *logos* is compared, produces an effect unrelated to its immediate sensation, not for any individual, but for mankind in general. Similarly, the sophist's *logos* produces an argument that is aimed at being true for all others. Whether or not this "defense" is faithful to Protagoras's own thought, and there are those who think it is,[14] it supports the argument that the *aisthēsis* of language is not the subjective objectification of each person separately but of people joined together by a common system of discourse. The sophist-rhetor's *logos* differs from any individual's perception of the truth in proffering notions which are true for others but which, like the product of any *technē*, are not yet part of the common understanding. Protagoras's ideal rhetorician would seem to have more in common with the eighteenth-century notion of an educated (*gebildet*) person of "taste" than with Plato's notion of the sophist as solipsistic.[15]

The relevance of Protagoras's "aesthetic" system to sophistic and rhetorical theory in general ought to be apparent. The sophist-rhetor's goal, unlike the philosopher's, is not knowledge of reality but the communication of a perceivable truth. The sophist, as Protagoras insists in his "defense," does not replace a false account with a true one, but persuades his audience that his account is also theirs and, conversely, that their own account is not what they really believe to be true. It is possible, Protagoras says, to "replace" (*metaballein*) one opinion with a better one, but not with one that is truer. Ultimately, it may be questioned whether philosophy, although its intention is different, offers anything else. Indeed, the pretense of rejecting one person's account as false in an effort to discover the truth may be the rhetorical gesture par excellence, and one whereby rhetoric is replaced with a mode of discourse more persuasive, if not more true.

Finally, it is also possible to discern in Protagoras's "aestheticism" what later became the rhetorical emphasis on the *form* of discourse. By the time Aristotle came to write his monumental treatise on *Rhetoric*, this will have become the dominant feature of rhetoric.[16] Because Protagoras's criterion for the truth of any statement is that it appears to be true, and because language is intrinsically true, the sophist *qua* rhetor will not fail to focus on language as itself truth. Attention to what later was called style (*lexis*) is a natural consequence of Protagoras's system, for its effect on an audience cannot be separated from the truth of discourse. But these consequences are more apparent in Protagoras's successor, Gorgias of Leontini; Protagoras's attention to language took the form of the first attempts at separating the grammatical parts of a sentence, as well as elaborating the different parts of an entire discourse.[17] The sophists' intense interest in rhetoric was based on their systematic equation of meaning with language, *logos* with *legein*, although for Plato this was simply the assimilation of one counterfeit occupation to another.[18]

*

Protagoras's man-as-measure statement is arguably the most famous single statement in the history of Western philosophy, and it owes much of its popularity to the apparent lucidity of its meaning: "pantōn chrēmatōn metron estin anthrōpos, tōn men ontōn hōs estin, tōn de ouk ontōn hōs ouk estin. [Of all things the measure is man, of things that are that they are, and of things that are not that they are not.]"[19]

The common understanding of this fragment follows the relativistic or humanistic idea that the "proper study of mankind is man" (and woman). This interpretation is also, more or less, the one mentioned by certain critics and philosophers one would not normally label naive. For example, Hegel, in his admittedly far from penetrating account of early Greek thought, interprets the statement as meaning that "everything has a relative truth only."[20] Curiously, this interpretation is precisely the one that Plato, who (as we have seen) parlays the statement's apparent relativism into an absurd subjectivism,[21] never considers. Later scholars, trying to resolve this tension, have been at odds over the precise meaning of Protagoras's "extremely obscure statement,"[22] although everyone seems to find some degree of relativism inherent in the fragment. Traditional interpretations of Protagoras's meaning, which have variously tended to ascribe humanism, idealism, scepticism, subjectivism and other nonrhetorical dogma to the sophist, have ignored the sophistic context of Protagoras's other statements as well as the fact that Protagoras calls mankind the measure, and not the measur-*er*.

Sound scholarship has long since called attention to the problems inherent in determining what Protagoras meant by nearly every word in the *homo mensura* statement, with the possible exceptions of *pas* ("all") and *ouk* ("not"). In most cases, however, the obvious translations of these problematic words, or what would have been obvious in the fifth century, are also the correct ones. By *chrēmata* Protagoras simply meant "things," whether common material objects or more abstract matters, and so the term can be equated with the more usual *pragmata*. Indeed, the pleonastic formula *panta chrēmata* is itself widely attested (see, for example, Herodotus 1.32); similar expressions of this formula can be found in Theognis, Mimnermus, and Anaxagoras.[23] Sextus, in his account, also makes this identification: "metron men legōn to kritērion, chrēmatōn de tōn pragmatōn, hōs dunamei phaskein pantōn pragmatōn kritērion einai ton anthrōpon. [. . . meaning by 'measure' the standard of judgment, and using the word *chrēmata* rather than *pragmata* for 'things.' So he says, in effect, that man is the standard of judgment of all things.]" Others may also be cited.[24]

Metron, however, does depart somewhat from its usual meaning of a quantitative index, but the figurative sense is made clear by calling *anthrōpos* the "measure" and by stating that it is *all* things that are measured. Indeed, Aristotle informs us that Protagoras explicitly rejected the objective validity of quantitative measures: "For the circle touches the straightedge not at a point, but as Protagoras said it did when he refuted the geometers" (*Metaphysics* 3.2.997b32).[25] Burnet accepts the attribution of this argument to Protagoras and cites the then-topical discussion concerning the incommensurability of the diagonal with respect to the side of a square.[26] Moreover, Dupréel notes that many of the Greek words for measured units refer to anatomical dimensions.[27] Both would agree that, in making man the unit for measuring "all things," some of which have no measure, Protagoras emphasized his relativistic idea that measures are distinctly human configurations that do not determine objective reality.

"Things which are and are not," which refer back to *chrēmata* are thus not "existent realities" but things which are and are not true for man (*anthrōpos*). Further proof of this is supplied by the context, for man can hardly be the measure of nonexistent things. As Protagoras makes clear in his statement "On the Gods" ("Concerning the gods I cannot know either that they exist or that they do not exist"), when it comes to the existence of things outside the mind one can only say nothing at all.[28] Finally, evidence that *hōs* should be translated by the conjunction ("that") rather than by the adverbial "how" is also provided by Protagoras's parallel statement about the gods just mentioned, where, as has been frequently noted, "how" is strictly precluded by Protagoras's addition of the final clause.

All this combines to form the following rendering of Protagoras's most famous statement: "Mankind is the measure [criterion] of all things, both of those which are [true], that they are [true], and of those which are not [true], that they are not [true]." It should be noted that "On Truth," *Tēs Alētheias*, is one of the two titles mentioned for the work that began with the man-as-measure statement.[29] Protagoras is saying, then, that it is not according to some standard or reference outside mankind that things are measured or determined but according to mankind itself. This is where scholarly opinion, following Plato, usually turns its attention to inquire precisely who this *anthrōpos* is who determines reality, whether each person individually or, contrary to Plato's reading, humanity in general. But, to recall the riddle of the sphinx, man is not the question, but the answer: each man, any man, all men are doubtless what Protagoras had in mind by *anthrōpos*. The first question to be answered is instead, What does it mean to make mankind the *measure*, and not the measur-er, of reality? Does it mean anything more, or different from, the traditional view of the strictly relative nature of all human reality? And finally, how does the man-as-measure statement fit with the other statements attributed to Protagoras, especially those more overtly concerned with rhetoric like the *dissoi logoi*?

Dupréel's observation that the Greek words for measures are often derived from human proportions[30] provides the key to what may be called Protagoras's insight into the a priori nature of all human reality. We do not know reality, Protagoras's statement declares; rather, we register, *like a meter*, empirical impressions which are immediately converted into human understanding, much as a measuring stick can only give us multiples of a unit of measure that is peculiar to itself and cannot itself be measured. This is indeed different from calling man the measurer, because that would require that mankind has some relation to reality outside itself, whereas Protagoras wants to say that the reality outside man is a multiple, as it were, of the reality inside man. Protagoras argues much the same point in his statement concerning the existence of the gods quoted earlier: "Concering the gods I know nothing, neither that they are nor that they are not."[31] If there were gods, Protagoras is saying, we would be the last to know it—or maybe not even the last.

The common view that Protagoras's man-as-measure statement advocates a form of relativism falls short only insofar as it can imply an absolutism which is carefully precluded by Protagoras's statement. If everything were relative to the human mind that ordered it, this would not allow for the possibility that there could be anything other than the human interpretation of reality. From the perspective of Protagoras's "relative relativism," as it were, one could not say, as had Xenophanes,[32] whether the gods of oxen or horses or lions would look like them, since we know as little about such animals as we know about the gods.

Before discussing the implications of this for Protagoras's rhetorical interests, we need to explain the seemingly superfluous second part of the statement, which, after all, is longer than the first part already discussed. Any reading of the second half of the man-as-measure statement must begin by acknowledging its apparent redundancy in relation to the first part of the sentence, to its own two parts, and to the two parts of each of these.

If man is the measure of everything, why reiterate that he is the measure of things which are and are not? And, if man is the measure of things which are, must not the things which are not also be things which are, in so far as they are not? And, last but not least, if *anthrōpos* measures things which are and are not, of course he/she measures that they are and are not.

Protagoras adds that statements about both *ta onta* and *ta ouk onta* are equally possible in order to emphasize that humanity's reality has nothing to do with existence, which, as Parmenides proved, cannot not be. For, as already mentioned, if *ta onta* are understood as existent realities, man would be the measure "of non-existent things, [saying] that they don't exist," which is patently absurd. For Protagoras, unlike Parmenides, things which are not most definitely are a part of all the things which man measures. Thus, neither *ta onta* nor *ta ouk onta* are to be understood as existentially real, but rather as statements of truth and falsity. This emphasis on predication is why Protagoras adds the *men/de* clause, and why he also adds the two *hōs* clauses: mankind's relation to things which are and are not is strictly predicative, for it measures that things are and that they are not.

Since, as has already been argued with respect to the fragments discussed earlier, Protagoras's notion of reality is a function of language rather than the converse, statements of nonbeing are quite as valid and real as statements of being. Protagoras protracted the first part of the man-as-measure statement in order to show that the things of which he is speaking are not things "according to themselves" but predicates of man's perception of the world. If Protagoras challenged Parmenides with the validity of things which are not, he is not therefore opposed to Eleaticism on its own terms, but has merely redefined it. Instead of the metaphysical one which is and cannot not be, there is now the epistemological unit "man" which is required for every notion of being or nonbeing.

When the notion that "there is nothing besides perception" is combined with Protagoras's man-as-measure statement, we can then conclude that the *aisthēsis* of the earlier fragment is not really to be understood empirically. For if "there is nothing beyond perceptions," we now see that these impressions are nonetheless unrelated to the "real world." But what, one wonders, does the aesthetic grounding of knowledge in the man-as-measure statement have to do with Protagoras's preoccupation with language and with rhetoric?

Once one identifies humanity as the measure of reality, language has then to be acknowledged as the human measure that registers reality in distinctly human terms. This does not mean, of course, that other human senses do not perceive the world in nonlinguistic terms, just that language was privileged by Protagoras as the distinctly (if not uniquely) human way of *measuring* the world. Animals may indeed possess certain linguistic abilities, but it is only mankind which, through language, can measure the world. This brings us to the final, and for our purposes most important, fragment of Protagoras to be analyzed: if the measure that is human is language, it is also the case that this criterion is double, for "on every question there are two opposing statements—including this one."[33]

*

The notion that "everything is true," even if it were not explicitly ascribed to Protagoras, could be shown to follow from the two fragments already discussed, which were interpreted as referring to the primacy of the truth of statements over statements of truth. The explicit references to this notion, none of them fragments in the strict sense, might suggest the possibility that it stems from Plato's interpretation of the latter. However, because of the large number of such references[34] and the fact that it is an obvious corollary of the man-as-measure statement, its genuineness is rarely doubted: Vlastos refers to Plato's reference as an "unusually reliable statement of Protagoras' doctrine."[35] If this is the case, how is one to interpret another statement of Protagoras's that seems to argue the opposite, namely, that nothing is true because every statement is inextricably bound to its own refutation?

> prōtos ephē duo logous einai peri pantos pragmatos antikeimenous allēlois. Hois kai sunērōta. Prōtos touto praxas.
> [Protagoras was the first to say that on every issue there are two arguments opposed to each other; these he made use of in arguing by the method of questioning, a practice he originated.][36]

> P. ait de omni re in utramque partem disputari posse ex aequo et de hac ipsa, an omnis res in utramque partem disputabilis sit.
> [Protagoras says that one can argue equally well on either side of any question, *including the question itself whether both sides of any question can be argued*.] (Seneca, *Letters* 88.43; italics mine)[37]

This statement of the *dissoi logoi*, or "double meanings," does indeed seem to suggest the opposite idea from the notion that "everything is true": if everything one maintains is questionable, then nothing is true. However, because Protagoras's thought is essentially antilogical, or double, there is really no contradiction between these two statements; each is in fact little more than a restatement of the other. If "on every question there are two statements," then the opposite notion, that "everything is true," must also be valid. Conversely, if everything is true, then the opposite opinion must also be granted, which is exactly what is presented in the *dissoi logoi*.

Two obvious objections that have been raised regarding the *dissoi logoi* will, when resolved, shed much light on this controversial notion. If there are two *logoi* on every subject then, as Plato and numerous others since have maintained, there is also a second *logos* which rightly asserts the opposite—that there is only one true *logos*. The second objection is less easily dismissed: if there are two opposing statements on every question, then there will be more than two, indeed, there will be an infinite number, and so there are not really two such *logoi*, there is in fact no such *logos*.

The first objection, that, in the manner of Plato's "peritrope,"[38] Protagoras's notion "turns back against itself," is valid, yet it is still not really a refutation of the statement of the *dissoi logoi*. By a true *logos* Protagoras means any predicate that agrees with its own subject, and so whose truthfulness is always included within itself. The *dissoi logoi* are not, then, to be considered contradictory statements about the same *pragma* (in this case, that there are and are not opposing statements on every question), of which only one can be true, but antilogical statements about different *pragmata*. There can thus be two opposing, as well as only one, *logoi* or *logos* because Protagoras's antilogical *logoi* cannot really be opposed to each other.

But why, if every *logos* is intrinsically correct, does Protagoras speak of antilogical or opposing statements at all? Why is there a doctrine of the *dissoi logoi* at all when Protagoras's system would seemingly function more effectively without it? And, moreover, has not Protagoras readmitted the *pragma* as an object outside man by speaking of two opposing *logoi* about every thing (*de omni re*)?

The doctrine of "two meanings" does not subvert the Protagorean system and its basis in perception (*aisthēsis*), for the referential *pragma*, which is the truth of every statement, is also outside man, outside the unity of the *logos/pragma* which constitutes meaning. That is, to equate meaning with language, *logos* with *legein*, as Protagoras does, is already to inscribe the antilogical relationship between language and reality, *onoma* and *pragma* or *logos* and *ergon* within language and thought. To identify meaning with language is to make meaning, with its necessary reference to some *pragma* or idea, always other than itself, with the result that language is both referential and self-referential, the same and other than the world, always true and never true. Thus the doubling that makes every statement contestable is a necessary part of the truth of every statement. Protagoras's perceptual/aesthetic notion of the truth analyzed in the first two parts of this chapter includes the doctrine of the *dissoi logoi* within itself as its necessary corollary. One might even say that the objection that there is only

one *logos* on every question is the essential truth of the *dissoi logoi*, because, for there to be an antilogical *logos* that is equally true as the first,
there must be only one *logos*.

The double, then, is an essential part of the *logos* which is always true;
Protagoras's *logos* is itself a *dissos logos*. This "two" is also one, for meaning must first establish itself before it becomes contested, and every contes-
tation of that meaning is true and itself contestable. But (second objection)
does the endless repetition of two/one/two in turn imply that Protagoras's
notion of meaning resists being included within itself, that meaning is infinite and so meaninglessness? Theodor Gomperz, eager to reassert what
seems to be the quickly diminishing status of statements of truth within
Protagoras's system, would understandably like to interpret the statement
as implying something other than the infinite regress which he nonetheless
admits is its more obvious meaning.[39] He would like to have the statement
mean "on every question one can argue pro or contra equally well." The
essence of this reading is that there are two and only two antinomical *logoi*,
and that these join together to constitute the truth of any question. But
although this was certainly the more common interpretation of Protagoras's
notion for generations of later rhetoricians, one must doubt whether Protagoras would really have restricted the notion to two and only two
speeches. One way to answer this is to examine whether the other notion
of two really leads to an infinite regress, and to the kind of skepticism
Gomperz is eager to avoid.

Although no one, or even two, *logoi* would represent the truth, finalized and complete according to itself, there would always be a return of
meaning to itself within such a system. For any second *logos* is really a
double of the first, which means that, although it is opposed to the first, it
also repeats it in relation to a third, and so on, with the result that every
logos is itself the other which denies it, and so, although part of an infinite
regress, also meaningful in and of itself. The two of the *dissoi logoi* does
not need to be understood as two and only two in order to avoid an infinite
regress, thus turning the fundamental basis of the Protagorean system into
a shallow dialectic that finds truth in simple antitheses. If "a statement is
opposed to every statement," not only a unity of opposites, but an opposition of unity is at stake, for the antithetical *logos* posited is itself one of the
pantes logoi. Only by understanding the *dissoi logoi* in this way is it possible to maintain Protagoras's notion that every *logos* is true, for if truth is
defined as antithesis, no antithetical *logos* is true without the other.

The two notions just discussed, that "everything is true" and "nothing
is true," are the *dissoi logoi* of the *dissoi logoi*. For not only, as was argued
with respect to the man-as-measure statement, has the truth of statements

transcended the level of statements of truth and falsity, but it has also transcended the truth and falsity of statements. The Protagorean notion of "truth" that was previously described as the true meaning, or intention, of every statement can now be labeled falsity. But perhaps this "falsity" is itself false, should itself be called into question and referred to as the *doubt* which, again, is etymologically linked to the critical *double*. For, if there are two *logoi* on every question, it is also true that there is a question about every *logos*.

3 | The Parabolic Double
Christ's and Kafka's Parables of Parable

> I will open my mouth in parables, and will utter things kept secret from the foundation of the world.
>
> —Matt. 13:34

RECOGNITION OF THE problematic essence of figuration is one of the touchstones, if not the cornerstone, of recent deconstructive writings. As de Man, Derrida, Hillis Miller, and other deconstructive critics have repeatedly shown, there is no way to "grasp" such tropes as metaphor, for example, except metaphorically: "The notion of metaphor," writes Sarah Kofman in *Nietzsche et la métaphore*, "is itself only a metaphor" (65). But if a preoccupation with problems of figuration in general and metaphor in particular reflect characteristic deconstructive concerns with rhetoric, philosophy and language, then parable (*parabolē, Gleichnis*) is as worthy of scrutiny as is metaphor in illuminating any critical debate about such matters. Although it has not received the same degree of attention as metaphor, parable too challenges any confidence in our ability to narrow the gap separating artistic/literary truth from itself in its essential doubleness.

The doubling of the phrase "parable of parable" can be read in at least two ways. First, and most clearly, it refers to a parable that is about parable. But, just as all metaphors that cannot be defined are "metaphors of metaphor," parables that cannot be reduced to a translatable message can also be considered "parables of parable." This means that such figures have no other object than their own unstable figurability, and that they are always only metaphors or parables of what they may be in reality. Because both these meanings will be shown to describe the two parables of parable discussed in this chapter, we must avoid the tempting term *meta-parable* if the prefix implies, as it often does, any self-referential closure. The critical double of aesthetic figuration neither allows nor precludes any closure.

Christ's Parable of Parable: The Sower

> As he taught he said: "Listen! A sower went out to sow. And it happened that as he sowed, some seed fell along the footpath; and the birds came

and ate it up. Some seed fell on rocky ground, where it had little soil, and it sprouted quickly because it had no depth of earth; but when the sun rose the young corn was scorched, and as it had no root it withered away. Some seed fell among thistles; and the thistles shot up and choked the corn, and it yielded no crop. And some of the seed fell into good soil, where it came up and grew, and bore fruit; and the yield was thirtyfold, sixtyfold, even a hundredfold."[1]

It is impossible to discuss parable in its more literary manifestations over the last two thousand years without careful grounding in the New Testament. However, comparison of Jesus' parables with the *mashal* of the Old Testament[2] or with Aristotle's rhetorical *parabolai*[3] only serves to demonstrate that Christ's originality is such that Jesus has been said to have reinvented the genre.[4] If one were so inclined, it could be argued that the originality of Christ himself is nowhere more apparent than in parable, since Jesus "never spoke to the people except in parable," and "the greatest and most effective Parable of all is Jesus' own life."[5] But just as one cannot discuss parable without discussing Christ's relation to the "genre,"[6] one also cannot discuss the latter without recognizing the millennia of biblical scholarship devoted to the parables, from the earliest allegorical treatments to the most recent applications of structuralist and poststructuralist methodologies.[7] The countless contributions of biblical scholars, while noted where relevant in the discussion of Christ's "parable of parable" which follows, are too numerous and significant to be treated inclusively here.

That the justly famous parable of the Sower (Matt. 13, Mark 4, Luke 8) is a double "parable about parable" can be shown in two ways. First, Christ's parable is about the hermeneutical difficulties of disseminating a message that promises only lesser degrees of "asymptotiveness," thus recalling the mathematical parabola as well as the literary parable. Second, immediately after the parable of the Sower, which itself begins the series of "parables of the Kingdom" (Mark 4:11), the disciples ask Christ why, in general, he speaks in parable (Matt. 13:10). Christ's explanation is significantly placed between the Sower proper and its interpolated allegorical explanation, thus suggesting that the parable of the Sower is part of the discussion about the parabolic dissemination of the Word in general. Because this discussion about parable that follows the Sower is so essential to it, we shall first discuss Christ's explanation to the disciples of why he speaks in parable and then turn our attention to the parable of the Sower itself.

Although efforts have been repeatedly made to decide on textual grounds between the different reasons Christ gives for why he speaks in parables,[8] a more fruitful approach might be to utilize the controversy as itself illuminating the texts from which it stems. In what is generally believed to be the earliest (but by no means original) Gospel, Christ explains to the disciples why he speaks to the people in parable:

> To you the secret of the kingdom of God has been given; but to those who are outside everything comes by way of parables, so that (as Scripture says) they may look and look, but see nothing; they may hear and hear, but understand nothing; otherwise they might turn to God and be forgiven." So he said, "You do not understand this parable [the Sower]? How then are you to understand any parable? (Mark 4:11)

Two things are sure to startle anyone not already familiar with the controversy surrounding these lines. First, the common notion that Christ spoke to the people in a direct, concrete way that even they would understand—in other words, that Christ chose parable as the "language of the masses"—is directly controverted here. Christ speaks in parable so that—*hina*—the people will not understand (*mē idōsin*). The second startling point is that not only ordinary men and women but even the supposedly initiated disciples are victims of Christ's enigmatic message.[9] Jeremias and Jülicher are among those who reject the notion that Jesus would have discouraged proper understanding; Perrin, Funk, and Kermode are among the many who insist upon it.[10] I think the "hardening theory" of Mark is what Christ intended, but before discussing the meaning of Mark's version of the Sower, I must first note certain significant discrepancies in the parallel versions of this section.

The parallel section in Luke (8:10) also has Christ speaking to the people in parable "so that they may look but see nothing," although the disparaging, if not despairing, reference to the disciples is left out. It is in the parallel section of Matthew 13 that we find the source of the more common, positive explanation of why Christ spoke in parables: "That is why I speak to them in parables; for they look without seeing, and listen without hearing or understanding." The important shift in conjunctions from the *hina* ("in order that") of Mark and Luke to *hoti* produces not purpose but causality: "I speak in parable because the people do not understand (*hina des Mc and Lc ist hier durch *hoti* ersetzt; was dort Absicht heisst, heisst hier Ursache).[11] It is not hard to see how Matthew's version can be the source of a more optimistic interpretation of Christ's use of parable, but, despite the fact that it is more flattering to our human ears, is it preferable to the very different versions found in Luke and Mark?

One way to prove the greater validity of Mark's and Luke's versions is to show that Matthew's theory of why Christ spoke in parable, despite the shift in conjunctions, is not very different from the "hardening theory" of the other two synoptics. The statements which precede and follow the statement in question belie its optimism. Before it Christ states: "To you it has been granted to know the secrets of the kingdom of heaven; but to those others it has not been granted." After the statement, the thoroughly pessimistic reference to Isaiah ends with the hope that the people's ignorance may continue: "You may hear and hear, but you will never understand." Have we painted ourselves into a hermeneutical corner (a version of the "hermeneutic circle") by reaching a conclusion about Christ's reply to the question "Why do you speak in parables" that does not bode well as to the serviceability of such a notion? Critics of the "obduracy theory" are right to hesitate before the blatant contradiction informing it. For how can Christ advocate the use of parables to learn about the secret of the kingdom and the use of parables to hinder such learning? This contradictory doubling, contrary to efforts to defend one or the other of its antinomies, is actually central to Christ's intention here and all such parabolic works in general.

In the final line of the Sower, Christ adds the famous warning, "If you have ears to hear, then hear." Unfortunately, we have heard that crucial formula so often that, as Isaiah predicted (Isa. 6:9–10), we tend to turn a deaf ear to this powerful paradox. Since our ordinary hearing is plainly being called into question by this warning, we must hear with another kind of hearing which is yet still hearing. But how do we ever know that we are listening with the second type of hearing referred to when one says, "You have ears but do not hear"? How can we ever be certain that we are hearing in one way and not the other?

If one were to answer this objection by saying that Christ obviously is exhorting us to interpret the parable with our "mind's eye" (or "ear"), as opposed to hearing what is really being said, this still does not resolve the paradox which is here at stake. For can we ever be sure that we understand the figurative message of the parable properly (another word for literally), and that we "see clearly" Jesus' meaning with our figurative "mind's eye"? The critical question is whether the parable of the Sower has any such translatable message that we know we are hearing, and, if not, just what the value of such parables in parable may be.

Questions concerning the haphazardness of Christ's sowing or the agricultural practices of the time[12] are of secondary importance if they do not address the general meaning as well as the allegorical detail of the parable's figurative intent. This general intention is to distinguish the four types of sowing as a progression of increasing fecundity, where the seeds come closer each time to unimpeded growth. Without sanctioning the entire allegorical interpolation of Mark 4:14 (recent biblical scholars reject this section as a later interpolation),[13] we can assume that the seeds represent the words of Christ himself: "The sower sows the word" (Mark 4:14). The parable thus compares different ways Christ's message can be received, and it might appear that there is nothing problematical here—no stones or thorns—with which to contend.

If such a facile interpretation is indeed without thorns or stones, that is because it is like the first type of sowing, which is the least tenable of all, which falls on "rocky ground." How, following the logic of the parable, does one ever know that any interpretation of Christ's words or acts is the right one and not one that, if it has not already been swept away, will soon be choked by thorns or blasted by the sun? How does one know that when one replies "because I know" this is not just what Christ meant by those who receive the Word too quickly: "As soon as they hear the word, they accept it with joy, but it strikes no root in them" (Mark 4:16)?

The critical question here is not "Which type of soil are you?" but "How do you know which type of soil you are?" Surely no one knows this for certain—which is tantamount to saying no one knows it at all. Recalling the etymological connection often referred to in this book between *doubt* and *doubling*, the parable seems to be saying that nothing meaningful will emerge without this grounding in uncertainty. The question raised above must, then, be answered in the negative: the parable of the Sower has no sort of translatable message that we know we are hearing. But, in answer to the second question concerning the serviceability of such a notion, it is only when one knows that there is no way of knowing what type of soil we might be that we paradoxically affirm our understanding of Christ's message by doubling as the dark, fertile soil spoken of in the parable. Just as the seed that flourishes does so by taking root under the ground, beneath the level of appearance, so the parable can only be understood when our lack of certainty is acknowledged. Only then does the double "parable in parable" take root, and surely that cannot be construed as negative.

It is worth recalling here that the word *parable* is etymologically related to the Romance root *parl-*, meaning "to speak" (Latin *parabolare*, French *parler*). For there is no interpretation of the Sower, or of the fertile soil that forms its essence, which stands outside the speaking of the parable itself as its proper interpretation. This is not to say, however, that the meaning of such parables as the Sower is ever self-evident. To say that the meaning of the Sower is in the parable itself is to acknowledge the *doubt* which is generated by the *doubling* of a parable where whatever one thinks the parable means must always fall short, just as the metaphor of the fertile soil, with its connotations of darkness and depth, necessarily implies. As this chapter's epigraph from Matthew 13 reveals, to speak in parables is to utter secrets that underlie, or double, the grounding or "foundation" of the world; the doubling of under-standing referred to in the Sower will never be able to be grounded in literal reality. Yet, since Christ's parable of the Sower is about just this process of undermining, our examination of Jesus' message can hardly be construed as negative. If being the fertile soil of Christ's Sower requires, as the metaphor implies, that we turn a deaf ear to the usual modes of apprehension, that would be necessary if we are to double the word with "the Word" and hear "without hearing."

Kafka's Parable of Parable: "Von den Gleichnissen" ("On Parables")

Recent writers on parable are as unlikely to discuss Kafka as someone who wrote in parables as, conversely, critics of Kafka are inclined to discuss parable *in stricto sensu*.[14] As far as many of the most prominent Kafka scholars are concerned (Emrich, Sokel, Politzer, and others), the parables proper, while not specifically dismissed as a marginal part of Kafka's work, are nonetheless treated as though they were—used, if at all, to lead into a discussion of either the stories or novels. One reason for this neglect, the unpublished state in Kafka's lifetime of all but a few of his parables notwithstanding,[15] is critics' tendency to reduce Kafka's thought to some thematizable idea or meaning. If one approaches literature as an expression of some explicit or implicit philosophical notion rather than as the process of self-denying doubling described here, one is bound to come to no little grief reading Kafka's parables.[16]

Another reason for the neglect of Kafka's parables is a backlash against the tendentious religious reading of Kafka begun by Brod.[17] But to speak of Kafka as either religious or atheistic (or agnostic), as Judaic or Christian, is surely to frame the argument so as to reach no useful conclusion with regard to a thinker who so studiously avoided antitheses as did Kafka.[18] Indeed, it is impossible to ignore the many Christian elements in Kafka's writings,[19] particularly when one is writing about parable, a genre which, as we have just seen, was radically redefined by the parables of the *New Testament*. The purpose of this discussion is to show that Kafka's double "parable of parable" "On Parables" ("*Von den Gleichnissen*") can be better understood by placing it in its proper religious context and by recognizing that, within such a context, parabolic meaning is necessarily double.

Claude David, the French editor of Kafka's *Oeuvres complètes*, provides a good example of the tendency to ignore the parabolic context (both religious and generic) of "On Parables." Indeed, David argues that *Gleich-nis* in "Von den Gleichnissen" does not mean "parable" at all: "It is clear that Kafka does not take the word in this sense [parable] here; the example that he cites, 'Go over' [*Gehe hinüber*], alludes only to an implicit comparison, an 'image' or, as one also says in French, a 'figure' of speech—of ordinary speech as well as the language of wise men or philosophers."[20]

Despite the fact that Kafka's French editor is here flying in the face of most other Kafka critics, as well as Luther's standard translation of the Greek *parabolē* as *Gleichnis*, it is strange to find the editor so opposed to the notion of *Gleichnis* as a "récit symbolique." If anything is "clear," it is that *Gleichnis* in "Von den Gleichnissen" has its specific biblical sense of parable and its more general sense of "figure of speech." Of course, the two are not exclusive: all parables are extended figures of a sort, but the difference between figure in its general sense and a text which is *in toto* figurative argues for the usual translation of *Gleichnis* as parable. Further, "Gehe hinüber," which the editor says refers to figures and not parables, is used in reference to a speech which explicitly points toward a transcendent truth. Figures like similes and metaphors could have more specific referents or appear in stories or poems which do not require one to "go beyond" to learn their lesson. Finally, Kafka is speaking here specifically of "the words of wise men," not of poets. This is not a distinction Kafka would have failed to appreciate, and this is why his parables are never parables of wisdom but parables about parables of wisdom.[21]

"On Parables" is dated at the end of 1922 and appears in the so-called "second black notebook" together with "Give It Up" and "The Married Couple."[22] All of these important works were written about the same time, but "Von den Gleichnissen" (the title was added later by Brod) is entered with the notebook turned around after a gap of a number of blank pages:

> Many complain that the words of the wise are always merely parables and of no use in daily life, which is the only life we have. When the sage says: "Go over," he does not mean that we should cross to some actual place, which we could do anyhow if the labor were worth it; he means some fabulous yonder, something unknown to us, something too that he cannot designate more precisely, and therefore cannot help us here in the very least. All these parables really set out to say merely that the incomprehensible is incomprehensible, and we know that already. But the cares we have to struggle with every day: that is a different matter.
>
> Concerning this a man once said: Why such reluctance? If you only followed the parables you yourselves would become parables and with that free of all your daily cares.
>
> Another said: I bet that is also a parable.

> The first said: You have won.
> The second said: But unfortunately only in parable.
> The first said: No, in reality: in parable you have lost.[23]

One might identify the complaint which opens this parable with the Lord's Prayer ("Give us this day our daily bread"): "Give us," say the many, "something which is applicable (*verwendbar*) to our daily lives (*täglichen Leben*)." But, unlike the speaker of the Lord's Prayer, Kafka's parable critic asks only for the stuff of which daily life is made. The more significant similarities are between this opening statement from "On Parables" and a famous passage from Kafka's diary (dated December 6, 1921):

> From a letter: "I warm myself . . . in this sad winter." Metaphors are one of the many things which cause me to despair (*verzweifeln*) of writing. The dependence of writing on the serving girl who heats the stove; on the cat which warms itself by the oven; even on the poor old man who warms himself; all these are self-sufficient actions, whereas writing is helpless, wanders outside itself, is a joke and despair.[24]

Kafka criticizes metaphor here, just as he criticizes parable in "On Parables," because it is not directly applicable to our daily lives and because its "lack of self-sufficiency" (*Unselbstständigkeit*) causes epistemological doubt and despair (*Verzweiflung*). In fact, Kafka's writings are never witty in the way he describes in this entry, and one would be hard pressed to find a metaphor like the above-mentioned "sad winter" in all of his writings. It would seem, then, that critics who want a realist or immanent Kafka would be justified in reading the parable as a defense of the parable critic's opening statement of disdain for such useless messages.

The initial complaint in "Von den Gleichnissen" is not one that can be dismissed lightly as mere philistinism, for it mirrors Kafka's scruples about figurative language in expressing a definite need for substance. However, it is also the case that Kafka's parables cannot be referentially determined in an effort to provide such substantive nourishment. Far from it. These "parables and paradoxes" are not reducible to messages that can be in turn applied to reality.[25] The problem before us, then, is how such nourishment can be gleaned from such ambiguously double ("ambiguously ambiguous") parables like "On Parables."

The word Kafka chooses for his example of the wise man's parable, *hinüber-gehen*, is one of those important words which loosely translate *meta-phor*, *trans-cendence*, *trans-gression*, and, of course, *trans-lation* (*Übersetzen*) itself. As was argued in chapter 1, recent criticism has developed I. A. Richards's notion that "all thought is metaphoric"[26] into a devastating critique of any attempt to understand individual metaphors or metaphor in general without recourse to "metaphors of metaphor" or "metaphors of metaphorization," which vitiate understanding.[27] The wise man's "Go over" in "On Parables" is not only a word for metaphor, or even a metaphor, but also a "metaphor of metaphor" in that we are not, as the sage tacitly admits, really going over anywhere: the wise man "does not mean that we should cross to some actual place . . . he means . . . something unknown to us."

What value do such nonreferential figures as "going over" have when we are not really going anywhere? It is important that we distinguish these open figures from the witty metaphors disdained in Kafka's letter. Metaphors such as the "sad winter," unlike the *Gleichnis* of "going over," are rejected because they fall back on some unintended attribute rather than pointing us toward the correct one. "Go over" may also fail to say exactly what it means, but it succeeds in pointing us in the direction of a transcendent reality that "cannot be more precisely designated": "Speech can only be used to indicate things beyond the sensible world, and so can never be used except as a comparison which brings us closer to them because, corresponding as it does to the sensible world, it concerns only possession and its relationships."[28] The sage's edict to "Go over" is just such an "indication" insofar as it points us in the direction of transcendence—pointing us toward pointing, as it were—rather than offering us any more substantive information on exactly what such a process entails. Kafka's famous *Verwandlung* ("metamorphosis" is yet another form of *hinübergehen*) into the form of a bug provides a more concrete example of how such transcendence outside the bounds of the literal is possible. If such a metamorphosis seems anything but transcendent, it should be noted that the story of Kafka's *käfer* (a thinly veiled disguise of Kafka's name) abounds in parallels to Christ's life, death, and resurrection.

Although it might be argued that the ultimate goal of such freedom from the literal is tantamount, in its denial of reality, to death, that Kafka welcomed thoughts of the ultimate doubling of life which is death as a release from the constraints of the literal has been discussed extensively by one of Kafka's most devoted critics, the French writer Maurice Blanchot: "In one of his journal entries Kafka makes a remark on which one might reflect: 'Returning home I told Max that on my deathbed I would be quite happy providing that my sufferings were not too great. I neglected to add (and did so later by design) that the best of what I have written is a result of this capacity to be able to die happy.'"[29] "Von den Gleichnissen" shows us that Kafka's welcoming of death is also evident in his parabolic writings, which can be considered "parables of death" insofar as they always "go over" by denying transcendence any transcendental *signifié*.

In the second part of the parable, the major "positivistic" criticisms of this notion of the doubling of parabolic transcendence are addressed. (It is no accident that this standoff is repeated in each chapter of this book; metaphor, parable, Freud's antithetical meanings, James's "figure in the carpet," and so on are all emphatically countered by well-known positivistic interpretations.) "All these parables" says the critic, "really say is that the incomprehensible is incomprehensible, and we know that already." The haughty tone of the critic's complaint is evidence of the weakness of his argument, but in the attempt to reduce the double "incomprehensibility of the incomprehensible" to a mere tautological repetition of the same the critical difference between the realist and the sage emerges. For the realist, the "incomprehensibility of the incomprehensible" means an identity of the incomprehensible with itself—the comprehensibility of the incomprehensibility—whereas, for the wise man, the same phrase refers to a doubling that denies, not the very notion of incomprehensibility, but the possibility of comprehending such a notion. There is a great deal at stake in such an argument. To claim, as does the realist, that we know all we shall ever know about such incomprehension would deny the value of artworks which continually enlighten us without ever being comprehensible. As I. A. Richards has said, "No one can say there is only this and this in the poem."[30]

When the realist presses the objection that such parabolic incomprehensibility will surely not "put bread on the table" (as the saying goes), the sage replies: "Why worry? You have only to follow the parables (*folgen den Gleichnissen*) and you will be free from the cares of the daily world." This answer, which refers us back to Kafka's notion of the "happy death," is only slightly ironic. Following parables frees us from the cares of the world because in "going over" the literal terms of life are no longer applicable, and once we have accepted the figurative nature of "our world" even the suffering of that world is subject to a higher truth. Kafka's world, I would maintain, nowhere gives evidence of the value of suffering except as redemptive.

Such freedom, both speakers agree, is itself parabolical ("I bet that that too is a parable") because no way exists to say exactly what parabolic freedom is without contradicting the very terms through which it is constituted. The parabolic double, like metaphoric and rhetorical doubling, can be defined only by contradicting its essential linguistic structure (again, it is significant in this regard that the word for speaking in Romance languages—for example, *parlare*—is derived from *parabolare*, when one might have expected "speaking in parable" to be derivative of speaking in general). This explains why the realist wins the bet on freedom being parabolical "in reality" and not "in parable." Yet the ending of the text does suggest a way to win the bet in parable, a way whose sinister implications give the conclusion of this parable its magisterial tone. The only way to "win in parable" is by dying, because only then will referentiality be transcended once and for all. Such genuinely ambiguous winning occurs often enough in Kafka's texts, as seen in the radiance that suffuses the protagonist's death in "Before the Law" or, more figuratively, in "The Hunger Artist," "The Most Insatiable," "The Judgment," and so on, but is definitely not the kind of winning the critic of Kafka's parables is betting on here.

Many similarities exist between Kafka's parable of parable and Christ's Sower, the first and foremost parable of parable in the Western tradition. In both we have wise men speaking in parable about parable to the uncomprehending many concerning a higher, transcendent truth. Just as Christ spoke in parable "so that [*hina*] the people will not understand,"[31] parable in "Von den Gleichnissen" is likewise described as defying understanding. Kafka's way of reconciling this apparent contradiction is to maintain that by not understanding what the parable means we can more closely "divine" its spiritual intent, as in the case of "going over" when we do not understand what such transcendence means. Similarly, only when we confess our not understanding the meaning of the parable of the Sower—our not knowing whether we are the seeds that sprout in shallow soil, or those that are later choked by thorns—is the seed of a truly transcendent meaning planted within us, and we can under-stand Christ's meaning without understanding.

Both of the "parables of parable" discussed here devolve upon a moment of doubt (etymologically related to *doubling*) or uncertainty that is essential to a "proper understanding" of the parables' spiritual intent. In the parable of the Sower it was said that the moment of truth, or grounding, was also the moment of uncertainty in answering such a question. Kafka's highly compatible notion is that the religious transcendence to which parable gives voice (*parabolare* > *parlare*) must remain precisely that, "parables of parable" which express a transcendent (metaphoric) truth as tropes "turning" away from and toward their literal meaning. Only by virtue of this critical doubt or doubling which signals a turning—away from and toward knowledge—can the truth of parables or, for that matter, all "sacred texts" (*heilige Schriften*) emerge.[32]

4 | The Tragic Double
A Dionysian Theory of Greek Tragedy

GERALD ELSE AND Brian Vickers[1] are justified in rejecting the speculations of Nietzsche, Harrison, Murray, and others insofar as such theories
pretend to enlighten us as to the so-called origins of Greek tragedy. Yet the
latter critics and their more recent followers (Dodds, Winnington-Ingram,
and Charles Segal, to cite the most eminent)[2] are equally justified in ex-
ploring the relevance of Dionysianism to tragedy and especially to Euripides' *Bacchae*, the only extant Greek tragedy about the god of tragedy, no
matter what one may think about the origins of the form. In marked contrast to Else and Vickers, Winnington-Ingram states that the *Bacchae* "is
about the religion of Dionysus and the behavior of his votaries." Yet, although he offers many valuable insights into Euripides' play, Winnington-
Ingram fails to explore the correlations between Dionysus, Dionysianism,
and tragedy in general. This causes him to neglect some obvious comparisons between the *Bacchae* and other plays (for example, if "Dionysus' revenge would have been shocking," would not Aphrodite's in the *Hippolytus* have been too?) as well as to reject Pentheus as the tragic hero of the
Bacchae and the play itself as a tragedy: "Yet tragedy does not seem the
right word nor Pentheus to be of the stature of tragic heroes; and any attempt to make such a hero of him is bound in one way or another to distort
the character as revealed by the text of the play."[3]

The simple fact that the *Bacchae* is a tragedy about tragedy, that is, a
tragedy about the god of tragedy, has either been ignored by the leading
critics of the play or merely alluded to in general terms. Charles Segal, who
has written more on the *Bacchae* in recent years than anyone, acknowledges that "like its god [Dionysus], tragedy comes into being at the point
where man's creative and destructive impulses cross,"[4] but he does not try
to establish on the basis of the plot, characters, and themes of Euripides'
drama about Dionysus a typology of the form which is applicable to a
number of other tragedies as well. Although a Dionysian theory of tragedy
might seem to offer nothing new, theories such as Segal's and those on
which it is based do not focus on the kernel of the tragic conflict in general:
the ambivalent repression—or doubling—of amoral Dionysian forces.

Facile references to the "paradoxical" essence of tragedy[5] do not adequately comprehend, for example, the unity of the tragic hero with the Dionysian forces he opposes in the *Oedipus*, *Hippolytus*, and *Antigone*, to mention only a few of the plays that follow the model of the *Bacchae* (these plays will be discussed in the second part of this chapter). The purpose of the first part of this discussion is to show that the central conflict of the *Bacchae* is founded on a critical doubling that pits its male hero, Pentheus, against the female followers of Dionysus (the Maenads and the androgynous Dionysus) whom he both despises and adores. Although modern tragedy is not discussed directly here (Steiner's bold declaration of the "death of tragedy" inadvertently reveals that tragedy has thrived on its so-called death)[6] this model of tragedy based upon the Greeks is believed applicable to later developments of the genre as well.

*

Another peril inherent in supporting a Dionysian theory of tragedy with reference to Euripides' last play is that, however much compatibility may exist between that theory and Nietzsche's, it will serve only to highlight Nietzsche's famous contempt for Euripides and disregard of the *Bacchae*. Although, as Vickers argues,[7] Nietzsche is merely "taking to its ultimate conclusion" the long-standing prejudice against Euripides common from Aristotle through A. W. Schlegel, this does not explain why Nietzsche would have deferred to critics he was more accustomed to attacking. Nor is it enough to say that Nietzsche's contempt for figures like Euripides, Socrates, Christ, and Wagner is in direct proportion to his admiration. To be sure, it would not be difficult to rescue Euripides from Nietzsche's offended preferences for irrationality and music, both of which are seen by other critics as all too prevalent in Euripidean drama. But without attempting to "reevaluate" Nietzsche's attitude toward Euripides (given Nietzsche's own "reevaluation of all values," that would not be difficult), I will argue a thesis that Nietzsche would not seemingly have endorsed: that the god of "deindividuation" he praises in nearly every line of *The Birth of Tragedy* is the same in spirit as well as in name as the god of Euripides' *Bacchae*.

Classical scholarship and Nietzsche are rarely in accord, but the scholarship shares Nietzsche's unwillingness to read the *Bacchae* as a play about Dionysus or Greek tragedy in general. At the extreme end of such unwillingness is Gerald Else's view that Greek tragedy has "nothing to do with Dionysus."[8] Although he admits that "modern theorists have been almost unanimously agreed that tragedy grew out of some choral or group performance of ritual nature" and that "if any single impression concerning the origin of tragedy is fixed in the minds of most literate members of Western society, it is that tragedy stems from Dionysus and Satyrs," Else maintains that "nothing either in the tradition . . . or in the extant plays, earlier or later, shows any trace of this 'Dionysian ecstasy.'"[9] At the literal level, Else ignores the majority of odes in the *Bacchae* and in a number of other plays as well; at the thematic level he seems unaware that the refusal to recognize Dionysus is an essential part of Dionysianism. Most classical scholars have ignored or rejected Else's "Penthean" theory (Segal never mentions him; Foley rejects his speculations about the origin of tragedy as irrelevant since "we know that Euripides' contemporaries thought of Dionysus as a theater god"; Grube and Sandys are among the many others who stress the importance of Dionysianism to the *Bacchae*), but the same critics have been almost equally unwilling to maintain any link between the role of Dionysus and Dionysianism in Euripides' play and tragedy in general.[10]

The *Bacchae* begins in the way much Greek literature begins, and not all of it tragic: *mēnin aeide Thea*, "Sing, goddess, about the wrath of humiliation." English readers of the *Iliad* are misdirected by the very first line of the epic when *mēnis* is translated (as by Robert Fitzgerald) as "anger," for *mēnis* is a specific form of wrath.[11] If we examine other instances of the word in Homer and later writers we see that it almost always refers to "rage over a slight," as when Agamemnon (*Iliad* 1.75) reacts angrily to the seer's advice that he give up Chryseis unrecompensed. Instances of *mēnis* are typically that of a god whose power has been belittled by a mortal, but Achilles and Agamemnon's *mēnis*, rather than an exception, serves merely to strengthen this definition.

The demonstration of Dionysus's *mēnis* in the *Bacchae*'s prologue is crucial to the development of Euripides' play.[12] Yet, as important as Dionysus's "wrath of humiliation" may be, it is not unequivocal, for we also learn in the prologue that Dionysus has come to Thebes to bestow his blessings upon it: "This city, first in Hellas, now thrills and echoes to my women's cries, their ecstasy of joy" (20–21). It is not necessarily contradictory that Dionysus should want to establish his religion in the same city which holds him most in contempt. However, it is contradictory that Dionysus should punish his detractors by bestowing the blessing of his worship upon them and reward his faithful followers by destroying them—at the end of the play Cadmus, whom Dionysus earlier referred to as having "won my praise: for he has made this tomb a shrine, sacred to my mother" (10), is all but destroyed by the self-same god. Such contradictory doublings stem from the amoral Dionysian forces that later culminate in the ambiguous conflict between the tragic hero and Dionysus.

The doublings and reversals in the *Bacchae* are nowhere more beautifully emblematized then at the moment of Dionysus's birth, which is also the moment of his mother Semele's immolation: "So his mother bore him once in labor bitter; lightning-struck, forced by fire that flared from Zeus, consumed, she died, untimely torn, in childbed dead by blow of light! Of light the son was born!" (88–93).

Combined at the moment of Dionysus's birth—itself, *pace* Nietzsche, *the birth of tragedy*—are sexual release (Zeus's and Semele's), creation (Dionysus's birth), and destruction (Semele's death). This can be called "emblematic" because the matrix of contradictory forces gathered at the moment of sexual release is essential to tragedy: "The myth of his [Dionysus's] birth . . . is the most sublime expression of his being."[13] I have already mentioned Dionysus's contrary motives with regard to Thebes, Cadmus's family and Cadmus himself. Yet another way of referring to the essential doubling of Dionysus is that his return to Thebes is part of that species of doubling which Freud refers to as the uncanny (*unheimlich*).[14] The city is both his place of origin, his "home," and the place where he is most strongly opposed as a stranger and impostor. As is often the case in instances of the uncanny, this ambivalence arises from the emotive or sexual dynamics of Dionysus's rejection by his mortal family. Like his great-nephew Oedipus, Pentheus also returns to Thebes to destroy a family that earlier tried to destroy him. This same uncanniness could be the reason Vickers and others note that "there is something sinister about the cool unmoved way in which he [Dionysus] destroys his enemy."[15]

As Charles Segal has pointed out, there are many such doublings and ambiguities that structure and destructure—de-con-struct—Euripides' play; but, as Dodds maintains, the worship of Dionysus is the basis for all such reversals:

> It is hard to guess at the psychological state that he [Euripides] describes in the two words ὠμοφάγον χάριν ["flesh-eating blessedness"]. But it is noteworthy that the days appointed for ὠμοφαγία were "unlucky and black days," and it appears that those who practice a comparable rite in our time experience in it a mixture of supreme exaltation and supreme revulsion: it is at once holy and horrible, fulfillment and uncleanness, a sacrament and a pollution—the same violent conflict of emotional attitudes that runs all through the *Bacchae* and lies at the root of all religion of the Dionysiac type.[16]

Omophagia is the Dionysian practice described in the *Bacchae* and elsewhere of eating the raw flesh that has been torn apart (*sparagmos*) by the god's followers. As Dodds further explains, "We may regard the *omophagia*, then, as a rite in which the god was in some sense present in his beast-vehicle and was in that shape torn and eaten by his people."[17] The doubling of such fundamental opposites as creation and destruction in this orgiastic celebration is strikingly revealed. At the moment of worshiping Dionysus his followers destroy him; to become the god (the process described by Dodds of becoming *entheos*, whence our word *enthusiasm*) they must also destroy him. The striking parallels between this rite and the Christian Mass, as well as those between Christ and Dionysus in general (both are "sons of God," both are conceived by "immaculate conception," both came to earth to set mankind free, both demonstrate a curious mix of power and passivity) have been curiously ignored by most critics but are too extensive and important to be examined here.

Euripides' descriptions are no less ample in their demonstration of the doublings that Dodds urges us to "keep in mind."[18] "Hard are the labors of the god" the Chorus begins, "but his service is sweet" (*Bacchae*, 68). Silence is coupled with song (71–73), city with country (108), youth with old age (694), docility with aggression (68, 680–735), hunter with hunted ("He wears the holy fawn-skin. He hunts the wild goat and kills it. He delights in raw flesh," 136). This "enigmatic combination"[19] joins religion with sacrilege, joy with suffering, and winter with spring (73–75). Violence is coupled with restraint ("Handle with holy care the violent wand of god," 113), and propriety with impropriety: "Then from them to Rhea's hands the holy drum was handed down; but stolen by the raving Satyrs, fell at last to me" (128). The character of Dionysus himself and Dionysus's relation to Pentheus continue this same process of self-undermining doublings.

Certainly in all of Greek literature there is no more ambiguous god than Dionysus: "Dionysus is different. His divine identity oscillates bewilderingly between extreme and even opposite characteristics."[20] Sexually, Dionysus can be called "ambiguously ambiguous," for although he is described in androgynous, bisexual terms, his oft-remarked effeminacy coexists with masculine attributes of power and assertiveness over both men and women. Dionysus's status as god and man is equally double. He twice says in the prologue (5, 54) that he has come to Thebes as a "god disguised as a man," but he is known here and in the various myths that recount his adventures almost exclusively through such disguises. Why, one must wonder, would Dionysus come to Thebes disguised as a man "to prove to every man that I am a god indeed" (47)? It is this hybrid status that causes Dionysus's convergence with Pentheus, who suffers Dionysus's own fate of *sparagmos* ("dismemberment"). As Hölderlin and others have pointed out, mortality and immortality, *morality* and *immorality*, are inextricably linked in tragedy.[21]

The essential doubling of the play is not Dionysus's own ambiguous nature, alternately passive and violent, benign and malevolent, but the affinity with his rival Pentheus, really his alter ego: "The ease of the god's victory is an index of the extent to which Pentheus was already his unconscious follower."[22] The doubling of the tragic hero and his nemesis constitutes a tragic typology that encompasses all the above reversals. It might seem that no two characters could be more unlike than Cadmus's two grandsons, and that Vickers's belief that comparing the two would be "suicidal" is justified.[23] Pentheus can be said to represent the desire to govern the city according to law or, at least, according to his own perception of the law. Dionysus, on the other hand, represents the unbridled forces of nature, which may or may not actually threaten the workings of the civilized state (Pentheus thinks they do, Dionysus and Teiresias say they do not).[24] How can two such different rulers be one?

A critical crux of the *Bacchae* is the moment when Pentheus suddenly ceases to oppose Dionysus and expresses his eagerness to participate in the Bacchae's revels (811ff.). Readings may explain away this transformation with specious dramaturgical suppositions or ignore it altogether, as do most critics of the play, but the change should be seen as confirming the essential doubling of the two characters. Pentheus becomes Dionysus, as shown by his suffering the god's *sparagmos*, because his obsessive opposition to the god is finally revealed as the repression of his own hidden desires. Pentheus is transformed into Dionysus so easily because he already is Dionysus, or wants to be. In opposition to this view, Vickers says, emphatically echoing Pentheus's own language, that "Pentheus' resistance to Dionysus has nothing whatever to do with his own sexuality repressed or otherwise."[25]

Another critical crux explained by the tragic double is the way Dionysus, at the play's end, reveals as many Penthean attributes as Pentheus reveals Dionysian ones. Vickers is aware of this second reversal when he writes: "The reversal in our sympathies is complete. Those who had some claims to revenge become, when they gloat over its fulfillment, objects of loathing." So too Bellinger, who writes: "As the first half of the play leaves us with the feeling that the mortal has been unjust to the god, so the second half leaves us with the feeling that the god has been unjust to the mortal." Even those sympathetic to Dionysus have admitted being repulsed by his "petty and immoral" behavior in the final scenes of the play (Winnington-Ingram, 20), but this has usually led to futile discussion about Euripides' rational opposition to what others see as his supposed conversion to Dionysianism. Far less debatable is the chiasmus of the two characters' attributes: our sympathy turns away from Dionysus and toward Pentheus just as, earlier, it had moved away from Pentheus toward Dionysus.[26]

When one sees these two characters as essentially doubles, the reason for this shifting in our sympathies is no less fundamental to tragedy than the paradoxical relationship between tragic joy and tragic suffering.[27] Pentheus earns our sympathy at the end of the play, and Dionysus loses it, because the repressed forces Dionysus represents must always be perceived as both beautiful and horrible and so both worshiped and abhorred. Pentheus is portrayed so sympathetically because the nucleus of his desire is shown to be the destructive Oedipus complex, here taking the form of Pentheus's dismemberment by his mother, Agave. The brutality of Agave's destruction of her beloved son as he reaches out to her for protection must justify Pentheus's earlier repression of his primitive Dionysian desires.

In many fifth-century Athenian dramas the tragic hero, usually male because he represents the *polis*, opposes one or more aspects of Dionysus, nature and the feminine. But for Pentheus as for Hippolytus, Creon, Oedipus, and others, such "opposition" turns out to be a *doubling* paradoxically derived from the very Dionysian forces to which it is opposed. For example, Oedipus's obsession with defending the law throughout Sophocles's play can be seen as a direct result of the fundamental law of nature he has already violated. Freud often said that humanity acquired its moral conscience as a result of the successful resolution of the Oedipus complex.[28] We can now paraphrase Freud and add that tragedies like the *Bacchae*, which are clearly based upon the *unsuccessful* repression of primitive Dionysian desires, are based upon the forces which civilization is based upon. It is for this reason that tragedy at once is Dionysian and has "nothing to do with Dionysus."

*

The *Antigone* would seem to be a good place to begin examining the validity of this Dionysian model of tragic doubling, for its primary conflict, allegiance to family or state, appears more abstract than the opposition between male and female, culture and nature, consciousness and the unconscious found in the *Bacchae*. But however valuable Hegel's ethical reading of the *Antigone* may be, it is as blind to the play's Dionysian elements and their affinities with the *Bacchae* as is Aristotle's formalistic reading of the *Oedipus*. For Creon's "function" in the play, in Propp's structuralist use of the term, is much the same as Pentheus's in Euripides' play or, for that matter, Oedipus's in *Oedipus the King*. All three kings are typologically related in their obsession with the authority of the *tyrannos* to decree and enforce the laws of the state in contradistinction to *the* gods. Hegel is incorrect in giving equal weight to Creon and Antigone in this regard, for Antigone's nobility is not that of the typical male hero of tragedy. Among more recent critics, failure to define the Greek "tragic hero" along such typological lines has led Winnington-Ingram and Charles Segal (as we just saw) to reject Pentheus, and Normand Berlin Creon, as the tragic heroes of their respective plays.[29]

Women also perform an essential, and equally consistent, function in Greek tragedy. Without entering into the dubious debate concerning the status of women in fifth-century Athens as evidenced by their prominent role in tragedy,[30] one can say that if women are not tragic heroes, they certainly share center stage with their male counterparts, if not as their equals, then as their doubles. Just as Dionysus is usually accompanied by women, so too the women of tragedy must be grouped with their effeminate god, joining him in typical opposition to the typical tragic hero. Like Dionysus, the women of tragedy are heroes (if one is to use the term) but in a different sense: they represent the liberating forces of nature that triumph over the repressive forces of culture: "Women and Dionysus are closely associated in several myths which involve threats to the *polis* and its values."[31] Although largely neglected, this pattern has not gone entirely unnoticed, especially outside its literary context. In her analysis of the changing attitudes toward women in the fifth century as reflected in vase paintings of maenads, Sheila McNally writes that "rationality created divisions between man's mental and his physical existence"; in more overtly sociopolitical terms Marylin Arthur repeats this view of the "greater fragmentation" of classical Greek culture and the correlative alienation of women.[32]

Antigone's resemblance to Dionysus in the *Bacchae* is particularly striking. Both stand in calm defiance of the laws as they, like Aeschylus's Prometheus, champion a more natural code of behavior and virtue (*themis* versus *dike*). Medea, Klytemnestra, Aphrodite, Phaedra, Antigone, and others all form a consistent typology: like Dionysus, all these women represent the "return" of natural forces normally repressed by its double, the law of the male ruler.

If conservatism is typical of the tragic hero, so is an obsessive opposition to Dionysus and the women who represent him. This may seem less convincing in the case of Creon, whose concern for loyalty is not so blatantly unmasked as is Pentheus's desire for transgression. But on closer examination we can show that Creon's concern with loyalty is no less a function of the desire for his repressed double than is that of Pentheus.

Writers on the role of women in tragedy have not noted this typological association of Antigone with Dionysus, or the male:female::culture:nature::Pentheus:Dionysus conflict from which it stems. As mentioned, one reason for this neglect is that the *Antigone* is traditionally seen as concerned with ethical versus sexual conflicts. Another reason is that Antigone, unlike Phaedra, Medea, and Klytemnestra, does not represent herself as a spokeswoman for her sex. But if Antigone is unaware of her predicament as a "women's issue," Creon's concern with Antigone's status as a women matches his obsession with enforcing the city's laws. His remarks on women, although less explicit than Hippolytus's famous diatribe (*Hippolytus* 616–68), are essential for demonstrating the relevance of our typology and the tragic doubling on which it is based.

The first of these remarks occurs midway through the play, where Creon is lambasting the recalcitrant Antigone before the Chorus after her second attempt to bury her brother: "This girl was expert in her insolence when *she broke bounds beyond established law*. Once she had done it, insolence the second to boast her doing, and to laugh in it. *I am no man and she the man instead if she can have this conquest without pain* (*Antigone* 480–85; italics mine).[33]

If, says Creon, Antigone is allowed to thwart his will, then she will be the man and he the woman. Creon is not being faithful here to his "classical" argument that the laws of the city must precede other, more personal obligations. He is maintaining something quite different, namely, that whoever wins in their dispute will be the man, and so it cannot be right if Antigone is to have her way. If this were the only instance of an utterly misogynistic argument undermining Creon's more abstract, ethical demands, it could be ignored, but there are other examples of this subversive logic that are even more compelling.

A few lines later, after their confrontation has reached the fevered pitch of a stichomythia, Creon concludes, "Then go down there, if you must love, and love the dead. *No woman rules me while I live*" (525–26; italics mine). Again, the logic of Creon's final line is that Antigone is wrong, not because of her beliefs or for opposing the sanctity of the city, but because she is a woman. At the end of this scene, after Creon and Antigone have been joined by Ismene, Creon's exasperation reaches its limit as he angrily dismisses the two sisters: "Now, no delay! Slaves, take them in. *They must be women now. No more free running.* Even the bold will fly when they see Death drawing in close enough to end their life" (577–81; italics mine).

If we didn't know better, we might assume this to be Pentheus railing against the dangers of women being allowed to run free (*Bacchae* 218–20), for, whatever else they may be guilty of, Antigone and Ismene are certainly innocent of "free running." Creon's "hysteria" may even be more neurotic than that of Pentheus, who was at least responding to the reality of having to contend with such "loose women." As the above two quotations also indicate, Creon's fear is far more indicative of his own inner fantasies of being controlled by women than of any realistic threat to Thebes's stability.

The final quotation demonstrating Creon's misogyny, and the play's typlogical links with other Greek tragedies like the *Bacchae*, is perhaps the clearest in showing that Creon's battle is not on behalf of the state against the individual but on behalf of man against his tragic double, the natural, Dionysian woman: "If men live decently it is because discipline saves their very lives for them. So I must guard the men who yield to order, *not let myself be beaten by a woman. Better, if it must happen, that a man should overset me. I won't be called weaker than womankind*" (674–80; italics mine). These lines, spoken to a "weaker" son far wiser than he, demonstrate that the oft-remarked ethical debate in the *Antigone* between religion and the state is what Freud would call "secondary revision," for Creon is willing to forsake the propriety of his actions if only he not be "beaten by a women"!

Creon's misogynistic utterances are particularly important for our purposes because they reveal the facade of his conscious motivations in enforcing the law, however these may be justified. Like the *Bacchae*, the *Antigone* is about conscious efforts to repress the unconscious, which can only succeed in manifesting the unconscious at the same time as the greatness of the conscious is demonstrated (the heroism, however flawed, of Creon, Oedipus, and Pentheus is not in question). In reference to the countless uplifting theories that see tragedy as ultimately reasserting cosmic justice or moral truth, I would defer to Clifford Leech when he says that in tragedy "there is nothing reassuring . . . no promise that a new chain of evil will not quickly ensue, no lesson that men or the gods have learned."[34] We can now conclude by briefly indicating the relevance of this pattern of tragic doubling, with its essential components of misogyny and Dionysianism, to *Oedipus Tyrannus* and the *Hippolytus*.

Like Pentheus and Creon, Oedipus and Hippolytus are otherwise pious rulers who transgress the will of *a* or *the* god(s). Less obvious is the fact that both kings (Hippolytus is the surrogate ruler of Troezen) are also repressive rulers who stand in opposition to, yet double, representative Dionysian forces of nature. Oedipus's obsession with defending the law throughout the play is a result of the fundamental law of nature he has already violated. Like Pentheus, Oedipus lashes out at those around him because he has already done what Pentheus is shown to want to accomplish: to destroy utterly the norms of society.[35] (It is significant that the double, androgynous figure of Teiresias is the "archetypal" victim of such "tongue lashings," here, in the *Bacchae*, and in the *Antigone*.) It is the criminal in Oedipus, in other words, that makes him so obsessed with defending the law and with representing the reverence in which it is held. Since Oedipus has transgressed the boundary separating humanity and nature, he knows the horrors that await the one who does not strive to repress them. Although not speaking directly about *Oedipus*, Roy Morrell refers to this transgression/repression mechanism at work in tragedy when he asks, "Does tragedy provide the individual in the audience with a means of expansion through empathy . . . and then, but only in the destruction of the hero free the individual, break his empathy . . . ?"[36]

Finally, although Theseus assumes Creon's and Oedipus's role as representative of the *polis*, Hippolytus follows the pattern of the Penthean tragic hero in all other respects, just as the play *in toto* follows the typological pattern of Dionysian doubling outlined here. Like Dionysus's *mēnis* ("wrath of humiliation") with which the *Bacchae* began, the *Hippolytus* also begins with an explosion of indignant rage. Aphrodite, who stands for many of the same forces Dionysus represents, is justifiably angered by a mere mortal's insulting disregard:

> *Hippolytus:*   The God of nocturnal prowess is not my God.
> *Servant:*   The honors of the Gods you must not scant, my son.
> *Hippolytus:*   . . . For your Cypris here—a long goodbye to her![37]

In much the same way that Creon, Pentheus, and Oedipus had championed justice, Hippolytus imagines himself as representing those "in whose very soul the seed of Chastity toward all things alike nature has deeply rooted, they alone . . . not the wicked" (*Hippolytus* 81–83). Just as the other rulers we have discussed were destroyed by their manifestation of the forces they strove to repress, Hippolytus's "chaste" imagination doubles more explicitly erotic imaginings such as Phaedra's. Compare, for example, the following passage to Phaedra's lines about "drawing a draught of fresh spring water in the tufted meadow" (208–11): "My Goddess Mistress, I bring you ready woven this garland. It was I that plucked and wove it, plucked it for you in your inviolate Meadow. No shepherd dares to feed his flock within it: no reaper plies a busy scythe within it: only the bees in springtime haunt the inviolate Meadow" (71–75).

The presence of eros is clearly felt in this exquisite description of picking flowers that dare not be picked. Indeed, later in Euripides' play Hippolytus's image of the bee is repeated in the Chorus's highly erotic ode on love, Aphrodite, and Dionysus: "Love distills desire upon the eyes, love brings bewitching grace into the heart of those he would destroy. . . . Love is like a flitting bee in the world's garden and for its flowers, destruction is in his breath" (525–65). These passages and many others suggest that Hippolytus's repressive desire for Artemis's "inviolate meadow" is already inhabited by Aphrodite's "flitting bee" of love.

Much more needs to be said about the doubling of opposing forces, particularly those of Artemis and Aphrodite, in Euripides' *Hippolytus*. But returning to our general paradigm of tragic doubling, we can now conclude that the male tragic hero "opposes" Dionysus and his female followers because he fears losing his authority to them, and that this fear is based less on reality than on the desire for that which the hero is attempting to repress (note the curious way that Creon, Pentheus, and Oedipus, for example, create their own misfortunes). In the *Bacchae* Pentheus's desire for the repressed is made manifest in the play itself; for this reason the *Bacchae* should be considered a "tragedy of tragedy" as well as a tragedy about the god of tragedy. Similarly, Oedipus's paranoid fears about the plots being laid against him were viewed as a reaction to the actual fulfillment of his own hidden desires, while Creon was shown to be concerned less with the legality of his case against Antigone than with his imaginary fear (and desire) that power be turned over to a "free-running" Dionysian woman. For Hippolytus the case, as already mentioned, is somewhat different, but the essential tragic pattern of a male hero threatened by his own repressed desires is still clearly evident.

5 | The Psychoanalytic Double

Psychoanalysis, Art, and
"The Antithetical Sense
of Primary Words"

> Contraries are constantly represented by one and the same element in
> the modes of expression used by the unconscious, such as dreams.
> —Sigmund Freud, "The Theme of the Three Caskets"

> All true effigies have a double, a shadowed self. "Art" fails the moment
> a sculptor believes that as he models he liberates a kind of shadow
> whose existence unsettles him.
> —Antonin Artaud, "Theatre and Culture"

DESPITE A TITLE that promises relevance to aesthetics as well as to psychoanalysis, Freud's "On the Antithetical Sense of Primary Words" (1910) has been virtually ignored by "new" and older Freudians, "new" and older critics alike.[1] This is largely because in 1951 the eminent linguist Emile Benveniste attacked the piece in one of the few, if not the only, critical appraisals of Freud's essay.[2] Benveniste's study, however, is not the devastating dismissal it appears to be and can even be used to begin a reevaluation of *Über den Gegensinn der Urworte*. After reexamining Freud's theory of psychoanalytic doubling in the light of Benveniste's criticisms, I will argue that "The Antithetical Sense of Primary Words" is relevant to other fundamental psychoanalytic notions, such as Freud's theory of bisexuality, and to Freud's discussion of poetic meaning in three of his essays on art: "On the Uncanny," "The Taboo of Virginity," and "The Theme of the Three Caskets."

        *

    Although Freud's "The Antithetical Sense of Primary Words" raises at least as many questions as it answers, Sarah Kofman wisely warns us against disregarding those texts which "often appear written in a rather haphazard manner, whereas they in fact obey a hidden logic all their own."[3] Kofman also states that Freud's writings on dreams are perhaps the best source for his understanding of art,[4] an observation borne out by

Freud's beginning the discussion of language in "The Antithetical Sense of Primary Words" by referring to observations made in the *Traumdeutung*:

> In my *Traumdeutung* I made a statement concerning one of the findings of my analytic work which I did not then understand. I will repeat it at the beginning of this review: "The attitude of dreams towards the category of antithesis and contradiction is most striking. This category is simply ignored; *the word "No" does not seem to exist for a dream.* Dreams show a special tendency to reduce two opposites to a unity. . . . Dreams even take the liberty, moreover, of representing any element whatever by the opposite wish, so that it is at first impossible to ascertain, in regard to any element capable of an opposite, whether it is to be taken negatively or positively in the dream-thoughts."[5]

Characteristic of his self-avowed "rationalistic, or perhaps analytic, turn of mind,"[6] Freud here defines dreams by making a statement about them that dreams cannot make themselves: "the word 'No' does not seem to exist for a dream." Moreover, this "law of contradiction" applies as well to poetic language insofar as that language is consistently related by Freud to dreams: "I cannot suppress the surmise that even the most extreme variations [of art] could be brought into relationship with this model [of the daydream] by an uninterrupted series of transitions."[7] The attitude of *art*, to paraphrase Freud's statement, toward the category of antithesis and contradiction is most striking: this category is simply ignored; the word *no* does not seem to exist. My intention here is to demonstrate that Freud viewed the language of the unconscious in general and art in particular as antithetically double. To be sure, there is nothing new in the notion that the unconscious and its manifestations are to be understood in linguistic rather than, say, mechanistic terms.[8] But Freud's view of the antithetical nature of "original" language has been virtually ignored.[9] Indeed, it was against such an elevation of linguistic doubling that Benveniste based his influential attack on Freud's essay.

During the same year in which Freud wrote his review-essay of the philologist Karl Abel's "Über den Gegensinn der Urworte" he had already expressed an interest in "searching in the direction of archaic regression . . . which I hope to master through mythology and the development of language."[10] This is the context in which Freud's review-essay must be read, for, as John Forrester explains in *Language and the Origins of Psychoanalysis,* "in the 1910's Freud was forced to give up the double determination of the linguistic usage of the present—that is, free association—and resorted to determination of symbolism through the pre-historic origins of language."[11]

In order to support the psychoanalytical notion, derived from the *In-*

terpretation of Dreams, that opposite, "repressed" meanings are joined in primitive thought and primitive language, Freud reproduces examples from Abel's article of words which were supposed to have originally included their own opposites: *bass* (well) relates to *bös* (bad); *cleave* corresponds to German *kleben* (to stick); German *stumm* is connected to *Stimme*; Latin *clam* (secretly) is linked to *clamare*; and so on. Writing some forty years later, the eminent philologist Emile Benveniste has a field day in ridiculing these etymological examples of "original words with a double meaning" by pointing to the different root systems lying behind these "same" words: "The Old German adverb *bass* 'well' is related to *besser* but has no connection with *bös* 'bad,' . . . English *cleave* does not correspond to German *kleben* 'to stick,' as Abel says, but to *klieben* 'to cleave' (cf. *Kluft*). . . . In the same way, in Latin, *clam* 'secretly' is linked to *celare* 'to hide,' and not at all to *clamare*, and so on." [12]

Although it is not my intention to rescue Freud from these "grave errors" of historical and comparative linguistics, Benveniste's dismissal is not altogether convincing. It is possible to detect a certain insecurity in Benveniste's insistence throughout this paragraph that the words in question "have nothing in common," are "not at all" linked, and "have no connection" with each other. But it is in his dismissal of "a second series of proofs, also erroneous" that Benveniste's defensiveness is most apparent. The "double sense of Latin *sacer* [as both] 'consecrated' and 'accursed'" is dismissed because

> the ambivalence of the notion should no longer surprise us since so many studies of the phenomenology of the sacred have made a cliché of its basic duality; in the Middle Ages, a king and a leper were both "untouchables," but it does not follow that *sacer* includes two contradictory senses; it was cultural conditions which determined two opposed attitudes toward the object described as *sacer*. [13]

That a king and a leper should both be referred to as "sacred" might not surprise Benveniste, but the medieval connection between the sacred and the accursed is no less surprising for being a "cliché." What is surprising is Benveniste's separation of "the object described as *sacer*" and what are vaguely referred to as "cultural conditions" from linguistic conditions of the word *sacred*. Such separations are characteristic of Benveniste's very limited view of language as an unambiguous system.

Having dispensed with Freud/Abel's specific examples of primary antithetical words, Benveniste then turns his attack on the general theory they purport to prove by declaring an axiom of *un*-ambiguity underlying "real language":

But it nevertheless remains that language is a system, that it obeys a specific plan, and that it is articulated by a set of relationships capable of a certain formalization. The slow but incessant work that goes on within a language does not operate at random . . . [but] in such a way as to renew or multiply distinctions that are useful at all levels of expression. . . . *It is thus a priori improbable—and an attentive examination confirms it—that these languages, however archaic they are assumed to be, escape the "principle of contradiction" by using the same expression for two mutually exclusive or simply contrary notions.*[14]

Benveniste views language as a "system" of "articulated relationships" that makes it "a priori improbable" that words would be ambiguous to the point of meaning their own opposites. This structuralist view rests on (at least) two highly suspect assumptions: first, that language always operates pragmatically ("multiplying distinctions *which are useful*"), and, second, that antithetical words are "a priori improbable" because language is "a priori" systematic. Benveniste's view of the unambiguous "system" of language must be considered alongside the views of other linguists who view ambiguity as "apparently a universal characteristic of linguistic surface structure."[15] Even if one were to accept Benveniste's notion that "real language" (72) functions this way, that would not refute Freud's compatible notion that "real language," the language of consciousness, obeys the law of noncontradiction while "original language," the language of the unconscious, does not. In other words, Benveniste criticizes Freud for theorizing about a view of language that disobeys the law of noncontradiction whereas it is precisely Freud's intention to consider language before it becomes "real."

Benveniste is right to reject Freud/Abel's false etymologies insofar as they were intended to provide historical evidence for the unity of opposite words like *bös/bass*. But this does not mean that Freud's view of unconscious, versus "real," language is untenable. Benveniste's argument is even compatible with Freud's in its view of "real language," and the two are also in agreement as to the antithetical nature of dreams, rhetoric, and art: "What Freud asked in vain of 'historical' language he could have asked to a certain extent of myth or poetry. Certain forms of poetry can be related to dreams and can suggest the same mode of structuring. They can bring about in the normal forms of language that suspension of meaning which dreams project into our activities."[16] Although Benveniste accepts the idea that oneiric logic is antithetical as Freud describes, and although he relates this in turn to "myth or poetry," Benveniste nonetheless insists that this has nothing to do with language: "Everything seems to take us far away from an 'actual' correlation between oneiric logic and the logic of a real language."[17] Yet, if one accepts that the relevance of antithetical relationships to art is not limited to certain explicitly dream-oriented, surrealist works like those of Breton (whom Benveniste, evidently unaware of Freud's disdain for surrealism, chides Freud for failing to consider in this essay), then the notion that "real language" has nothing to do with "oneiric logic" and its antithetical doublings is far less persuasive than Benveniste intends it to be.[18]

Benveniste's "refutation" also falls short when one acknowledges that Freud has claimed only to have found "confirmation" of the tendency of dream symbolism in early language ("dürfen wir *eine Bestätigung* unserer Auffassung vom regressiven, archaischen Charakter des Gedankenausdruckes im Traume erblicken").[19] Abel's error simply cautions us to understand *Urworte,* "original language," as "a 'language' so special that it is of the greatest importance to distinguish it from what we normally call language."[20] Yet this highly "specialized" language includes, by Benveniste's own admission, not only myth, poetry, and linguistic idioms but the whole of style and rhetoric:

> *For it is style rather than language* that we would take as term of comparison with the properties that Freud has disclosed as indicative of oneiric "language." One is struck by the analogies which suggest themselves here. The unconscious uses a veritable "rhetoric" which, like style, has its "figures," and the old catalogue of tropes would supply an inventory appropriate to the two types of expression. One finds in both all the devices of substitution engendered by taboo: euphemism, allusion, antiphrasis, preterition, litotes. The nature of the content makes all the varieties of metaphor appear, *for symbols of the unconscious take both their meaning and their difficulty from metaphoric conversion.*[21]

Benveniste has conceded much to Freud's notion of primary antithetical language. Although "metaphoric conversion" is not synonymous with antithesis, Benveniste's description of the "language" of the unconscious as stylistic and metaphoric makes Freud's hypothesis that the language of the unconscious is antithetical all the more credible. For rhetoric has long been identified with antithesis, whether implicitly, as when Aristotle defines metaphor as the "introduction of a word which belongs to something else" or explicitly, as in the case of the sophist-rhetor Protagoras's notion of the *dissoi logoi* ("For every argument there is an equally true opposing argument, including this one").[22] Indeed, the "ancient" definition of irony as "expressing something by its opposite, its *contrarium*" makes the connection between rhetoric and antithesis more explicit.[23]

Benveniste's separation of style and rhetoric from language (he twice puts the "language" of the unconscious in quotation marks), which must be understood as the use of words without style and rhetoric, must make one wonder whose notion of language, Freud's or Benveniste's, is more convincing. Although Freud erred in claiming to have found historical support for the original doubling of antithetical terms, Benveniste's notion of "real language" as an unambiguous "system" devoid of antithesis, rhetoric, and style limits the relevance of Benveniste's views while, at the same, elevating the importance of antithetical meanings to the "language" of myth, art, and the unconscious. The way is now cleared for a reconsideration of the importance of the antithetical doubling of primary words to psychoanalysis in general and to its view of art in particular.

*

Laplanche has done an exemplary job in showing how the "objects" of psychoanalysis must be understood in rhetorically antithetical terms. Taking his lead from Freud's notion that "we have been in the habit of regarding the connection between the sexual drive and the sexual object as more intimate than it in fact is," Laplanche describes just how perilous the notion of a sexual "object" can be. And, Laplanche is careful to add, this means not only that the object of sexuality may be anomalous as in the case of perversions but, taking object in its epistemological sense of "objectively real," that "the object can be, without prejudice, a *fantasmatic* object and that it is perhaps essentially such."[24]

Although Laplanche does not himself do so, his analysis of the "objects" of sexual drives can be applied to Freud's notion of the antithetical sense of primary words. Following Freud's interest in "sensual sucking," *Lutschen,* as a process which begins as nutritive and ends as sexual, Laplanche views the object of sexual desire as hopelessly lost between the two: "Can we be sure whether it [the object of *Lutschen*] is still the milk or already the breast?"

> Thus the sexual object is not identical to the object of the function, but is displaced in relation to it; they [nutrition and sexuality] are in a relation of essential *contiguity* which leads us to slide almost indifferently from one to the other, from the milk to the breast as its symbol. "The finding of an object," Freud concludes . . . "is in fact a re-finding of it." We would elucidate this as follows: the object to be rediscovered is not the lost object, but its substitute by displacement; the lost object is the object of self-preservation, of hunger, and the object one seeks to re-find in sexuality is an object displaced in relation to that first object. From this, of course, arises the impossibility of ultimately ever rediscovering the object, since the object which has been lost *is not the same* as that which is to be rediscovered. Therein lies the key to the essential "duplicity" situated at the very beginning of the sexual quest.[25]

According to Laplanche's interpretation of Freud's famous statement, it is because we never find the original object, but only a later repostulation of it, that the original object can never be found but only refound. Once the breast has merged with the identification of the whole mother, it may be refound in the thumb, penis, et cetera, which is as much the "original object" of sexual desire as the breast failed to be, since the breast is only "contiguous" to the milk which it provides, the nipple it contains, and so on. "The object which has been lost is not the same as the object to be rediscovered" because the sexual drive is part of a larger, original "life instinct" that is different from the sexual drive per se.

It is possible to invoke the "ignorance of the category of antithesis and contradiction" referred to in "The Antithetical Sense of Primary Words" and in *The Interpretation of Dreams* in order to understand infantile sexuality in its original relation to the "life instinct." Indeed, one could make the case that the entire realm of sexuality as Laplanche describes it, which is "simultaneously the same and different" from the instinctual "life process" from which it emerges, is double, for the nutritive—Laplanche uses the term *cannibalistic*—instinct must continue to inform adult sexuality at the same time as it is denied. If "sensual sucking" (*Lutschen*), which Freud repeatedly saw as "the prototype of every relation of love," is defined as the pleasure derived from eating without eating, then sexuality *in toto* can be defined as the discovery ("re-finding") of objects which are antithetically related to their "true object." Voyeurism, for example, is clearly antithetical in this sense, for it too derives pleasure from an act that is the opposite of its "true" act.[26]

Another obvious place to test the relevance of Freud's notion of the antithetical doubling of primary words is his theory concerning "the antithetical sense of primary sexuality," bisexuality as the origin of human sexuality. Freud's notion of original bisexuality, adopted early in his career from Fliess, was to remain a staple feature of his thought. In an essay of 1931, "Libidinal Types," Freud wrote: "The precipitating occasions [of neurosis] are . . . conflicts between the three great psychical agencies, *conflicts arising in the libidinal economy by reason of our bi-sexual disposition*, conflicts between the erotic and the aggressive instinctual components."[27] In "Hysterical Fantasies and Their Relation to Bisexuality" (1908) Freud made this bold claim for the importance of bisexuality even more explicitly: "An hysterical symptom is the expression of both a masculine and a feminine unconscious sexual fantasy."[28] The claim is especially bold when one recalls that among "hysterical symptoms" Freud includes daydreams, nocturnal dreams, and the whole array of unconscious manifestations; thus, bisexual doubling is potentially as significant in the etiology of neuroses as sexuality itself:

> The connection between the [hysterical] symptoms and the phantasies makes it easy to arrive, by psycho-analysis of the former, at a knowledge of the components of the sexual instinct dominating the person concerned, which I have described in my *Drei Abhandlungen zur Sexualtheorie*. In some cases, however, investigation by this means yields an unsuspected result. It shows that for many symptoms it is not enough to resolve only one unconscious sexual phantasy or even a number of them, of which one, the most important and fundamental, is of a sexual nature; to resolve the symptom one has, on the contrary, to deal with two sexual phantasies, of which one has a masculine and the other a feminine character, so that one of these phantasies has its source in a homosexual trend. This new statement does not alter our seventh formula; an hysterical symptom must necessarily be a compromise between a libidinal and a repressing force, but incidentally it may represent a combination of two libidinal phantasies of an opposite sexual character.[29]

Freud alludes here to a kind of "Chinese box" arrangement in which the bisexual opposition exists within the libido component of the opposition between the "libidinal and a repressing force." What, then, are we to make of this more profound opposition which exists within the libido itself, which "marks the highest degree of complexity in the way in which an hysterical symptom can be determined"? Indeed, what is one to make of this phenomenon when Freud frequently stressed the "anatomical distinction between the sexes"?[30]

Freud's notions of the doubling of original language and original bisexuality must stand or fall together. Corresponding to the passage from *The Interpretation of Dreams* quoted earlier about the impossibility of asserting oppositions in dreams are a number of statements in the same text that "assert of many dreams, *if they are carefully interpreted*, that they are bisexual, since they unquestionably admit of an 'over-interpretation' in which the dreamer's homosexual impulses are realized—impulses, that is, which are contrary to his normal sexual activities."[31] As Jean-Michel Rey states in his brilliant study "De la bisexualité," "No criterion of judgment is provided [in dreams] which could validate the difference between the sexes."[32] While Freud would certainly deny that phallic and vaginal symbols do not exist as such in dreams, sexual difference progressively disappears within the folds of unconscious thought, folds that gradually envelop the dreamer's own sexuality as well as that of the particular symbol involved: "It is true that the tendency of dreams and of unconscious phantasies to employ sexual symbols bi-sexually betrays an archaic characteristic; for in childhood the distinction between the genitals is unknown and the same kind of genitals is attributed to both of them."[33] To the extent to which sexuality is essentially such an unconscious, "primary" process for Freud, any attempt to assert a difference within the realm of sexuality, "sexual difference," will result in a double "event which proves what is denied in its denial" ("un événement qui se produit en se déniant."[34] We can demonstrate the validity of this curious maxim by looking at three famous examples of symptoms which turn out to be bisexual, and at the theory of "castration fear" and "penis envy" on which they supposedly depend.

A woman's stroking, braiding, and otherwise manipulating her hair symbolizes the missing penis whose absence is *denied* through covering up, simulation through braiding, replacement by the fingers, and so on, as well as *affirmed* by virtue of the hair's similarity to the female genitalia.[35] Weaving of the hair (or, as Freud also says, weaving in general) thus conceals as well as reveals the absent penis and so exemplifies the notion that there are no masculine or feminine symbols per se. From the male perspective, "the multiplication of symbols of the penis signifies castration," and the presence of the phallus, as in the case of fetishism, is a sign more of its absence and the fear of castration than of presence.[36] The presence or absence of the penis, then, is less a way of distinguishing between the sexes than a sign of their original doubling, for it is as much present in its absence ("penis envy") as it is absent in its presence ("castration fear").

In typical fashion, Freud was even more correct than he indicated when he suggested that it is impossible to distinguish between the sexes at the level of sexual symbolism. In Freud's article "Medusa's Head" (1922), and Neil Hertz's remarkable discussion of the same in *The End of the Line*,[37] the apotropaeic power of the Gorgon's head emblazoned on a shield is seen as a symbol of power over castration as well as fear of the same. The symbol of the Gorgon's head, which combines both masculine and feminine attributes (note the superabundance of snakes), reveals phallic superiority and its denial to be one and the same. The antithetical doubling of opposites like the male and female genitalia inevitably results in a chiasmatic "penis fear" or "castration envy," for the object of desire of the erect penis is the "castrated" vulva: "If the head of Medusa replaces the representation of the female genitalia, or, rather, if it isolates its terrifying effect from its pleasurable one, one can recall that showing the genitalia is elsewhere just as well known as apotropaeic."[38]

My purpose in analyzing these two examples is to show that bisexuality, the antithetical doubling of those most primary of words, male and female, is part of that unconscious substratum that undermines any assertion of sexual difference in art, dreams, symptoms, and so on. One of the few places where Freud seems to argue *against* the importance of bisexuality in the unconscious is in his study "'A Child Is Being Beaten': A Contribution to the Study of the Origin of Sexual Perversions" (1919).[39] And so, before concluding this discussion, we will consider Freud's supposed objection to a characterization of the unconscious as bisexual.

In "A Child Is Being Beaten" Freud is concerned with the pleasure "frequently" derived by many of his patients from the fantasy of a child being beaten. The *woman's* fantasy of a male child being beaten is discovered to be the result, not of any jealousy toward the male and satisfaction at observing him punished, but of relinquishing her incestuous desire for the father only to the extent of adopting a masculine unconscious persona (186). In other words, the unconscious, due to repression, has produced a more easily tolerated masculine persona (but not tolerated enough to escape punishment) in order to allow the fantasy of a relationship with the father to continue.

The *male's* fantasy of a child being beaten turns out to be equally bisexual, for the male is viewed as assuming a *feminine* role in being beaten (loved) by the father (mother):

> In the case of the girl the unconscious masochistic phantasy starts from the normal Oedipus attitude; in that of the boy it starts from the inverted attitude, in which the father is taken as the object of love. . . . The boy, on the contrary, changes the figure and sex of the person beating by putting his mother in the place of his father; but he retains his own figure, with the result that the person beating and the person being beaten are of opposite sexes. (195)

The man's original fantasy, then, is identical with that of the woman, to be loved by the father. This should surprise those who adopt a more simplistic reading of Freud and assume that the original male and female fantasies are sexually coded, with, for example, the male desiring the mother and the female the father. In Freud's analysis the same fantasy is viewed as masculine on the part of the girl insofar as she identifies with the male and feminine on the part of the boy. What is more, the girl is also still a girl given the continuation of her Oedipal fixation on her father, and the boy is also still a boy in the original fantasy, which is that of a male child being beaten.

Freud then turns (section 6, 191–201) to two theories, those of Fliess and Adler, which posit repression as a function of "repression of the opposite sex" and "repression of the feminine." What Freud finds unacceptable in Fliess's theory (Adler's theory is similarly dismissed) is that the male is viewed as originally a male whose repressed unconscious is female: "The dominant sex of the person, that which is the more strongly developed, has repressed the mental representation of the subordinated sex into the unconscious" (197). Freud's analysis, however, of the male and female fantasies of "a child being beaten" revealed that the unconscious is in reality bisexual, with repressed fantasies that are capable of doubling as male and female for both sexes: "In the last resort we can only see that both in male and female individuals masculine as well as feminine instinctual impulses are found, and that each can equally well undergo repression and so become unconscious" (199). Freud thus rejects as too "simplistic" Fliess's identification of the male with his possession of a penis: "Such a theory as this can only have an intelligible meaning if we assume that a person's sex is to be determined by the formation of his genitals" (197). To conclude, in "A Child Is Being Beaten" Freud rejects not the identification of repression with bisexuality but the reduction of unconscious doubling and the identification of repression with sexuality, with one sex or the other.

*

The remainder of this chapter will be concerned with the relevance of Freud's notion of the doubling of "primary words" to the psychoanalytic interpretation of art. That poetic meaning is "primary" and stems from the repressed unconscious is a familiar tenet of Freud and his followers. As with dreams, poetry expresses itself in "oblique words behind which one must recognize *the original meaning of desire*" ("les sens primitif du désir").[40] Sophocles' *Oedipus the King*, for example, is permeated with veiled (and not so veiled) expressions of Oedipus's "original" double desire to kill his father and marry his mother. Whether or not we accept that, like dreams, art is an expression of the repressed unconscious will depend on the reader's tolerance for psychoanalysis in general. My intention is only to show that such repressed, "primary" meaning in art is always antithetically double. It may even prove to be the case that by accepting the latter notion the former may appear less reductive.

The psychoanalytic essay on art which has been discussed by literary critics more than any other in recent years is "On the Uncanny" (1919), Freud's analysis of fictive horror as the return of childhood desires.[41] But if we examine this essay from the vantage point of "The Antithetical Sense of Primary Words," we find that the foreign/familiar dichotomy on which the uncanny is based (the German *unheimlich*, "uncanny," literally means "not of the house" as does its own opposite, *heimlich*, which also means "of the house") turns on the doubling of these two opposing forces in the unconscious. What is foreign is so because it is really familiar, "of the house," and then, by virtue of repression, is feared as a threat to what is really its own identity: "the unheimlich is what was once heimisch, home-like, familiar" (153). For example, later repression of our original infantile narcissism returns to haunt us in the form of ghosts, doubles (*Doppelgän-ger*), talking dolls, and the like. Such a process might be likened to that of "the purloined letter" in reverse: rather than a letter which is hidden by not being concealed, here something familiar is pretending to be concealed.

The uncanny is an "antithetical primary word" par excellence, for it is both the "strangely familiar" as well as the "familiarly strange." Once again it appears that Freud was more correct than he realized, for his theory can be applied to E. T. A. Hoffmann's "Der Sandmann" even beyond the point where Freud's own reading leaves off. The dreaded figure of Cop-pelius is not only associated with but also is his own double, the beloved father whose authority the son Nathaniel splits off from his "good father" in order to continue his narcissistic childhood fantasies. Throughout the story Nathaniel is persecuted by the evil father-figure Coppelius for failing to relinquish narcissistic desires readily apparent in Nathaniel's love for the automaton Olympia, as well as in his final leap from a lofty tower in order to escape both his fiancée, Clara, and the dreaded Coppelius. And, the first time Nathaniel sees Coppelius conferring with his father in their home is when Nathaniel sneaks out of bed late at night to observe the two clandes-tinely.

As a word that also means its own opposite, "the uncanny" perfectly illustrates Freud's notion of the doubling of unconscious meaning. For the effects of the uncanny described in Hoffmann's story are all derived from the same disturbing unity in the unconscious of the foreign (Coppelius, the automaton Olympia) and the familiar (the father, the fiancée). Moreover, a chiasmus can also be formed that doubles these opposing terms even fur-ther, for Clara, like Coppelius, represents the repressive "reality principle" eschewed by Nathaniel, whereas Nathaniel's father, like the hollow doll Olympia, steadfastly refuses to condemn his son's solipsism. Either way, the uncanny effects of Hoffmann's story depend on double figures that turn into their own opposites.

In his essay "On the 'Uncanny'" Freud questioned why beloved child-hood desires (like a doll coming to life) should return to haunt us as adults. Similarly, "The Taboo of Virginity" (1918) begins by asking why virginity should be revered by some cultures and feared by others (or, revered and feared in the same culture).[42] Freud's explanation of this ambiguity is that original intercourse as it is informed by the unconscious is also a terrifying experience resulting from the "wounding" of the female by the male who penetrates her. And it is frightening for both sexes, because the resulting anger of the injured female is perceived as a threat of similar injury to the male. Emerging, then, from Freud's sketch of this "primal scene" of sexual intercourse is a palimpsest that resembles the story of Judith and Holofernes.

Like Sophocles' version of *Oedipus*, in the Apocrypha version Judith can be seen as motivated by the highest moral concern, that of saving her people, and not by sexuality or sexual revenge. For Freud, however, "the taboo of virginity and some part of its motivation has been portrayed most powerfully of all in the well-known figure of Judith in Hebbel's tragedy" (203). And, lest one think that the psychoanalytic reading applies only to Hebbel's *Judith und Holofernes* version and not to the story of the Apocrypha, Freud informs us that "with the sensitive intuition of a poet Hebbel probably divined *the primordial theme* that had been lost in the tendentious story [of the Apocrypha], and only gave back to the content its earlier currency" (204; italics mine). Judith, according to Freud, is not "a" but "the" virgin; she represents for Freud our *original* attitude toward sexuality. And original *Ur*-sexuality, like original words (*Urworte*), turns out to be originally antithetical, or double.

The "antithetical meaning of original intercourse" is that of the hatred, fear, and anger that accompany sexual desire. Hebbel's Judith is the prototype of this because her beauty and desirability cause fear and impotence in her first husband ("My beauty is like deadly nightshade, enjoyment of it brings madness and death") while her defloration results in the castration of her lover, symbolically represented by Holofernes' beheading. The antithetical doublings of desire and impotence merge because possession of the object of desire is originally a dangerous endeavor. And if the initial impotence is overcome and the object attained, there is still the "castration anxiety" which ensues as a result of possessing the previously intact, independent object of desire. Although one might assume that Freud's interpretation of Hebbel's *Judith* would be used to support a feminist reading of the same, recent feminist literary theory rightly cautions us against such an unambiguous interpretation. One writer, however, has suggested that Freud's essay is itself vitiated by the very taboos it describes, and so is antipathetical to any feminist agenda.

Anyone reading Mary Jacobus's feminist essay on Freud's "Taboo of Virginity" ("Judith, Holofernes and the Phallic Woman") will experience strong dramatic undercurrents in the text itself that reflect those of the Judith/Holofernes story.[43] The purpose of Jacobus's reading is to take revenge against Freud for his acts of "violence against literature" in general and women in particular.[44] Since Jacobus's view that Freud's violence is the result of "univocal" theorizing which eschews "undecidability" runs directly counter to the notion of psychoanalytic doublings offered here, her view of Freud's essay, and of psychoanalysis in general, warrants special attention.

Jacobus begins by accusing Freud of "slyly invoking" feminism in the essay "On Femininity" when he characterizes the objection that psychoanalysis does not serve women's "eagerly coveted equality with men" as "a knife that cut both ways." Freud's point is that, while the "Oedipus-complex" may itself stem from a "masculinity complex" in its "innate inclination to disparage and suppress women," this equally "feminist" and "psychoanalytic argumentation" (Freud's words) "cuts both ways" because the objection can itself be seen to support the existence of the masculinity complex. Jacobus calls Freud "sly" in this regard because, although he refuses to take sides in the feminist controversy, he admits that the basis of psychoanalysis is masculine.

Jacobus's second main objection is that Freud repeats "primitive man's" error of converting psychic fears into real ones: Freud "proposes the startling idea that women actually do pose a threat to men after sexual intercourse, and especially on the first occasion" ("Judith, Holophernes, and the Phallic Woman," 116). When Freud goes on to attribute actual aggressiveness to women in response to their loss of virginity, he has evidently forgotten that such a projection of psychic fears into real ones is fallacious: "For Freud himself, it seems, the projected danger is as real as for primitive man" (116).

Third, Jacobus invokes Sarah Kofman's "indictment of Freud's violence against literature" (117) to support her view of Freudian theory as "univocal," as essentially opposed to "the oscillation of meaning or 'irresolution' which both Freudian theory and the little boy must repress in order to make sense of what they see" (122). Likened to a "little boy" (just as, earlier, he was likened to a primitive man) who represses the possibility of castration by disparaging women, Freud "univocally" assumes, among other things, the reality of the castrating woman.

Although Jacobus's powerful study deserves lengthier analysis, it is possible to respond to the essay's three main objections as follows:

First objection: that "Freud 'slyly invokes feminism' while at the same time validating psychoanalysis' sexist constructs." Freud's point in the passage Jacobus cites from "On Femininity" is that, while the feminist might object to psychoanalytical constructs like those of the castration and Oedipal complexes as harmful to women's equality because they illustrate men's "innate inclination to disparage and suppress women," such objections can also be said to validate the constructs of psychoanalysis (this is the "knife's" other edge). That is because psychoanalysis studies precisely those primitive, unconscious modes of behavior that result in the suppression of women. Freud is not, then, indicating any disagreement with feminism, yet he is acknowledging that disparagement of women is a feature of many of the complexes psychoanalysis studies. Jacobus considers this "sly," by which she must mean that Freud is guilty of saying one thing and meaning another. But is it slyness to say that psychoanalysis cannot itself take sides in the feminist controversy, while being, at the same time, in favor of feminism as a political goal? Jacobus's main point throughout her essay is that the Freudian sword does *not* cut both ways and so eschews "undecidability," but Freud's point in "On Femininity" is that "the use of analysis as a weapon of controversy can clearly lead to no decision."

As Jacobus herself notes, a literal translation of Freud's phrase in "On Femininity" (and in "Dostoyevski and Parricide") is that of a "stick with two ends," not that of a "double-edged sword." Nonetheless, Freud is still attacked for wielding such a "weapon": "Analysts with feminist views might be tempted to reply that psychology itself has emotional desires; or at least that the 'knife that cuts both ways' may slice unevenly for men and for women. Significantly, Freud's borrowed metaphor equates psychoanalysis itself with what had by this time become its centrally informing concept, the castration complex" (111). Again, the sword, or knife, is Strachey's, *not* "Freud's borrowed metaphor." In order to prove the centrality of the castration complex (and its violence to women) Jacobus must, first, "beat Freud's stick into a sword" and, then, beat that double-edged sword into one that "slices unevenly."

Second objection: that "Freud reifies primitive man's psychic fear of the castrating woman." There is nothing unusual in Freud's consideration of an actual/psychic aggressiveness on the part of women that corresponds to men's own fears. The male's "castration anxiety" is just as "anhypothetical"[45] a hypothesis as the woman's "penis envy." Moreover, the passage Jacobus alludes to which contains Freud's "startling idea" is much more ambiguous than her reference reveals, for in it Freud's mention of "a danger which really does exist" is inextricably linked to the notion of a purely psychical danger: "I will anticipate the result of such an examination by saying that a danger of the kind does really exist, so that with his taboo primitive man is protecting himself from a danger—a psychical one, it is true—which his intuition had quite correctly divined [*der Primitive sich mit dem Tabu der Virginität gegen eine richtig geahnte, wenn auch psychische Gefahr verteidigt*]."[46]

Equally offensive to Jacobus in this regard is Freud's attribution of a specific motive—"penis envy"—underlying women's supposed aggressiveness. For "though Freud *goes through the motions* of searching elsewhere for the causes of female hostility . . . *he fastens finally on the girl's desire to possess the penis*" ("Judith, Holofernes, and the Phallic Woman," 116; italics mine). But Freud's reference to "penis envy" cannot be said to efface the other motives he mentions. Jacobus omits from her "dismal litany" of other motives Freud's emphatic inclusion of an Oedipal motive also said to underlie woman's resentment ("A husband is, so to speak, never anything but a proxy, never the right man," 199), and which Sarah Kofman too sees as operative in Hebbel's *Judith*. Kofman sees in Hebbel's play "a perfect illustration of woman's hostility unleashed by the attack on her virginity" (84), thereby utilizing another of Freud's "dismal" motives as well as supporting his view of women's resentment over the "loss" of their virginity.[47]

Third objection: that "Like a little boy's, Freud's ideas are too one-sided, or 'univocal,' and so do violence to literature's multiplicity of meanings." Anyone familiar with the three books Sarah Kofman has written on Freud and, in particular, on Freud's interpretations of art, must wonder at Jacobus's characterization of Kofman's as "among the most telling indictments of Freud's violence against literature." This misrepresentation of Kofman's views and attitude toward Freud, which are decidedly constructive and even reverential throughout, must make one wonder if Jacobus isn't misrepresenting Freud too, as well as unfairly polarizing his theory along strict gender lines. Likening Freud to a little boy is the same as saying that Freudian theory is infantile. Unfortunately, this puts Jacobus herself into a position of parental authority which her notion of "undecidability" would like to do without.

The following passage from Sarah Kofman's book on Freud and art can help in responding to the larger question of Freud's supposed insensitivity to "oscillations of meaning," especially in art-related matters:

> We can draw a certain number of conclusions from Freud's method of reading [artistic works]. First, Freud's conception of truth is a new one. . . . truth is given only in its distortions and is constructed from those distortions. There is no originary text that the others supposedly translate; rather, one is always referred from one text to another, one version to another, produced by the differential play of a single universal fantasy that is structured in that play. . . . André Green shows very well what the relation is between distortion, repetition, and interpretation: "Destined to let itself be deciphered by interpretation and to wander in distortion, truth repeats itself relentlessly in order to be recognized and hide itself

indefinitely." . . . *The signifier, even as it relentlessly announces itself, distorts itself and eludes any unequivocal, global, and definitive grasp.*[48]

How can a double "method of reading" that denies closure at the same time as it pursues a meaning that is never fully present be described as too "univocal," as insensitive to "oscillations of meaning"? Indeed, it would not be hard to make the case that a method of reading overtly informed by the concept of "undecidability" is itself the more univocal. Freud's readings, Kofman continues, deny paternal authority—symbolized by Holofernes—through interpretive acts of violence which "cut both ways," for they are "inscribed in a chain of substitutes" which "reveal and mask" their meaning at one and the same time.

The final essay on art to be read from the perspective of "The Antithetical Sense of Primary Words" is Freud's famous study of "The Theme of the Three Caskets" (1913).[49] Freud takes as his point of departure questions raised by Bassanio's puzzling choice in *The Merchant of Venice* of the third, leaden casket to win "the fair and wise" Portia for his bride. In resolving this contradiction, Freud first notes that the motif of a dangerous choice, usually among three women, to find one's beloved is in fact a universal one: "we have here *an ancient theme*, which requires to be interpreted and traced back *to its origin*" (64; italics mine). (The reader will recall that this is exactly what Freud said about Hebbel's version of *Judith und Holofernes*.) The choice in *King Lear* among Regan, Goneril, and Cordelia is seen as a variation on the same theme, the only difference being that the myth is slightly altered so that, as an old man, Lear chooses between his three daughters ("An old man cannot very well choose between three women in any other way: thus they become his daughters," 66). The seemingly antithetical relationship between Bassanio's youth and Lear's old age is, as we shall see, essential to a proper understanding of each.

The problem Freud still faces in "The Theme of the Three Caskets" is understanding why, in *The Merchant of Venice*, the third casket of good fortune should also be leaden. When combined with the "plainness" or "muteness" often demonstrated by "third women" like Portia, Cordelia, and Aphrodite, Freud reaches the startling conclusion that the third woman of the "ancient theme" represents not only good fortune but death ("Muteness in dreams is a familiar representation of death," 67). But the question Freud now raises is even more disturbing: why should anyone choose death in choosing good fortune?

> It is with deep dissatisfaction that we find how unintelligible insertion of the new interpretation makes the situations we are considering and what contradictions of the apparent content then result. The third of the sisters

should be the Goddess of Death, nay, Death itself; in the Judgment of Paris she is the goddess of Love, in the tale of Apuleius one comparable to the goddess for her beauty, in *The Merchant of Venice* the fairest and wisest of women, in *Lear* the one faithful daughter. *Can a contradiction* [Widerspruch] *be more complete? Yet perhaps close at hand there lies [a solution for] even this, improbable as it is—the acme of contradiction.* It is certainly forthcoming if every time in this theme of ours there occurs a free choice between the women, and if the choice is thereupon to fall on death—that which no man chooses, to which by destiny alone man falls a victim. (71–72; italics mine)

Freud continues this passage with an explicit reference to the main idea of "On the Antithetical Sense of Primary Words," and then adds significantly to his earlier tenet:

Contradictions of a certain kind, replacements by the exact opposite, offer no serious difficulty to analytic interpretation. We shall not this time take our stand on the fact that contraries are constantly represented by one and the same element in the modes of expression used by the unconscious, such as dreams. But we shall remember that there are forces in mental life tending to bring about replacement by the opposite, such as the so-called reaction-formation, and it is just in the discovery of such hidden forces that we look for the reward of our labors. (72)

The "hidden forces" allow us to replace something by its opposite only because of an original—or, to use Kofman's less strictly chronological term, "originary"—doubling: "The Goddess of Love, herself, who now took the place of the Goddess of Death, *had once been identical with her.* . . . the replacement by the wish-opposite of which we have spoken in our theme is built upon *an ancient identity*" (72–73; italics mine). Although the choice of beauty is typically seen as a denial of death, Freud is suggesting here that it is also an election of death insofar as the two are "originarily" unified in the unconscious; hence Portia's leaden casket. This leads Freud to formulate a convincing theory of Lear's choice, for as an old man near death Lear insists all the more adamantly in having the young and beautiful Cordelia for his own. It is because of the hidden presence of its antithetical sense, death, that there is something "uncanny" in beauty: "The fairest and the best, she who has stepped into the place of the Death-goddess, has kept certain characteristics that border on the uncanny [*die an das Unheimliche streifen*], so that from them we might guess at what lay beneath" (73). If the doubling of beauty and death is "original" in the unconscious, then the implications of this for our better understanding of the "antithetical" beauty/death *topos* are very far reaching indeed.

It is important to indicate, if only in passing, the obvious relevance of this idea to Freud's discussion of *eros* and *thanatos* in *Beyond the Pleasure Principle* (1920).[50] The "breakthrough" of Freud's supposed revision of his previous theories in *Beyond the Pleasure Principle* centers on the notion of a "death drive" whose goal is not pleasure but quiescence, the return to an inanimate condition (*thanatos*) which exists alongside the desire for satisfaction (*eros*). The original antithetical unity described in "The Theme of the Three Caskets" of the "great Mother-goddesses" who are both "goddesses of life and of fertility, and death-goddesses" (73) must be understood as the same doubling of opposing forces, *eros* and *thanatos*, described in *Beyond the Pleasure Principle*. Although there the two forces are viewed by Freud as "opposed from the very first" (34), they are also later described as one and the same: "The pleasure principle seems actually to serve the death instincts" (57). This unity of *eros* and *thanatos* schematized in *Beyond the Pleasure Principle* is demonstrated more concretely in the enigmatic choice of a beautiful young woman who also represents death in "The Theme of the Three Caskets." The more implicit discussion of "The Theme of the Three Caskets" is actually more informative than *Beyond the Pleasure Principle* in showing that the choices of death and a beautiful young woman can be identical insofar as the goal in both cases is to achieve an absolute end to desire. *The desire for the perfect woman, in other words, also fulfills the death drive in promising an end to the search for sexual satisfaction.* *Beyond the Pleasure Principle* professes to address nothing less than "the riddle of life,"[51] which it does indeed answer when considered alongside the riddle Bassanio answers in "The Theme of the Three Caskets." The answer to the riddle of life is that life is a riddle, a paradoxical doubling of two opposing terms such as that of life and leaden death.

I hope to have succeeded in rescuing Freud's "On the Antithetical Sense of Primary Words" from the neglect prompted by Benveniste's positivistic dismissal, and to have demonstrated the importance of Freud's theory of the doubling of primary language to the essays on art discussed here as well as to Freud's thought in general. Like "The Theme of the Three Caskets," the essays all demonstrate the continued importance of antithetical doubling throughout Freud's work.

6 | The Critical Double

Figuring Out Henry James's "The Figure in the Carpet"

Jumble: (prob. onomatopoetic: cf. bumble, mumble, fumble, rumble, stumble, tumble) to mingle together or mix up in confusion or disorder.
—*Oxford English Dictionary*

HENRY JAMES'S ENIGMATIC novella "The Figure in the Carpet" (1896) concerns two critics' attempts to read literature correctly, and so any discussion of James's tale should begin by examining the status of its own attempt to fathom "The Figure in the Carpet." Is it possible, one might ask, to read the title as referring to James's own novella, thus doubling the story "The Figure in the Carpet" with the figure in the carpet sought after in the story?[1] Wolfgang Iser's famous "reader-response" theory of "The Figure in the Carpet" warns us against such a possibility as taking James's title too literally.[2] But since being too literal about something is often to ignore its accepted figurative meaning—its literal figurative sense—two questions arise. What is the proper (namely, literal) reading of a title, and, is the proposed reading of James's title really literal, too literal, or figurative? Although a less suspicious (but no less suspect) reading could easily ignore these problematics, given a text that explicitly addresses itself to the problem of reading or misreading (and, to be sure, this explicit questioning is itself in question), it is well worth pausing to consider how one is to read the title of James's novella.

A discussion of James's ambiguous title cannot, of course, substitute for a more detailed analysis of the status of fictional titles in general. Such a study could begin with the intriguing question of why artworks, especially those which are "Untitled" but including those whose titles relevantly declare their irrelevance (Magritte's *Ceci n'est pas une pipe*), have titles at all, and then inquire when and how titles came into being, how they have been perceived by artists and their audience, and so on. Whether referring to some implicit idea or explicit thing that in turn refers to the entire text as a kind of figurehead (or, considering the necessary gap or separation that joins it to the text, as a kind of *caput decapitatum*), one thing at least is clear: the literary title is never literal. The double, figurative signification of all "fictional titles" refers to their naming function as well as to the

93

impossibility of fulfilling that same function. The figurative literary title names the work without naming it because, from the time commentators named Homer and his works, titles have referred to literary works whose essence, as literature, cannot be in any way defined. This is not to say that the *Odyssey* is not about Odysseus, but this "about" is just the kind of figurative deflection that is at issue.

It would seem, then, that it is indeed possible to read a literary title too literally; to read "The Figure in the Carpet" as naming or identifying the text itself as the figure in the carpet would be no less foolish than to read the *Odyssey* as about ("exclusively concerning") Odysseus. One cannot say that the tale is literally the figure in the carpet; but given the convoluted doubling of Vereker's pronouncements within the text about a figure that is concealed within the text, this identification is possible, if anything but literal.

One of the more outstanding anomalies of titles is that they are that part of a written text that is specifically meant to be quoted, spoken, or referred to; it is thus entirely possible to say that the story is "The Figure in the Carpet." Not literally, for that is the reason behind the title's being placed *entre guillemets*, its existence bracketed, but figuratively. The title is a metonymy that only refers to the entire novella figuratively by eliding the rather large gap that separates it from the text. Carrying one step further the more orthodox technique whereby a metonymic point of reference is chosen as the title from within the tale, James allows for the possibility that the title may stand for the entire text synecdochically (cf. "The Beast in the Jungle," "The Lesson of the Master," and "The Great Good Place"). If such a possibility remains merely figural and not literal, it is still important that "The Figure in the Carpet" is the figure in the carpet figuratively speaking.

The title forms the beginning of a pattern of tropes, or doublings, that constitute the figure of "The Figure in the Carpet." As a figure within the text, or carpet, the title manifests its figurative sense metonymically by eliding the gap (which is also a gap in meaning) that separates it from the text. "Il n'y a pas," quipped Gide, "au fond, de *figure in the carpet*," which, if he is referring to the absence *du fond* which characterizes such doublings as the title, is all too true.[3]

The Figures of "The Figure in the Carpet"

The very first reference to some sort of figure in the carpet is made early in the text, when the narrator is asked to write a review of Vereker's latest book:

"Speak of him, you know, if you can, as *I* should have spoken of him.
. . . he gives me a pleasure so rare; the sense of "—he mused a little—
"something or other."

I wondered again. "The sense, pray of what?" "My dear man, that's
just what I want *you* to say!" . . .

. . . Corvick at all events wrote me from Paris a little ill-humouredly.
Mrs. Erme was pulling round, and I hadn't at all said what Vereker gave
him the sense of. ("The Figure in the Carpet," 136)[4]

The central problem in James's tale is related to the two senses of the
word *sense*. Corvick has *a* "sense" of what will later be taken up by Vereker
as his own sense of *the* sense, or essence, of his works. On the one hand,
Vereker and Corvick are clearly referring to the meaning, or essence, of the
former's work. On the other hand, the notion of there being a sense behind
Vereker's work is something Corvick as well as the others have only a sense
of. Even in Vereker's case, this double "sense of a sense" is revealed in his
inability to state or explain fully but only to hint at the supposed figure.
He does this in a series of figures that succeed in giving the narrator and
the reader *a* sense, but not *the* sense, of what he is talking about:

"By my little point I mean—what shall I call it?—the particular thing
I've written my books most *for*. Isn't there for every writer a particular
thing of that sort, the thing that most makes him apply himself, the thing
without the effort to achieve which he wouldn't write at all, the very
passion of his passion, the part of the business in which, for him, the
flame of art burns most intensely? Well, it's *that*!"

. . . "Your description's certainly beautiful, but it doesn't make what
you describe very distinct." (141–42)

Additional doublings as "the passion of his passion" are sufficiently
unreadable for readers, like the narrator, to be on their guard against letting
Vereker's enthusiasm carry them away. Just as the passion Vereker is referring to is, like the double "sense of a sense" just referred to, distinguish-
able and indistinguishable from itself, so too the innermost portion of the
"flame of art" serves to remedy one "outermost" figure with another: the
flame of art, by itself, is deemed somehow insufficient. Repeating the pattern of figurative doubling that has constituted the "moments of truth" in
every instance of critical doubling I have discussed in this book, the figurative ground is placed in the curious position of having to rely on figures to
represent, or misrepresent, a metaphorical referent whose truth is also its
falsification. Figures like the "passion of his passion" are a model of the
doubling at work in the other figures *of* the figure in the carpet as well, for
"passion" becomes at once that which is, and that which is not, Vereker's
meaning. This catachrestic doubling, whereby "the figure [in the carpet] is

precisely a figure" which incorporates meaninglessness within its meaning,[5] is the "key" to understanding how we are to read these figures as well as the entire story: "It was something, I guessed, in the primal plan; something like a complex figure in a Persian carpet. He highly approved of this image when I used it, and he used another himself. 'It's the very string,' he said, 'that my pearls are strung on!'" (149).

This quotation demonstrates that the important figure of the Persian carpet, which is later singled out and repeated, is not exclusively privileged within the text. This is not surprising, because to prefer any of the forty-odd figures used to describe Vereker's meaning would mean that *the* figure is not also *a* figure—that the figure is not what it is. But if figurative meaning is contained in figures that fail to contain it, this particular figure of the figure in the carpet aptly refers to some form that is at once concealed within the text, or carpet, and yet is also formed by the same. This doubling, which places the figure where it is not, is compatible with other figures that seem to contradict it, such as the one Vereker quickly adds to the narrator's notion of the Persian carpet: "It's the very string that my pearls are strung on."

Although this latter image may seem to contradict the figure in the carpet (figure:carpet::string:pearls?), by approving of both figures Vereker is *suggesting* (and there can be no other way to refer to figural "reality") that such doublings are the necessary result of the falsification inherent in a literary meaning that can only contain itself in figures which fail to contain it. That is the reason behind the chiasmus that joins Vereker's pearls, not to the sought-after figure, but to the carpet: James "pearls" are revealed by the very pearls that conceal them.

Another aspect of the figure of the string of pearls should also be questioned: Is James referring to the diegetic transference of meaning of the narrative as such? Could Vereker be alluding to the structural relation of every separable part, or moment, to every other within the work, and then, on a larger scale, to the relationship of any particular work in an author's corpus to every other? If so, such synecdochical relationships would still be figurative, for we cannot possibly distinguish the relationship, say, of Vereker and his wife to Corvick and his, or of these to other artists and wives in James tales, from an indeterminate number of other relationships. Once the so-called string is identified it becomes but one more pearl, the extension and repetition of any single facet of the text as it appears and reappears throughout the work.

The desired figure, or ground, of literature, is contained in figures that misrepresent the former and, most important, represent a figural reality whose misrepresentation is part of its essence. Two final groups of figures will demonstrate again a process from which, unfortunately, there is always something essential missing.

> "Is it a kind of esoteric message?" His countenance fell at this. . . . "Ah my dear fellow, it can't be described in cheap journalese!" . . .
> "This extraordinary 'general intention,' as you call it—for that's the most vivid description I can induce you to make of it—is then, generally, a sort of buried treasure?" His face lighted. "Yes, call it that, though it's perhaps not for me to do so." (143, 145)

This first group contains two figures ("a kind of," "a sort of") which, by virtue of Vereker's apparent rejection of the one and approval of the other, can be usefully examined together. It is easy enough to see why, on the basis of what he has already said, Vereker disdains the former. An esoteric message implies that his writing is encoded and so contains, implicitly, another text; that notion is repugnant to Vereker because his meaning, although secret, is "a secret in spite of itself." Somehow, the message is in the text as it appears before the reader ("It dots every i, it places every comma"). Insistent as Vereker may be on this point, he is unable to convince the narrator who, as a representative of the vulgar journalese to which Vereker is referring, never transcends this conception of an "esoteric message." Put differently, the weakness in the narrator's first supposition is that it cannot be taken other than literally, for it is hard to see how decoding could be understood at all figuratively.

Not so the comparison to a buried treasure. Here Vereker approves; "his face lighted." While the first figure of the encoded message elicited Vereker's disdain because, being too literal—too true—it could only be false, here the figure cannot be taken as other than figuratively double. As a "buried treasure" the metaphysical "ground" is absent as well as unable to be simply unearthed or decoded. As a "secret in spite of itself" (143), the doubling of a "buried treasure" neatly refers to the text as its own hidden meaning, which conceals or denies itself at the very moment of its revelation, or shining ("His face lighted").[6]

The final group of figures is proffered by Vereker himself:

> "It stretches, this little trick of mine, from book to book, and everything else, comparatively, plays over the surface of it. The order, the form, the texture of my books will perhaps someday constitute for the initiated a complete representation of it. So it's naturally the thing for the critic to look for."
> . . . "But you talk about the initiated. There must therefore, you see, *be* initiation."
> "What else in heaven's name is criticism supposed to be?" (142–43)

These two descriptions, although emanating from the same source, seem to contradict each other: on the one hand, there is a total rejection of "surface" and reference to an "initiation," but on the other, Vereker demands attention to those aspects of an artist's work (order, texture, form) usually regarded as most superficial. It is not really the case, however, that Vereker is denying the surface of the text. For "over the surface" is ambiguous; it can mean that everything else obstructs the surface. In other words, to say that "everything else plays over the surface of it" could refer to a surface—text or texture—whose meaning is obfuscated by less superficial, more obscure aspects or interpretations which conceal the text as surface. This ambiguous possibility is reinforced by Vereker's further explanation about how, if the parts of each book (the form) and, analogously, the separate books (the order) are woven together (the texture), they "may constitute a complete representation of it."

If one keeps both these statements in mind, especially the way they contradict as well as support each other, then the figure *in* the carpet is the figure *as* the carpet. *For the "complete representation" (the figure) that emerges out of the text is in fact synonymous with the text itself in its most superficial, "textual" manifestations ("it dots every i . . . ").* This is why James privileges the figure of the figure in the carpet, for, perhaps more than any of the other figures, it refers to this peculiar doubling of a process which is both the text itself and separate from the text. The hidden figure, the "buried treasure," is hidden precisely because it is the surface, thereby revealing the characteristic tendency of literary and figurative meaning to conceal itself within the very form that is its most complete representation.

The Figures in "The Figure in the Carpet"

One way to understand the complex interrelations between the four principal characters of "The Figure in the Carpet"—the figures in "The Figure in the Carpet"—is through the four-cornered rhetorical figure of the chiasmus, itself a kind of figure in a carpet. In its simplest formulation, a chiasmus is merely the syntactical rearrangement of a parallelism which, because it is not sufficiently complex, can be usefully confused to sustain the reader's interest. The *Oxford English Dictionary* quotes an especially appropriate example in this regard—"Frequentia sustentatur, alitur otio"—and goes on to explain: "This is a good instance . . . of the figure called chiasmus, in which the order of words in the first clause is inverted in the second."[7] The chiasmus usually involves the figurative opposition of more literally opposing pairs: "*Chiasmus* (marking with diagonal lines like a X) is the crosswise arrangement of contrasted pairs to give alternate stress."

Smythe, in the section of his *Greek Grammar* devoted to grammatical and rhetorical figures, goes on to exemplify this: *hen sōma echōn kai psuchēn mian*, "having one body and a soul that is one, too."[8] In each example he cites, Smythe shows the chiasmus to be dependent on a clear opposition: you/I, word/deed, master/slave, and so on.

Notwithstanding the movement away from contrasting and even opposing pairs of terms, the classical chiasmus does not yet involve a double "opposition to opposition," for the X formed by joining the means and extremes of two parallel phrases can be structured in ways that do not necessarily reverse the order of predication, although that is certainly possible. The classical chiasmus can even yield the most logical results: *pan men ergon pan d' epos legontas te kai prattontas* (literally, "doing every deed and uttering every word"). More recently, however, this potential for the chiasmus to reverse reversals, to double the doubling of two pairs of terms in related opposition has emerged as an epistemological tool in the hands of ingenious deconstructors like Jacques Derrida, J. Hillis Miller, and Paul de Man, who are interested in charting certain rhetorical or literary modes of thought. This version of the chiasmus, which is part of the ongoing deconstructionist project of writing a rhetoric of philosophy, is no longer the purely syntactical rearrangement of the "literal" chiasmus described above.

Paul de Man's discussion of the chiasmus in Nietzschean rhetoric is critical for understanding this deconstructive reevaluation of the classical figure:

> Once again, the reversal of polarities has not led to a restoration of literal truth. . . . This could hardly have been expected. The original pairing of rhetoric with error, as we encounter it from the *Course on Rhetoric* to *The Will to Power* was based on the cross-shaped reversal of properties that rhetoricians call chiasmus. And it turns out that the very process of deconstruction, as it functions in this text, is one more such reversal that repeats the selfsame rhetorical structure.[9]

Also exemplifying the doubt, or doubling, inherent in Nietzsche's chiasmatic discourse is the passage referred to where de Man discusses Nietzsche's deconstruction of cause and effect in *The Will to Power*:

> The outer, objective event in the world was supposed to determine the inner, conscious event as cause determines effect. It turns out however that what was assumed to be the objective, external cause is itself the result of an internal effect. What had been considered to be a cause, is, in fact, the effect of an effect, and what had been considered to be an effect can in its turn seem to function as the cause of its own cause.
>
> The two sets of polarities, inside/outside and cause/effect, which seemed to make up a closed and coherent system (outside causes produc-

ing inside effects) has now been scrambled into an arbitrary, open system in which the attributes of causality and of location can be deceptively exchanged, substituted for each other at will. As a consequence, our confidence in the original, binary model that was used as a starting point is bound to be shaken. The main impact of this deconstruction of the classical cause/effect, subject/object scheme becomes clear in the second part of the passage. It is based, as we saw, on an inversion or reversal of attributes which, in this particular case, is said to be temporal in nature.[10]

Because the X of a chiasmus must, by definition, involve the four corners of an encompassing quadrant, we can consider the chiasmus as a kind of figure in a carpet (as we have already seen, the so-called figure in the carpet can never be seen as anything other than "a kind of figure in a carpet"). This can be demonstrated by showing how such a schema follows the course, and canceling (X-ing) out of de Man's and Nietzsche's arguments. The four corners of the figure are provided by the two opposing terms (*subject* and *object*), and by two predicates (*effect, cause*) which follow, and so are the equivalents of, their subjects:

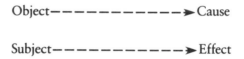

The first reversal of this quadrant occurs with the rejection of a banal empiricism by means of a temporal reversal whereby Nietzsche challenges the origin of perception ("The chronological reversal which makes the cause reach consciousness later than the effect"), yielding

At this point the essential turns in the argument should be carefully noted, for they will serve as a model for the following discussion of the "intensely odd successions"[11] and connections that form the turns and twists of James's tale. Having stated that "what had been considered to be a cause is in fact the effect of an effect, and what had been considered to be an effect can in its turn seem to function as the cause of its own cause," de Man reveals the infinite irony inherent in such a position. When he explains that the two coordinates have "now been scrambled into an arbitrary, open system in which the attributes of causality and of location can be deceptively exchanged, substituted for each other at will," that means that the chiasmus X's out the "carpet" while maintaining it, for the possibility persists that the empirical "cause," now the "effect of an effect" may once again become the cause, and the subjective "effect," the "cause of its own cause," might once again become the effect—if it were not already the cause: "Readers of *The Will to Power* know that this critique by no means pretends to discard phenomenalism, but puts us on our guard against the tendency to hypostatize consciousness into an authoritative ontological category."[12]

This digression into the various levels of interpreting the chiasmus was needed to clarify the way I will use the figure here. The referential figure that will now be applied to "The Figure in the Carpet" not only involves a reversal of polar opposites, but the double "reversal of reversal" as well, where the joining of opposing predicates serves to affirm as well as deny all of them. All of the figures *of* the figure in the carpet discussed in the first part of this chapter can be considered chiastic in this sense, for they all involve a reversal, not only of the usual rules of predication, but of their own figurative reversals as well. For example, the string was shown to be the figure of the pearls to which it was also opposed, just as the inside of the text was shown to be the invagination of its own superficial form. We shall now see how the four principal characters of the story, the figures *in* "The Figure in the Carpet," also form a chiastic pattern that is not only synonymous with *the* figure in the carpet but with literary figuration in general.

James focuses more of his attention on the figures—characters—involved in the quest for Vereker's meaning than on the unresolved quest itself: "The story dramatizes the experience of unreadability, or, rather, since this experience can only be named in figure, it presents figures for it, not least in the recurrent pattern of interpersonal relations which form the human base for the story's allegorizing of its own unreadability."[13]

The parallel relationships that will provide the four corners of our carpet can be drawn between Corvick and his fiancée (and minor novelist), Gwendolen Erme, and between the narrator (conspicuously nameless, but more on that later) and Vereker. The story begins with Corvick's having to give up his intention to review Vereker's latest book in order to continue plighting his troth to Miss Erme, whereupon it falls to the narrator to take up Corvick's task. Just as Corvick's pursuit of Gwendolen Erme turns out to be more difficult than first imagined (and, in the end, turns back into an attempt to capture Vereker just as the narrator's pursuit of Vereker turns into a final pursuit of Gwendolen), the nameless narrator's efforts to "capture" Vereker also turn out to be more prolonged than first envisioned.

One might object that in the schema as discussed thus far Gwendolen

Erme was described in two different ways: as the erotic parallel of the narrator's interest in Vereker, and then as a writer herself. We are also told that it was Corvick's critical interest in Gwendolen as a writer that prompted their affair,[14] and so her dual status is certainly no minor matter. However, when Vereker sets the stage for the final resolution of his mystery by saying, "Marriage may help," he does not then, or ever, refer to Gwendolen's status as a writer, but only as a woman. Similarly, the narrator later reinforces Vereker's suspicions of a parallel between Corvick's romance and literary discovery, but he too does so without drawing any explicit connection between Gwendolen's writing and the climactic discovery. Her second book, *Overmastered*, seems (to the narrator at least) to bear no relation to any revelation preferred her by her husband on their wedding night. Why, then, does James make Gwendolen an author when this is seemingly irrelevant to her role in the narrative? When answered, the question of why James makes Gwendolen a novelist might help to reveal the reason for the juxtapositions of personal and artistic relationships which, as we have seen, structure the entire story.

James's references to Gwendolen's career as a writer repeat the chiastic middle formed by Corvick's suspension between his pursuit of Gwendolen and Vereker. Because the two pursuits are really "two and the same" James makes Gwendolen a writer but then must, in the same breath, characterize her just as he does the other women in his novellas who merge the erotic with the artistic ideal (May Bartram in "The Beast in the Jungle" and Stransom's fellow worshiper in "The Altar of the Dead," among others). The larger question, then, is why James merges the artistic and erotic pursuits:

> He [Corvick] had instantly told Gwendolen [about the existence of the secret], *but Gwendolen's ardent response was in itself a pledge of discretion.* The question would now absorb them and would offer them a pastime too precious to be shared with the crowd. They appeared to have caught instinctively at Vereker's high idea of enjoyment. Their intellectual pride, however, was not such as to make them indifferent to any further light I might throw on the affair they had in hand. They were indeed of the "artistic temperament," and I was freshly struck with my colleague's power to excite himself over a question of art. He'd call it letters, he'd call it life, but it was all one thing. In what he said I now seemed to understand that he spoke equally for Gwendolen. ("The Figure in the Carpet," 149–50; italics mine)

> They would scarce have got so wound up, I think, if they hadn't been in love: poor Vereker's inner meaning gave them endless occasion to put and to keep their young heads together. (151)

Here the terms of Corvick's impending solution are explicitly laid out. His critical abilities are characterized by an "artistic temperament" which "equates art and life." Although the stock equation of art and life might strike us as all too familiar, the fact remains that Corvick's sexual involvement with an artist which, in turn, brings about the solution of Vereker's meaning is essential to the story. Less than familiar is the fact that art and life are unified, not by the supposed synthesis provided by a shallow aestheticism or equally shallow realism, but by Corvick's puzzling insistence on pursuing Gwendolen chiastically through Vereker and Vereker through Gwendolen.

Corvick's "homonymous" relation to Miss Erme and to Vereker is clarified by the separation that precipitates Corvick's solution. In order to remove himself from his obsessive involvement with Vereker's secret, Corvick leaves Gwendolen and Vereker and takes himself to India (compare Marcher's similarly motivated trip in "The Beast in the Jungle"):

> [The narrator:] "How strange of George to have been able to go into the thing again in the midst of such different and such powerful solicitations!"
>
> [Gwendolen:] "He hasn't gone into it, I know; it's the thing itself, let severely alone for six months, that has simply sprung out at him like a tigress out of the jungle. He didn't take a book with him—on purpose; indeed he wouldn't have needed to—he knows every page, as I do, by heart. They all worked in him together, and some day some where, when he wasn't thinking, they fell, in all their superb intricacy, into the one right combination. The figure in the carpet came out." (156)

Corvick's separation from Gwendolen is equally "severe," for he tells the narrator: "On my saying the last time I saw him something that bore on the question of his separation from our young lady, he brought out with an emphasis that startled me: 'Ah I'm not a bit engaged to her, you know!'" (154). Gwendolen explains only after Corvick has solved the riddle that the whole matter was carefully contrived to consummate the final resolution:

> That brought me back to the question of her marriage, prompted me to ask if what she meant by what she had just surprised me with was that she was under an engagement.
>
> "Of course I am!" she answered. "Didn't you know?" She seemed astonished, but I was still more so, for Corvick had told me the exact contrary. I didn't mention this, however; I only reminded her how little I had been on that score in her confidence, or even in Corvick's. (159)

In addition to the critical separation from Gwendolen and Vereker that precipitates Corvick's "union" with both, Gwendolen's description of the precise manner in which the secret occurs to Corvick while in India is equally significant: "We knew the change would do it—that the difference of thought, or scene, would give the needed touch, the magic shake. We had perfectly, we had admirably calculated. The elements were all in his mind, and in the *secousse* of a new and intense experience they just struck light" (156).

This *secousse*, or "magic shake," consummates Corvick's relationships to both parties whom he had intentionally denied in going to India. The obvious sexual imagery of this figure notwithstanding, such a "shaking up," which also aptly describes the chiastic workings of a "superb intricacy" which figure in the story, is all that is needed to rearrange Corvick's name phonemically into Vereker's. And, it is the same *secousse* that succeeds in joining Corvick to Vereker as well as to Gwendolen, whom he immediately marries upon his return.

We cannot discuss the importance of the figures of "The Figure in the Carpet" without discussing the prominent presence of death as it figures into the search for and revelation of Vereker's secret. The most important instance of this is the way Corvick dies immediately after divulging the secret to Gwendolen on their wedding night, but the relationship between art, love and death figures prominently elsewhere in the story too, as when Mrs. Corvick refuses to reveal the secret after her husband's death.

> She had conveyed to me in abundance that she was tongue-tied by her perversity, by her piety, that she would never break the silence it had not been given to the "right person," as she said, to break. The hour, however, finally arrived. One evening when I had been sitting with her longer than usual I laid my hand firmly on her arm. "Now at last what *is* it?"
>
> She had been expecting me and was ready. She gave a long slow soundless headshake, merciful only in being inarticulate. This mercy didn't prevent its hurling at me the largest finest coldest "Never!" I had yet, in the course of a life that had known denials, had to take full in the face. I took it and was aware that with the hard blow that tears had come into my eyes. So for a while we sat and looked at each other; after which I slowly rose. I was wondering if some day she would accept me; but this was not what I brought out. I said as I smoothed down my hat: "I know what to think then. It's nothing!"
>
> A remote disdainful pity for me gathered in her dim smile; then she spoke in a voice that I hear at this hour. "It's my *life*!" As I stood at the door she added: "You've insulted him!"
>
> "Do you mean Vereker?"
>
> "I mean the Dead!" (165)

This passage is more difficult to understand in relation to Corvick's understanding of Vereker's secret than Gwendolen's explanation of her separation from Corvick, for it abbreviates certain notions expressed more fully in other novellas, such as "The Altar of the Dead" (the present story might be said to reflect the rest of James's work in the same way that the figure in the carpet supposedly runs through all of Vereker's). There the similarly honored and capitalized Dead are not really dead, for they give the highest meaning to the lives of those of whom they "died possessed"— that is, of those whom they loved and were loved by in return. The Dead thus give life to the living, and the living cease to live except to memorialize their Dead:

> He had formed little by little the habit of numbering his Dead; it had come to him tolerably early in life that there was something one had to do for them. They were there in their simplified, intensified essence, their conscious absence and expressive patience, as personally there as if they had only been stricken dumb. When all sense of them failed, all sound of them ceased, it was as if their purgatory were really still on earth; they asked so little that they got, poor things, even less, and died again, died every day, of the hard usage of life.[15]

What is the connection between Corvick and Gwendolen's love, the secret "figure in the carpet" which we have already seen is in some sense homonymous—the same and different—with that love, and now, Gwendolen's keeping the secret of art to herself out of reverence for her "Dead" husband? It is extremely significant that, in Gwendolen's speech just quoted, James underlines "*life*" and capitalizes the "Dead," neither of which can really be spoken. What Gwendolen, who now confronts the narrator with the secret much as Vereker had done earlier, means by her *life* is revealed in this passage to be the same as its antithesis, the Dead (as well as the secret) by virtue of an impossible unity that exists all the same, and so can only be figured out, or in, figuratively, in this case with the two markings. James speaks here and elsewhere of the personalized Dead, not of an impersonal Death. As with Freud, *eros* and *thanatos*, life and death, merge in James's view of love as an impossible unity, a unity based on absence.[16]

Corvick's accidental death, the exact terms of which have yet to be discussed, is but one of the many instances of this important theme in "The Figure in the Carpet." By the end the text is literally strewn with corpses: not only Corvick's and Gwendolen's, but Vereker's and his wife's, as well as the narrator's brother, who, we are told, died "at the feet of a great master." One of the most interesting questions posed by the text is the death of Gwendolen's mother, which, we are repeatedly told, the couple are anxiously awaiting before they can be married (for example, the narrator comments that "Corvick would marry her [Gwendolen] if her mother would only die"). Mrs. Erme's death, like the couple's marriage, is meant to parallel the discovery of Vereker's secret: all three occur together, to which one might as well add Corvick's death, for it occurs on the very day after his marriage.

Although we never meet Gwendolen's mother, Mrs. Erme's presence throughout the tale is keenly felt. It is her illness that most directly generates the narrative, for Gwendolen has urgently requested Corvick to come to Paris to help nurse her mother after her latest collapse, thus causing Corvick to find a substitute critic for Vereker's latest work. The triad of art-*eros-thanatos* is already established at the beginning: the solution of Vereker's riddle and the death of the mother are both necessary for the marriage to occur.

When Gwendolen receives news from India that Corvick has solved the problem, she informs the narrator that the resolution of the other problem—her mother's opposition to their marriage—is sure to follow:

> She [Gwendolen] made her case slightly more intelligible by returning presently: "What the taste of things has been is that we felt of course bound to do nothing in mamma's lifetime."
>
> "But now you think you'll just dispense with mamma's consent?"
>
> "Ah it mayn't come to that!" I wondered what it might come to, and she went on: "Poor dear, she may swallow the dose. In fact, you know," she added with a laugh, "she really *must*!"—a proposition of which, on behalf of everyone concerned, I fully acknowledged the force. (159–60)

The ambiguities of this passage, with its sinister innuendo, are hardly removed when Gwendolen writes the narrator with news of her mother's death:

> She wrote me that her mother had yielded to long-threatened failure of the heart. She didn't say, but I took the liberty of reading into her words, that from the point of view of her marriage and also of her eagerness, which was quite a match for mine, this was a solution more prompt than could have been expected and more radical than waiting for the old lady to swallow the dose. I candidly admit indeed that at the time—for I heard from her repeatedly—I read some singular things into Gwendolen's words and some still more extraordinary ones into her silences. (161–62)

We will get nowhere by trying to understand the "singular things" to which the narrator is referring. But by understanding the crucial role death plays throughout the story, we can at least fathom the reason for this ambiguity.

The thing most directly responsible for Mrs. Erme's death is Corvick's solution of the figure in the carpet; that is what determines that the two shall marry immediately, and that is what determines that the problem of the mother's resistance can no longer be tolerated. If Mrs. Erme's death seems too convenient, even contrived, it is purposefully so. Her heart attack inevitably follows the outburst of passion that results from Corvick's solution, Gwendolen's excitement over that and her marriage, because the "heart attack" that undoes the mother is synonymous with the passion that undoes the two lovers and that also undoes the solution of Vereker's riddle. Gwendolen was aware of this, aware that her marriage would have the necessary result, and for this reason she is in a sense guilty of the sinister motives the narrator suggests.

These "intensely odd successions," as the narrator calls them, are clarified by the description of Corvick's death the morning after he has consummated his marriage *and* revealed the secret to Gwendolen. It is foolish to think that Corvick transfers the secret to Gwendolen on their wedding night and then, the next day, accidentally dies. If Kafka could call the ending of "The Judgment" "symbolic detumescence,"[17] the description of Corvick's death on the couple's honeymoon is even more clearly the result (or continuation) of the couple's wedding night, when Gwendolen saw the "idol unveiled":

> The happy pair went down to Torquay for their honeymoon, and there, in a reckless hour, it occurred to poor Corvick to take his young bride for a drive. He had no command of that business. . . . in a dogcart he perched his companion for a rattle over Devonshire hills, on one of the likeliest of which he brought his horse, who, it was true, had bolted, down with such violence that the occupants of the cart were hurled forward and that he fell horribly on his head. He was killed on the spot; Gwendolen escaped unhurt. (162)

To take the impossibly pedestrian view that Corvick dies because James cannot reveal the secret begs the question on a number of grounds, not least of which is James's reason for choosing to eliminate Corvick in this manner, at this time, and so forth. Corvick's death is the climax of the erotic parallel to his quest, and it emphasizes how seriously James means the chiastic parallels—the "figure in the carpet"—between love, literature, and death to be taken. Just as the revelation of Corvick's artistic secret was described in explicitly sexual terms (the *secousse*, or "magic shake," is about as explicit as James ever gets about sexual matters), so here the honeymoon and subsequent spill is best understood in term of the model of metaphoric transference referred to repeatedly throughout this work. As we have seen, the doubling of two different terms involved in any metaphorical exchange results in a momentary union that can only signify the death, as it were, of each—a "dead metaphor" is evidence of the inevitable aftermath of this impossible union by killing off the differences between the two terms involved. According to this model, the passionate transference of Vereker's secret to Gwendolen repeats both the "magic shake" that unveiled Vereker's secret and the jolt that threw Corvick out of the dogcart. Like the figure of the chiasmus itself, the figure in the carpet requires just such a *jumbling* of opposite terms that denies any literal unities at the same time they are being metaphorically asserted. Corvick's apparent lack of mastery over the vehicle he is steering is nothing of the sort. Rather, if Corvick is "overmastered" (the title of Gwendolen's last book, written after she has learned of Vereker's secret), it is because one must allow for the power of the metaphorical *vehicle* (I. A. Richards's term for the metaphoric signifier) to destroy one in the very act of artistic and/or critical mastery.

The Figure in "The Figure in the Carpet": The Nameless Narrator

As the story reaches its finale, only the narrator of all the original personages remains:

> I continue to trace with a briefer touch our intensely odd successions. Three weeks after this came Vereker's death, and before the year was out the death of his wife. That poor lady I had never seen, but I had had a futile theory that, should she survive him long enough to be decorously accessible, I might approach her with the feeble flicker of my plea. Did she know and if she knew would she speak? It was much to be presumed that for more reasons than one she would have nothing to say; but when she passed out of all reach I felt renouncement indeed my appointed lot. I was shut up in my obsession for ever—my gaoler had gone off with the key. (168)

Although the deaths of Vereker and his wife, and then of Gwendolen, are given much less attention than those of Corvick and his mother-in-law, this very arbitrariness must occasion their interpretation. The key to their demise is, in the narrator's words, their making off with the key to his obsession. The deaths of everyone who might have told of Vereker's secret is not arbitrary when one considers that, with respect to the narrator, it is the very secret that has died. But if it is granted that James's purpose in establishing the "odd succession" of deaths is to leave the narrator in the dark concerning Vereker's secret, the question then is, Why must the narrator be left in the dark? Knowledge of the figure has been linked throughout this chapter to a series of figures *of*, and figures *in*, "The Figure in the Carpet" which are based on chiastic reversals of oppositions, or doublings. The ultimate form of this "reversal of reversal" is undoubtedly the one that reverses the opposition between death and life, with death informing life in much the same way that Corvick comes to understand Vereker's secret by separating himself from it physically, and through his marriage to Gwendolen. Unable to see that knowledge of the figure is linked to the "odd succession" of deaths which surround him, the hardheaded, positivistic narrator is interested in Vereker's secret only if it can be apprehended directly, without any figurative displacements. Like Marcher in "The Beast in the Jungle," the narrator converts the figure into a conscious obsession that keeps him from the very object of his obsession. The chiastic doublings, especially that of life and death, are beyond him, and so he alone survives the end of James's novella, but without any knowledge of its meaning.

The narrator's failure is finalized at the end of the novella by Gwendolen's preference for Drayton Deane, yet another critic, as her second husband. As is the case with Corvick, the narrator's relation to Gwendolen is essential to his understanding of the figure, and so his complete failure at trying to establish a relationship with her mirrors his patent inability to fathom Vereker's secret (she even mocks the narrator with the comment that "one fine ignorance is as good as another" when he complains about her support for Deane). As the personification of a life opposed to art, love, and death, he alone, of those four characters who make up the chiasmus, survives the end of the tale. But the figure of the nameless narrator is no more a pawn to a strict opposition with Corvick than is Gwendolen. Indeed, there is much to be said on the narrator's behalf. Although his criticism falls short of the mark in comparison with Corvick's, the narrator acknowledges, at least, his inability to do better. Speaking more generally, the character of the hardheaded positivist who coolly maintains his demand for objectivity in the face of urgent matters of artistic and even metaphysical import is an essential figure throughout James's entire oeuvre, and so one which cannot be lightly dismissed.[18] Finally, because the narrator's "real start," as he explains it in the opening line, is synonymous with the narrative itself, it is hard to view him as merely marginal or in strictly negative terms. What, then, is the relation of the nameless narrator to that figure which, likewise, cannot be named?

It is helpful to compare the reason why the narrator is unable to name himself to the reason why the narrative cannot name its own figure. Like a person, a character does not naturally refer to his or her name for the simple reason that it is reserved for others. In other words, to do so would be to treat oneself as another, which normally (or better, abnormally) only occurs at moments when one speaks words of encouragement, anger, complaint, and the like to oneself as though one were another. And if referring to one's own name is potentially neurotic, to name oneself is impossible:

one can't name the "source" or "origin" of names without using a name, thus concealing the desired origin. The nameless narrator, the principal figure *in* the "The Figure in the Carpet," cannot name the figure because he is the figure in the carpet. Unfortunately, rather than realizing this proximity to the secret by acknowledging his namelessness, the narrator does the opposite. He falsifies a name for himself by creating a nonexistent difference between his ignorance and that of another hapless critic, the equally benighted Drayton Deane.

The narrator's "revenge" is the final point of the story. When Drayton Deane, the obtuse critic Gwendolen chooses as her second husband, writes a review of Vereker's final work, the narrator automatically assumes that Deane's recent marriage to Gwendolen must insure him of success:

> I began with due promptness to look for the fruit of the affair—that fruit, I mean, of which the premonitory symptoms would be peculiarly visible in the husband. Taking for granted the splendour of the other party's nuptial gift, I expected to see him make a show commensurate with his increase of means. I knew what his means had been—his article on "The Right of Way" had distinctly given one the figure. As he was now exactly in the position in which still more exactly I was not I watched from month to month, in the likely periodicals, for the heavy message poor Corvick had been unable to deliver and the responsibility of which would have fallen on his successor. (168)

All the elements appear to the narrator to be in place for a solution. But this is precisely the problem. The narrator's positivistic approach has again led him to look for the secret in a literal, scientific formula (the repetition of the once successful "marriage = figure" equation) rather than in the unexpected *secousse* that led to Corvick's success. One can point to a number of James's tales where the pairing of women having decidedly superior artistic and imaginative abilities with men of less refined sensibilities supports the opposite conclusion, that the successful pairing of Corvick and Gwendolen is anything but formulaic.[19] But the question remains: why does James end his novella with the nameless narrator staring into the great blank face of another critic whose pathetic ignorance becomes "almost my consolation . . . quite my revenge"?

James is not, as Wolfgang Iser and others would have it,[20] ridiculing the existence of the figure in the carpet, for the highly suggestive title of Gwendolen's final opus, when combined with *Deep Down* (the "intricate" earlier work in which Gwendolen had "lost herself"), does reveal vital information about the secret that both surviving critics ignore. They indicate, when taken together, that the kind of mastery the narrator enjoys over Drayton Deane is not enough, since to be "overmastered" implies mastery as well as something more, the double "mastery of mastery."[21] Corvick could not have mastered the story without Gwendolen's mastery over him, and the fact that Corvick's name and Vereker's are little more than phonemic rearrangements of each other also points to the secret as an "intricate pattern" in which one must lose oneself. The ending of the story reveals the narrator to be at the very antipodes from the kind of doubling involved in being "overmastered" or "intricated" in the other:

> I told him in a word just what I've written here. . . . I saw the immediate shock throb away little by little and then gather again into waves of wonder and curiosity—waves that promised, I could perfectly judge, to break in the end with the fury of my own highest tides. I may say that to-day as victims of unappeased desire there isn't a pin to choose between us. The poor man's state is almost my consolation; there are really moments when I feel it to be quite my revenge. (172–73)

In this climactic confrontation with his personal double[22] the narrator comes face to face with another critic suffering his own humiliation: "There is not a pin to choose between us." Why, then, does the story end with the utterly false position of the narrator revenging himself against himself? The narrator's "consolation" stems, first of all, from his projection onto Drayton Deane of his own failure. His "revenge," in turn, emphasizes the false separation that permits the narrator to feel better: Deane's suffering is perceived as canceling out his own. The narrator is allowed to salvage his ego by means of a totally false mastery, for although he is the same as Deane, he uses the sight of the latter's ignorance to abolish his own. James ends the novella with this unmasking of the narrator to show us why he cannot, and will not, figure out the figure in the carpet. The narrator represents the inability to do so because he is unable to be "overmastered," unable to relinquish his egotistical desire for what James reveals to be an utterly false mastery.

At the end we witness the cautionary spectacle of an obtuse critic asserting a difference between himself and another where there is none, rather than denying a difference where there really is one, as had been the case with Corvick and Gwendolen, the pearls and string, art and eros, and, of course, the figure and the carpet. Here as elsewhere James seems to be saying that art has nothing to do with the *vulgarities*[23] of life such as the lowly carpet, but everything to do with the almost *alchemical* process whereby life transforms itself into its own artistic double.

7 | The Deconstructive Double
Sign and Symbol in the Aesthetics of Paul de Man

The relationship between the literal and the figural senses of a metaphor is always metonymic, though motivated by a constitutive tendency to pretend the opposite.

—Paul de Man, *Allegories of Reading*

Any treatment of de Man that underrates the sheer strangeness of his work, the resistance it puts up to all our commonplace homely assumptions about language and experience, is a reading profoundly at odds with the character of that work.

—Christopher Norris, *Paul de Man*

THAT PAUL DE MAN'S major writings are all centered around his theory of figuration will come as no surprise to anyone familiar with his works. We even have the author's own statement that "the Yeats chapter [of his 1960 doctoral thesis] was already a rhetorical analysis of figural language *avant la lettre*, anticipating a mode that would later become predominant for me. Like Monsieur Jourdain's proverbial prose, I was apparently doing rhetorical analysis before I knew that such a thing existed by name." [1] Yet, despite the fact that de Man's interest in the "intralinguistic resources of figures" such as image, symbol, trope, allegory, and prosopopeia is too obvious to have escaped critical attention, no one has yet begun to analyze the "two poles" of figurative meaning (image/emblem, symbol/sign, anthropomorphism/trope, symbol/allegory, metaphor/metonymy, [2] and so on) around which most, if not all, of de Man's writings can be said to turn. [3] My goal here is not to prove the interchangeability of all these analogous terms, which will be shown to be fairly obvious, but rather to demonstrate that de Man's persistent emphasis on all these interchangeable doublings involves the "constitutive tendency" (referred to in the first of the chapter epigraphs) of metonymy to appear as metaphor, the sign as symbol, emblem as image, and so on. De Man is interested in the constitutive doubling of the sign in all its manifestations insofar as it intrinsically denies its own meaning ("including this one," to add once again the Protagorean qualifier we have invoked so often).

Because all of de Man's major writings require the kind of close, careful analysis he applied to others, I have chosen passages from three works to illustrate this problematic: the portion of de Man's doctoral dissertation republished as "Image and Emblem in Yeats" in *The Rhetoric of Romanticism*; "Sign and Symbol in Hegel's *Aesthetics*," and the essay on Nietzsche included in *Allegories of Reading* entitled "Rhetoric of Tropes."[4] And, since the doubling in question is equally evident in all the major essays, it will be necessary at times to introduce some of these other writings in order to clarify a particular problem.

A word about my title: the obvious play on de Man's title "Sign and Symbol in Hegel's *Aesthetics*" should not be seen as an open act of defiance against recent critics, such as Christopher Norris and Jonathan Culler, who have based their readings of de Man on his supposed attack on the ideology of the aesthetical.[5] Insofar as the seductiveness of the aesthetic referred to in de Man's book *The Resistance to Theory* is the same seductiveness of the symbol discussed here, I am not challenging the notion of de Man's opposition to both those categories. But the aesthetic as a category of literary/artistic signification is not limited by de Man to ideology: "It is by no means an established fact that aesthetic values and linguistic structures are incompatible."[6] My titular reference to de Man's "aesthetic" is intended as an acknowledgment that, however much de Man may have rejected "aesthetic ideology," he never saw himself as anything but a critic— one who concerned himself with works of art and art-related matters that are hardly to be viewed as unaesthetical.

*

Whether through Aristotle's statements that a proper use of metaphor is a gift of nature, or Rousseau's notion that the use of tropes is closer to our original nature, figurative language has often been viewed as the "language of the heart," of nature in opposition to the literal language of culture.[7] Oddly enough, calling a person, metaphorically, a lion is judged more natural than calling that person by his or her name. Even within the general realm of figurative language more recent writers such as Gaston Bachelard and Paul Ricoeur have followed Goethe, Coleridge and others in privileging image, symbol and metaphor over their more rhetorical and less natural counterparts such as emblem, sign and allegory.[8] This is because the former have "mimetic referents" which are "natural objects" as opposed to the latter, which "have given up all pretense at being natural objects and have become something else. They are taken from the literary tradition and derive their meaning from traditional or personal, but not from natural associations" ("Image and Emblem," 165).

According to de Man, Yeats's view of natural images as "nothing but disguised, not yet understood emblems" "represents a radical departure from one of the main tenets of the Western poetic tradition": "This tradition conceives of the *logos* as incarnate and locates divine essence in the object, not in the unmediated *word* of God" ("Image and Emblem," 168; italics de Man's). For example, de Man singles out a passage from *Ideas of Good and Evil* where Yeats explains the allegorical associations of flowers like the rose, the lily and the poppy as arising from "their colour and their odour, and their use":

> The other day, . . . I sat for my portrait to a German Symbolist in Paris, whose talk was all for his love for Symbolism and his hatred for allegory. . . . he would not even put a lily, or a rose, or a poppy into a picture to express purity, or love, or sleep, because he thought such emblems were allegorical, and had their meaning by a traditional and not by a natural right. . . . I said that the rose, and the lily, and the poppy were so married, by their colour and their odour, and their use, to love and purity and sleep, and had been so long part of the imagination of the world, that a symbolist might use them to help out his meaning without becoming an allegorist.[9]

From the symbolist's point of view, words ought to originate "as flowers originate" (Hölderlin), a view de Man sees as characteristic of those romantics whose pantheistic ontology seeks to return humanity and language to nature.[10] Yeats's painter is unwilling to include objects whose meaning is determined allegorically "by a traditional and not by a natural right." Since the passage in question concerns words whose meanings originate "as flowers originate," Yeats is understandably reluctant to go along with the symbolist's banishment of the rose, the lily, and the poppy from his vocabulary. Yet a "very characteristic shift" occurs in Yeats's apparent defense of the symbolic link between the material perception and "a certain experience of consciousness, such as purity." Contrary to the supposed synthesis between subject and object, between the flowers' appearance and meaning, Yeats also alludes to the flowers' "use" as generating their meaning. This produces a "distortion in Yeats' argument" because it effectively realigns allegory with emblem in the above-mentioned sense of "receiving meaning from traditional or personal but not from natural associations." De Man's point could be made even more forcefully by adding that the connections between odor and color and purity and love, respectively, are hardly natural.

By noting that allegorical / emblematical meaning originates from its use, de Man is not stressing a utilitarian explanation of, for example, the lily's association with purity or the poppy's association with sleep, but the flowers' figurative referent as derived from language, or linguistic consciousness:

> The permanence of the odor and the color resides in the thing itself, while that of the use resides in the will of man, or of a god acting through man. The former leads to a (problematic) vision of unity that transcends the opposition between object and subject, while the latter finds unity preserved in language as the carrier of a divine, and therefore permanently repeated, pattern of experience; it postulates as an act of faith that the divine is immediately and audibly present to human consciousness in the very entity—language—that is the distinctive attribute of this consciousness. ("Image and Emblem," 168)

One might be surprised to find that we have replaced the symbolic "pantheistic" view which would return language to Nature with another more allegorical divinity, but I would defy any of the critics of de Man's supposed secularization of the word to read this passage without giving its three references to the divine their due.[11] The purity of the lily is allegorically divine because it arises from "a god" and yet is synonymous with "the mind of man," with language as the vehicle of consciousness. De Man stumbles over the doubling between man "or" a god because poetic language, as exemplified here by the uncanny association of the lily with purity, is seen as simultaneously the product of both. If there is some relevance to de Man's supposed "secularization of the word," it is that the divine association of the lily with purity occurs through the "use" of language as the vehicle of consciousness, rather than the converse. Since all allegories are double insofar as they name what cannot be named (*allegory* means "speaking otherwise"), the divine meaninglessness of a pure lily, for example, is inseparable from more dangerous confusions such as the one de Man notes here between "man or a god."

Two other, less explicit statements provided in this passage regarding the revalorization of emblem and allegory need to be examined. The first is de Man's passing reference to the audible presence of language: "It [emblematicity] postulates as an act of faith that the divine is immediately and audibly present to human consciousness in the very entity—language — that is the distinctive attribute of this consciousness." It is no mere witticism to say that the audible quality of language, to which de Man frequently alludes, cannot be understood except as a doubling of the *inaudible* quality of language.[12] The sound of language is something we almost never hear because, as in the allegorical association of the lily with purity, the tropological, substitutive structure of language produces an audible "refer-ent" that is never an object or the thing itself but primarily an act of speak-ing, or language. This is not to say that language is a meaningless sound, but that in its meaningfulness the sound of language is the doubling echo, so to speak, of its own meaninglessness. De Man's essay on autobiography is perhaps his most articulate description of this *muteness* inherent in lan-guage, and so we will turn to that essay in considering the "audible pres-ence" of language alluded to in "Image and Emblem in Yeats."

In "Autobiography as De-Facement" (1979) De Man is led to consider the epitaph as a model of linguistic figuration in general and of autobio-graphical writings in particular. Although most analyses of this genre would have us judge autobiography as either pure fiction or as legitimately refer-ential, the project of "self-life-writing" is better seen as a *sounding* based on a *sundering* between the two: "Death is a displaced name for a linguistic predicament, and the restoration of mortality by autobiography (the pro-sopopeia of the voice and the name) deprives and disfigures to the precise extent that it restores. Autobiography veils a defacement of the mind of which it is itself the cause."[13]

Just as the "I" discovers its rhetorical status as double in its own in-ability to say "I," so here the speaking, or writing, of the self in autobiog-raphy is based on a contradiction that gives the self, and language, its meaning (autobiography "veils a defacement of the mind of which it is it-self the cause"). To the extent that all language is based on tropological substitutions like the lily and purity, or the dead speaking through epi-taphs, or the self writing about itself allegorically through the language "of others," to this extent all language is "privative," and so reduced to silence. But it is just this inaudible presence that gives language its own peculiar, paradoxical doubling of discovering its proper voice, or audible presence, through the act of *writing*.

Another revealing reference in the passage from "Image and Emblem in Yeats" is to the *mechanical* quality of language.[14] This element of auto-maticity is present here only by virtue of the reference to allegory as a "di-vine and therefore permanently repeated pattern of experience" that is "immediately present." However, in the paragraph immediately following de Man adds that allegory disenchanted Yeats for a time after his initial fascination because "the emblem is revealed by a key and this key is given a priori, as the divine order itself." Unlike the symbol, which "has to dis-cover the link [between tenor and vehicle] anew, make it originate at this moment, purity originating 'as flower originate'" ("Image and Emblem," 171), the link between the emblem and its meaning is always already there, and so is "permanently repeated" and "divine." De Man's privileging of the mechanical sign over the organic symbol is a persistent feature of his theory of figuration. It is imperative, then, that we look at some other references to this phenomenon in de Man's essays in order to determine what is at stake in such a curious preference.

While the first part of de Man's essay "Semiology and Rhetoric" concerns the undermining of grammar by rhetoric in the final lines of Yeats's "Among School Children," the second half concerns the converse: the undermining of rhetoric by grammar as typified by a passage from Proust where "the *mechanical, repetitive* aspect of grammatical forms is shown to be operative in a passage that seemed at first sight to celebrate the self-willed and autonomous inventiveness of a subject."[15] All of the terms which are for de Man typically associated with the unified *symbol* are here (and in the more detailed analysis of this same passage from Proust reserved for a later chapter)[16] clustered around this "self-willed and autonomous subject." Metaphor (insofar as the term connotes the mastery of analogy and the denial of difference), necessity, identity, totality, presence, essence, action, truth, beauty, primacy, "*genetic history, and, most notably, the autonomous power to will of the self*" ("Semiology and Rhetoric," 16; italics mine) are all opposed to "contingent figures of chance" like metonymy, which de Man sees as merely "masquerading" as the other terms.

A curious masquerade indeed, which has its guests arriving dressed up as their natural, "autonomous" selves.[17] And no one is more perfectly attired in such a manner than the natural, "psychological," autobiographical Proust. The passage in question celebrates Marcel's "autonomy" by describing his preference for reading inside the dark, cool seclusion of his room to going outside. The superiority of Marcel's choice is shown by breaking down the opposition with the warmth, light, and activity of the outside through a series of metaphors that effectively unite the two worlds. For example, the sound of bees heard outside the room is "connected to summer by a more necessary link; born from beautiful days, resurrecting only when they return, containing some of their essence, it does not only awaken their image in our memory; it guarantees their return, their actual, persistent, unmediated presence" (*Swann's Way*; quoted in "Semiology and Rhetoric," 13).

De Man is surely correct when he argues that the sound of the bees, described as "necessarily linked" to summer, is to be taken as metaphorical, whatever one might say about its metonymical status elsewhere. It would be "sacrilegious," de Man concludes, to read such a passage as anything other than a celebration of the artist's superior symbolic imagination. Such ironic statements by de Man almost always precede just such an alternative reading.

Among the metaphorical ways Proust tries to level the opposition between inside and outside is the description of his solitude as "supporting,
like the quiet of a motionless hand in the middle of a running brook, the
shock and the motion of a torrent of activity." But underlying the obvious
metaphorical expressions of inner/outer unity de Man detects contingent
"semi-automatic" patterns of "impersonal precision." The phrase "torrent
of activity," which literally refers only to the brook's "flood of activity,"
is also, in French as well as in English, a cliché referring to "heated activity."
These two levels allow Proust to unite the opposing terms of hot and cold,
not

> based on substitution, such as metaphor, to a syntagmatic structure
> based on contingent association such as metonymy, *the mechanical, re-
> petitive aspect* of grammatical forms is shown to be operative in a pas-
> sage that seemed at first sight to celebrate the self-willed and autonomous
> inventiveness of a subject. Figures are assumed to be inventions, the
> products of a highly particularized individual talent, whereas no one can
> claim credit for the programmed pattern of grammar. Yet, our reading
> of the Proust passage shows that precisely when the highest claims are
> being made for the unifying power of metaphor, these very images rely
> in fact on the deceptive use of *semi-automatic grammatical patterns*. The
> deconstruction of metaphor and of all rhetorical patterns such as mime-
> sis, paraonomasis, or personification that use resemblance as a way to
> disguise differences, takes us back to the *impersonal precision* of gram-
> mar and of a semiology derived from grammatical patterns. ("Semiology
> and Rhetoric," 15–16; italics mine)

All figures, like metaphor and personification, that seem to imply the
control of an individual subject are in fact, like the "subject" itself, always
already programmed by the "impersonal precision of a semiology derived
from grammatical patterns." Or, as de Man says elsewhere, "every metaphor is a blind metonymy" because it is really a result of the contingencies
of language first, and the mastery of the subject second.[18] Likewise, the
mechanical "use of semi-automatic grammatical patterns" is "deceptive"
because such contingent figures of chance are always being personalized—
personified—by the claims of the authorial subject. De Man's version of
the deconstructive doubling of language is focused on the way the mechanical, "impersonal precision" of language is deceptively constituted so as to
appear to be its opposite; every metaphor is a blind metonymy, every symbol is a blind sign, and so forth.

De Man's discussion of Baudelaire's "On the Essence of Laughter" in
"Rhetoric of Temporality" sheds light on the crucial automaticity identified with the sign in all its manifestations (emblem, allegory, metonymy,

irony, and so on). The passage I am interested in concerns *falling* as an example of what Baudelaire calls "absolute comedy" and, elsewhere in the same essay, "irony." De Man's discussion again hinges on the distinction between symbol and sign. The doubling (*dédoublement*) that underlies the comic irony of the fall involves an empirical, nonhuman world of nature where, to the extent to which it exists at all, language is synonymous with the things it represents, and "a world constituted out of, and in, language." "Language thus conceived," de Man continues, "divides the subject into an empirical self, immersed in the world, and a self that becomes like a sign in its attempt at differentiation and self-definition."[19] The operative term here is *attempt*: because the signic self is nonempirical, the subject's attempt at "differentiation and self-definition" is necessarily ungrounded.

When someone who uses language in the latter, empirical fashion, such as a poet or philosopher, falls, it merely reminds him or her of having already "slipped" into the belief of a grounded, empirical self. A certain arrogance or pride "before the fall" (Baudelaire's "fall" as analyzed by de Man thus retains its theological significance)[20] is seen as inevitable, because once the empirical self is grounded, as it must be, the ground is viewed as that which humanity has risen above. De Man stresses, the impossibility for even the most sophisticated artist or philosopher to avoid falling into this trap, for knowledge of being ungrounded is achieved only through the act of falling. The *sign* is thus identified with the inevitable grounding that results from the fall as much as the fall results from grounding. The artist who realizes the madness of grounding meaning on words and so "invents a form of himself that is mad" only adds to the madness by pretending to be lucid.

The mechanical doubling of the sign is evident throughout this section in a number of ways. First, the nonsymbolic act of falling practically defines spontaneity, which also gives it an automatic quality. Second, the fall is capable of imbuing the poet/philosopher with a new signic sense of language as double, as not only metaphoric but ironically so. For the sign that is immediately grounded after the experience of being ungrounded (through the fall) cannot help but continue to refer to the world through language that has been stripped of the ability to do so. The automaticity of the sign is thus an important new way of talking about the sign as double: the sign (versus the symbol) lacks a referent, but cannot help referring automatically to that selfsame lack.

Another passage from "Image and Emblem" also contains the first of de Man's famous interpretations of the final lines of "Among School Children."[21] The argument in which de Man was engaged before turning to those celebrated lines concerns Yeats's supposed "return to the world of natural images" in his mature poems, and the resultant tendency among Yeats's major critics (Ellman, Kermode, and others) "to see Yeats as the poet who went further than any in overcoming the separation between mind and matter" ("Image and Emblem," 188). Arguing against this tendency, de Man adduces the refrain from part 6 of "Meditations in Time of Civil War" ("O honey-bees, / Come build in the empty house of the stare") to exemplify Yeats's still vital emblematic tendencies: "The refrain expresses the vain and desperate hope of Western, romantic poetry, that divine presence will return in nature, a hope from which Yeats, too, can not disentangle himself, although he knows of the existence of another road" (193).

Honeybees are emblematic for Yeats (from Porphyry) of the "pleasure arising from generation" (192) in the natural world, of the "profane perfection of mankind," whose major poet for Yeats is (again, emblematically) Homer. Contrary to readings of this refrain that would find comfort in the bees' continuation of the birds' divine knowledge,[22] de Man "sacrilegiously" interprets the lines as lamenting the loss of divine, emblematic meaning manifested in the mechanical, repetitious activity of the birds. Emblematic meaning "finds unity preserved in language as the carrier of a divine *and therefore permanently repeated* pattern of experience" ("Image and Emblem," 171–72; italics mine). That the honeybees are themselves emblematic in referring to "the pleasure arising from generation" only adds to de Man's conviction that Yeats is more interested in the "half-real wisdom of daemonic images" (that is, emblems) than in a reconciliation between nature, with its "corruption of generation," and the atemporal linguistic consciousness of emblems.[23]

This same opposition between the natural (imagistic) world of the honeybees and the linguistic (emblematic) world of the birds is addressed in the similarly apostrophaeic final lines of "Among School Children":

> O chestnut-tree, great-rooted blossomer,
> Are you the leaf, the blossom or the bole?
> O body swayed to music, O brightening glance,
> How can we know the dancer from the dance?

As in the earlier poem, here too one might be tempted to read these famous lines as celebrating the symbolic unity of sensuous experience (the bole, the dancer) with the larger, encompassing form of which it is a part (the tree, the dance). But the lines also refer us to the discussion in *Ideas of Good and Evil* where the natural, symbolic unity between the lily and purity was contrasted with an emblematic unity that is unnatural and based on language—more specifically, on the structure of the sign insofar as it has no natural appearance. The usual reading interprets the final lines as a rhetorical question that unrhetorically denies any separation between word and referent. But it is also possible to read the lines literally (not 'One cannot tell . . . ' but 'How can one tell . . . ?') as celebrating the emblematic/linguistic form of the dance and of the tree which demand to be distinguished from their merely natural appearance. In other words, the natural, Cratylistic association of the *signifiant* (the dancer) with the *signifié* (the dance) is opposed by de Man to an "emblematic" reading which asks "with some urgency" how we might separate the human and the natural (the dancer, the bough) from a linguistic meaning that has no relation to the natural. Such a separation is desirable because linguistic/emblematic "meaning" is deemed, like the repetitious activity of the stare, to be unrelated to the immediate human sphere of activity.[24]

"Among School Children" puts into the form of a rhetorical question a linguistic doubling that can never be resolved. Just as the dancer can only be said to get in the way of the very dance of which he or she is a part (and this getting-in-the-way is itself the dance), the structure of allegorical meaning is such that, in referring to "something other than" that to which it actually refers (the dance versus the dancer), it also refers to something other than itself. The lily's purity cannot be understood without the lily, but nor can it be understood with it. De Man later states in this essay, "In pure emblem . . . the body is precisely what is not embodied" ("Image and Emblem," 223). The natural, bodily component does not, then, disappear in a system that favors the emblem over the image and, more generally, language over perception. However much the figural is able to dispense with the mimetic, it is inevitable that *the* dance, whose implications are infinite and divine, double as *this* dance, with *these* dancers. Yeats's reference to "a body swayed to music" takes on the more sinister implications de Man speaks of elsewhere in the dissertation with reference to Yeats's disdain for physical sensuality—implications which, one might add, are also evident in Fergus's deathly invitation to join his tragic dance, as well as in the "aged man's" condemnation of "that sensual music" in "Sailing to Byzantium."

*

In his essay on Proust, de Man used the term "impersonal precision" to describe how the "mechanical, repetitive aspect of grammatical forms is shown to be operative in a passage that seemed at first sight to celebrate the self-willed and autonomous inventiveness of a subject" ("Semiology and Rhetoric," 15–16). This sense of "impersonal precision" characterizes de Man's interpretation of Hegel's theory of the sign ("Sign and Symbol"), for it too demonstrates the automatic, machinelike quality of language characteristic of metonymy in Proust and emblem in Yeats. The sign, according to Hegel, has nothing to do with what the subject "I" says it is insofar as language is strictly citational, with its meaning determined by others. Because of this, even the "I" as sign has nothing to do with the *I* as personal subject, resulting in the doubling of an "I who cannot say I," or, of an "I which is not who I am."[25] Hegel describes the sign and the thinking subject, the "I," which purveys it, as both "self-effacing in the much more radical sense that the position of the I, which is the condition of thought, implies its eradication."[26] Rather than revealing the mastery of a subject, the sign and language in general are shown to imply their own "paradoxical self-effacement." According to de Man, it is in an attempt to forget this theoretical self-erasure that Hegel posits the aesthetic-symbolical as a category of thought which must "mean what it says," given Hegel's famous definition of art as the synthesis of image and idea. The need to define art as symbol is merely the result of the loss of mastery in the concept of art as sign.[27]

That the stakes in this escape from the sign are high is apparent in the crucial final pages of this essay, where de Man connects the ideological valorization of the symbol to a "dialectics of internalization" that preconditions the way we think about art and literature. "Secularized versions of the Fall" that permeate the attempts of many pre- and postromantic writers to regain a natural state of internalization can be seen as ways to avoid the mechanical exteriorization of a sign which doesn't actually say what it means. De Man refers to the "problematic of the sublime" as a regrounding of subjectivism at the expense of external reality which, like its linguistic analogue, represents the recovery of inner symbolic meaning at the expense of an external doubling of language that involves rhetorical slips, turns, and falls one cannot master.

Just as the sign described by Hegel is imageless (*bildlos*) in its purely linguistic character, so too memory (*Gedächtnis*), "the learning by rote of names, or of words considered as names," is distinguished from the referential nature of *Erinnerung* (remembrance) and the symbol: "The synthesis between name and meaning that characterizes memory is an 'empty link' [*leere Band*] and thus entirely unlike the mutual complementarity and interpenetration of form and content that characterizes symbolic art." As "a mental faculty that is mechanical through and through," *Gedächtnis* shares a machinelike quality with the sign due to its impersonal and arbitrary functioning.[28] Also like the sign, *Gedächtnis* has a self-effacing quality because of its machinelike functioning as but an "empty link" between the actual objects of remembrance: "In memorization, in thought and, by extension, in the sensory manifestation of thought as an 'art' of writing, 'we are dealing only with signs [*wir haben es überhaupt nur mit Zeichen zu tun*].' *Memory effaces remembrance (or recollection) just as the I effaces itself. The faculty that enables thought to exist also makes its preservation impossible.*"[29]

De Man's goal in all this is to show that the doubles of the symbol and *Erinnerung*, the sign and *Gedächtnis*, have a mechanical, self-effacing quality against which the personal, natural qualities of symbol and *Erinnerung* seek to define themselves. "Memory is a truth of which the aesthetic is the defensive, ideological, and censored translation" because the linguistic process of thought that makes, for example, imagistic tropes and literature in general possible is conveniently forgotten as we move away from the text in order to better see or understand it.[30] Images like the "I" and metaphor are "defensive, ideological, and censored translations" because they pretend to interrupt the process of thought and language that produced them in the first place.[31] Since language cannot be identified with the objects it produces, it must double them by *constructing* and *destructing* figures like the prosopoetic "I" and the metaphorical rose. This is why, in "Image and Emblem in Yeats," the emblematic connection between the lily and purity was shown to be preferable to the (supposedly) metaphorical unity between the rose and love.

De Man turns Hegel's famous pronouncement that "art is a thing of the past" into a true statement that means the opposite of what Hegel intended. That art, "like memorization, leaves the interior of experience forever behind" means that, as material inscription, it can never be fully present to itself.[32] Like allegory, art can never say "I," can never say what its subject is, though its subject is all that it can ever say that it is. "Allegory functions like the defective cornerstone of the entire [Hegelian] system" because it reveals the separation of subject from predicate—the "empty link" of *Gedächtnis*—which it is the goal of art always to deny, as through the subject of the allegorical narrative. If criticism has a "bad name," de Man concludes, it is because it is identified with the signic, allegorical, linguistic functions whose forgetting, or self-effacement, we are most eager to erase. To take de Man's notion one step further, only when such allegorical criticism is taken at least as seriously as the mimetic power of the "organic" work of art will criticism lose its bad name. The simultaneously grave and giddy tone of de Man's writings is not due to any "existential pathos": de

Man knew his attack on mimesis would probably add to his status as a pariah while eventually freeing him from the stigma attached to the critic.[33]

*

Given his persistent attack on "genetic" patterns involving "subject, intent, negation and totalization,"[34] a pattern that underlies the preference for symbols and images over allegories and signs, de Man's preference for the genitive preposition in his titles—the "genetic pattern" of the *of* in de Man's writings—might seem surprising, or even contradictory. But when we consider more closely the way the *of* functions in titles like "Rhetoric of Tropes," "Rhetoric of Temporality," and "Allegories of Reading," it is apparent that no such historical narrative, even the pseudohistory of Nietzsche's *Birth of Tragedy*, is ever implied. Rather than basing rhetoric on tropes, for example, de Man uses titles like "Rhetoric of Tropes," which refer instead to the impossibility of denying tropes their double meaning. The same is true when de Man uses allegory in such genitive phrases as *Allegories of Reading* or "allegory of errors" ("Rhetoric of Tropes," 118). These phrases refer to the fact that the text as double cannot tell us what it means even as it is doing precisely that, just as the "I cannot say I" even as it is doing so. Similar to the definition of doubling given in this work, the *of* of de Man's titles calls genitive meaning into question even as it is being asserted. The more de Man's writings call referentiality into question the more they recognize not only the necessity but the importance of such referents, for criticism is "unable ever to escape from the rhetorical deceit it denounces" ("Rhetoric of Tropes," 115). It is highly appropriate, then, that the writer who called the authority of the subject most into question should himself carry the *of* of genetic reference in his own name—a name which, moreover, is one of the few to escape the tyranny of capitalization.

The true nature of the important relationship between Yeats and Nietzsche has not yet been written,[35] but any attempt to do so should consider that the writers to whom de Man turned at the beginning and end of his career were both seen as elevating the emblematic function of language over the referential function of objects.[36] In "Rhetoric of Tropes" de Man is no longer concerned, as he was in the study of Yeats, with demonstrating the privilege of emblem over image and language over reality. Rather, de Man is drawing out the implications of basing meaning on language and the eloquence of rhetoric on the displacements of tropes (as opposed to the converse). Given Nietzsche's declaration, in "Über Wahrheit und Lüge im aussermoralischen Sinn," that all truth is figurative, is it possible to retain some philosophical grasp on what threatens to become the meaningless sands of a world reduced to "literature"? And, if not, what is the status of texts such as Nietzsche's that describe the truth of this predicament?

In order to demonstrate how Nietzsche bases meaning on a rhetorical view of linguistic doubling, de Man focuses on Nietzsche's attack on phenomenalism in favor of a more rhetorical (specifically, metaleptical) view of causality. Hardly to be content with traditional views of subjective versus objective truth, Nietzsche utterly confounds the classical polarity by defining objective causality as an effect of the subject, with subjectivity in turn as the effect of some other objective cause:

> The outer, objective event in the world was supposed to determine the inner, conscious event as cause determines effect. It turns out however that what was assumed to be the objective, external cause is itself the result of an internal effect. What had been considered to be a cause, is, in fact, the effect of an effect, and what had been considered to be an effect can in its turn seem to function as the cause of its own cause. ("Rhetoric of Tropes," 107)

The problem, as de Man sees it, stems from confounding temporality's chronological ordering with logical ordering. The mind errs by positing a temporal sequence that determines cause and effect because the subjective "effect" can also be seen as the cause of the effect that supposedly precedes it.

Nietzsche's view of figurative language matches de Man's view of allegory, the sign, and language in general. "The entire process of [causal] substitution and reversal is conceived by Nietzsche, and this is the main point for us in this context, as a linguistic event" (108). Against phenomenalism, Nietzsche views as *linguistic* this erroneous process of substituting causes for effects and effects for causes. By language Nietzsche means rhetoric, and by rhetoric, metonymy (the "prototype of all figural language," 109). Truth is linguistic, and language metonymic, because whatever is assumed to be true is always a substitution for something else. Such a process of substitution is metonymic rather than metaphoric because there is no truth for which the substitution is really a substitute.

De Man's analysis of Nietzsche's language-based universe is a rewriting of his own view of language as sign versus symbol. Just as Nietzsche's antiphenomenalism leads him to view truth as a rhetorical process of tropological substitution, de Man systematically rejects any naturalism—symbolic or otherwise—that would base language on meaning, rather than the converse. Yet this does not mean anything so simple as denying the referential status of language; to affirm, or deny, the rhetorical nature of language would be to completely miss de Man's and Nietzsche's point. That point, in de Man's terms, is that language as sign is far more automatic, and hence meaningless, than any transcendental model would allow.

This focus on language allows us to view the world that exists before language as the truth, but as the "un-truth" which is forgotten by the falsification of language imposed in the name of truth. If the status of truth, then, is neither true, since it is rhetorical, nor false, since there is no truth to which it can be compared, then the skilled liar who is able rhetorically to "misuse the established linguistic conventions by arbitrary substitutions or even reversals of names" (Nietzsche, quoted in "Rhetoric of Tropes," 112) is demonstrating the same exemplary power of language as that shown by the skilled rhetorician, politician, or philosopher. A difference exists between a bad liar and a good philosopher, but who would prefer a mediocre philosopher to an excellent liar? The difference is immediately apparent in the figure of Nietzsche himself, who, in "On Truth and Lies in an Extra-Moral Sense" as throughout his writings, is able to tell lies that are closer to the truth than many more scrupulous accounts. For example, the "minute" of human reason scornfully described in "Truth and Lies" ("Es war die hochmüthigste und verlogenste Minute der 'Weltgeschichte'") could also, following Nietzsche's logic, easily last an eternity. And the idea of "leaf" achieved by deceitfully eliminating all the particular leaves can also be considered, as Nietzsche himself demonstrates in the course of the essay, the very triumph of reason. The fact that Nietzsche tells us the truth about lying does not stop him from lying about telling the truth.

Nietzsche is not just demeaning truth or glorifying literature, for literature is itself a kind of truth, or, to use Nietzsche's term, a "gay science" which discovers meaning as compatible with its own de(con)struction.[37] The various doublings that were shown to inform de Man's other writings are here reduced to their most general form, that between literal, referential truth and an "allegory of errors" that de Man sees as "the very model of philosophical rigor" ("Rhetoric of Tropes," 118). The errors of confounding the lily with purity, of calling the I "I" or of naming the dancer from the dance confirm Nietzsche's goal of revealing language to be an automatic, catachrestic process of calling things by their wrong names. This error is further described as an "allegory" by de Man because, like Schlegel's "permanente Parekbasis," the supposed recognition of that erroneousness is itself a kind of error: no nonrhetorical, nonlinguistic position of truth exists from which one can properly judge "truth and lies." The recognition of rhetorical doubling necessarily leaves the reader "suspended between the truth and the death of this truth" (115).

Whether through their emphasis on irony, emblem, allegory, or sign, de Man's deconstructive writings are inseparable from the recognition of rhetoric, whereby such devalorized figures all double the supposedly greater reality of things themselves.[38] Time will tell whether this linguistic awareness produces the kind of textual "supermen" de Man envisioned as resisting the mimetic fallacy that confuses the dance—the "impersonal precision" of meaning that is mechanical and so unaccounted for—with the dancer. Or whether, like Nietzsche, de Man moved criticism in a direction where further progress was blocked by the clarity of the path lying open before us.

8 | The Comparative Double

Romanticism, Figuration, and Comparative Literature

The "great argument" for comparative literature has always been, René Wellek repeatedly maintained, the necessity of studying literature as one, as a unified totality.[1] The common notion that comparative literature is simply the study of literature in more than one language is incomplete, because an English comparatist who also studies French or German, for example, should not, and probably could not, do so without bringing his or her particular point of view to bear. The comparative study of a foreign literature is carried out in the belief that it must also be understood from the standpoint of the native literature, and that the native literature should also be examined from the expanded foreign point of view. Most, if not all, of the problems inherent in definitions of the discipline of comparative literature[2] ("To what shall I compare thee?") are a function of this stated or unstated telos which is the proper goal of comparative literature: if the unity or totality of all literature is its project, comparative literature seems doomed at the outset to a lack of completion that is devastating in its own terms. As Victor Lange states: "Als Universitätdisziplin hat sich 'comparative literature' allein dort behaupten können, wo ihre Grenzes soweit und damit so anspruchlos gezogen wurden."[3] The purpose of this chapter is to argue for this same lack of completion as resulting from the necessary (and highly productive) doubling of comparative literature's romantic, figurative basis.

Before examining Wellek's notion of comparative literature as the study of literature as such, it is important to consider the view of another school of criticism that sought to define the field of comparative literature in much less ambitious terms. Although the most apparent roots of comparative literature, like that of many nineteenth-century disciplines, are in romanticism,[4] the "French school" (Baldensperger, Van Tieghem, Carré, Gruyard, Trousson, and others) attempted to divert the comparative study of literature along more empirical, less idealistic lines. Baldensperger's study of *Goethe en France* (1904) is hailed by that school as a classic example of the comparatist's methodology, but it was only as late as 1931 that Van Tieghem published the manifesto that sought to define the French version of comparative literature for the first time. This lag of more than a quarter of a century is significant, for Van Tieghem's treatise was published closer in time to the demise than to the origin of the French school whose doctrine it outlines for the first time.

In order to define clearly a proper methodology for comparative literature, Van Tieghem, who is the originator of terms like *thematology, genology,* and a host of other Hellenic neologisms, is forced to eliminate all aesthetic, critical, and speculative inquiry into the meaning of literature:

> Le caractère de la vraie littérature comparée, comme celui de toute science historique, est d'embrasser le plus grand nombre possible de faits différents d'origine, pour mieux expliquer chacun d'eux; d'enlarger les bases de la connaisance enfin de trouver les causes et les plus grand nombre possible d'effets. *Bref, le mot comparé doit être vidé de toute valeur esthétique et recevoir une valeur scientifique.*
> [The true character of comparative literature, like that of every historical science, is to encompass the greatest possible number of different facts concerning origins in order to explain better each of them, and to enlarge the basis of knowledge in order to discover causes and the greatest possible number of their effects. *In a word: "comparative" ought to be void of all aesthetic value and receive a strictly scientific meaning.*][5]

The rationale behind this scientific ideal is understandable. As soon as one admits "close readings" or other ways of understanding the particular work of art within the domain of comparative literature, a veritable army of related concerns is destined to emerge from its hollow underbelly. How, Van Tieghem wonders, can a comparatist be expected to account adequately for the *explication de texte* (for example, Rousseau's *Julie*) and then for that of the related works (Richardson's *Clarissa*) to which it is being compared? For surely an attempt to understand the particular work of Rousseau will include an understanding of his other works, its place within Rousseau's life, the place of those within the broader horizons of French culture and literature of the eighteenth century, of that age within French literature in general, and of that literature within other European literatures, non-European literatures, and so on and so forth. Then one must do the same all over again for Richardson, as well as for Goethe, to chose only the most celebrated authors of eighteenth-century *romans epistolaires*.

So it is understandable if Van Tieghem wants to eliminate a concern with understanding particular literary works. He is even on safe philosophical ground in not wanting to compare two utterly unique particulars. So-called parallel studies of different representations of one particular genre or motif (the trajectory of tragedy from Aeschylus through Beckett, doomed lovers à la Tristan and Iseult, and so on) which rely on the reader's intuition of a similarity based on an interpretation of the particular text are to be rejected for similar reasons if they forsake revealing actual points of contact (hence the metaphor of parallelism). The scientific ideal of comparative literature envisioned by Van Tieghem must, then, restrict itself to the study of *influences*, which are the historically verifiable transmissions of literature "across state lines," as it were:

> Si, en parcourant la littérature française, on porte son attention vers ses contacts avec d'autres littératures, on s'aperçoit immédiatement de leur nombre et de leur importance. L'histoire littéraire telle que nous l'avons décrite a constamment à s'occuper d'influences, d'imitations et d'emprunts. . . . le jeu des *influences* récues ou exercées est un élément essentiel de l'histoire littéraire.
> [If, in surveying French literature, one were to focus one's attention on its contacts with other literatures, one would immediately perceive their great number and importance. Literary history such as we have described it must concern itself exclusively with influences, imitations and borrowings. . . . the play of received or exercised *influences* is an essential element of literary history.][6]

Enter René Wellek, who is rightly appalled at this violent elimination of all the essential concerns of comparative literature and at the restriction of comparative studies to the discovery of actual historical contacts or influences. However, Wellek too is suspicious of the alternative to this empiricism, for he too sees parallelism as a threat to the methodological validity of the discipline he wishes to defend:

> Comparison is a method used by all criticism and sciences, and does not, in any way, adequately describe the specific procedures of literary study. The formal comparison between literatures—or even movements, figures, and works—is rarely a central theme in literary history, though such a book as F. C. Green's *Minuet*, comparing aspects of French and English eighteenth-century literature, may be illuminating in defining not only parallels and affinities but also divergences between the literary development of one nation and that of another.[7]

I believe Wellek is correct in saying that "actual comparisons," the literal comparison of two individual works or writers, are "rarely central" in the study of literature. Hence the slight but oft-repeated misgivings Wellek expresses about the name "comparative literature": *the practitioner of "comparative" literature does not actually compare literatures.* But, if the comparatist doesn't actually compare, how shall we define such a method, to what shall we compare it? Shouldn't we do away with the name altogether?

On closer examination of Wellek's twenty-year attempt to answer this question, we see that he does not in fact eliminate the process of comparison or parallel studies from their particular relevance to comparative studies. To be sure, such approaches are exiled from the comparatist's "central focus" (as a metaphor for the subdued light of literary recognition from an outside source, *illuminating* may be preferable anyway) for the obvious reason that they all neglect their "truly literary" subject matter, the individual work of art. But Wellek does not, despite his links to the New Critics of the 1940s and 1950s, revert to a more formalist, "closed" approach to literature. Like any comparatist, Wellek is not only concerned with the individual work but with its relation to other literatures, historical currents, and other disciplines which all exist outside the borders of the so-called closed text. That is, the comparatist must do a close, or closed, reading of particular literary texts, thus remaining true to the aesthetic essence of the text, but must also study such "external relations" as its historical context as well as its relation to other texts, other authors, other literatures, other disciplines, and so on, all of which are "illuminated" by as well as illuminate the individual text itself. Wellek even "out–Van Tieghems" Van Tieghem, for, at one point in *Theories of Literature*, he argues that the comparatist must not only study the literary relationships between nations but between regions within any given nation, because before one can understand a national literature one must understand its regional substructure.[8] If, to paraphrase Wellek, one is going to study only external relations "across state lines," one had better start with states and not countries. Wellek's point, although not explicitly stated, is that matters are not made any less complex by trying to isolate the external from the internal in literary studies.

The notion of "suggestion" or "illumination" is the critical aspect of Wellek's approach, but, unfortunately, he does no more than suggest or illuminate its essence. In the light of literary scholarship since 1965 (the date of Wellek's last article on comparative literature), we can take Wellek's idea further. In insisting throughout his career on the "nonneutral" literary value of the particular work of art Wellek was preparing the ground for the more recent insistence on the figurative, or to use Wellek's term, symbolic status of literature and all approaches to literature. Because literary and, in general, artistic "meaning" is double, the individual literary text is capable of meaning anything while denying any strict identification with everything it means. Hence Wellek insisted repeatedly on comparative literature as the study of literature as one totality while at the same time claiming that the study of parallels, of comparisons as such, can be only marginal concerns.[9] The study of parallels between any two writers, or the study of genres, periods, and motifs, can be valid only if the individual differences between the different works are revealed by the comparisons that "bring them together" in the first place. In other words, I compare *x* and *y*, not only to find out what they have in common, but to understand *x* and *y* individually. This is what Wellek means by the study of literature in its totality. As in the case of Erich Auerbach, whose work, with Ernst Curtius's, Wellek holds up as an ideal for comparative studies,[10] the "unity" that the comparatist reveals between Homer and the Old Testament, for example, separates as well as joins the individual works being compared. (The problematic of borderlines is crucial to comparative literature, for borderlines share this paradox of joining and separating at one and the same time.) The comparison cannot be central for Wellek because it serves ultimately merely to *illuminate* the individual work and so also denies any strict or central unity.

*

The figurative doubling of literature is the essence of *comparative* literature, the study of literature in its totality. The writings of two early romantics, Friedrich Schlegel and Mme de Staël, will help us to demonstrate this. Explicit pronouncements of the symbolic, figurative value of literature were an essential, perhaps the central, concern of these early romantics, and it is surely no accident that these same figures are commonly credited with heralding the cry that resulted in the formal discipline which we are now studying.[11]

A preoccupation with romanticism appears endemic to the comparatist project, and the reasons for this are at least twofold: modern comparativism has its roots in the romantic notion that "the time has come to leave national prejudices behind and hasten the epoch of world literature" (Goethe),[12] and romanticism has its roots in a concern with the symbolic relation between individual and universal that necessitated the comparatist's outlook:

> Er [der Dichter] muss streben, seine Poesie und seine Ansicht der Poesie ewig zu erweitern, und sie der höchsten zu nähern die überhaupt auf der Erde möglich ist; dadurch dasser seinen Teil an das grosse Ganze auf die bestimmteste Weise anzuschliessen strebt: denn die tötende Verallgemeinerung wirkt gerade das Gegenteil.
> [The poet must continually strive to expand his poetry and his view of poetry, and to have it approximate the loftiest possibility on earth by endeavoring to integrate, in the most specific way, his part with the entire body of poetry: deadening generalizations result in just the opposite.][13]

To understand comparativism it may well be that we must properly understand romanticism, and vice versa. One place to begin this project is the famous Fragment 116 of Friedrich Schlegel, which offers a dazzling analysis of *Romantische* as *Universalpoesie*:

> Die romantische Poesie is eine progressive Universalpoesie. Ihre Bestimmung ist nicht bloss, all getrennte Gattungen der Poesie wieder zu vereinigen und die Poesie mit der Philosophie und Rhetorik in Berührung zu setzen. Sie will und soll auch Poesie und Prosa, Genialität und Kritik, Kunstpoesie und Naturpoesie bald mischen, bald verschmelzen, die Poesie lebendig und gesellig und das Leben und die Gesellschaft poetisch machen.
> [Romantic poetry is a progressive universal poetry. Its mission is not merely to reunite all separate genres of poetry and to put poetry in touch with philosophy and rhetoric. It should at once mingle and amalgamate poetry and prose, genius and criticism, the poetry of art and the poetry of nature, rendering poetry living and social, and life and society poetic.][14]

The purpose of romantic poetry is not only to reunite the various poetical genres, and poetry with philosophy and rhetoric. Its telos is also to "mix and melt down" a series of classical oppositions between poetry and prose, genius and criticism, naive and artistic poetry, and, finally, to make poetry lively and life poetic. The English translator of this fragment translates *mischen und verschmelzen* as "mingle and amalgamate," whereas the context of this metallurgical metaphor also allows the more antithetical notion of "combine and disintegrate," or, more literally, "mix and melt down." Schlegel's point is that the romanticist both joins and separates the numerous divisions that continue to exist in poetry.[15] The structure of Schlegel's thought here is chiastic, for the romanticist *converts*, and does not actually compare, the various components within as well as without poetry. Poetry should be philosophic, philosophy should be poetic, prose should be poetic, poetry prosaic, life artistic, art lively, and so on. We can thus begin to see what Schlegel means by those two key terms with which he begins: *progressive* and *universal*. The various forms of artistic expression are not to be contained within static boundaries, but must be able to merge and become one *as well as* maintain their separate integrity. If poetry is to be philosophic and philosophy poetic, this does not mean a synthesis but rather a *doubling* whereby the "universal" succeeds in maintaining its individual identities.

Progressive in Schlegel's system also means that "die romantische Dichtart is noch im Werden; ja das ist ihr eigentliches Wesen, dass sie ewig nur werden, nie vollendet sein kann [the Romantic type of poetry is still becoming; indeed, its peculiar essence is that it is always becoming and that it can never be completed]."[16] The perfection of a genuine synthesis is never a part of Schlegel's system. Rather, the individual works, genres, et cetera cross their boundaries and those of related disciplines, of related national literatures, and so forth, all in the fulfillment of their own individuality. Romanticism is seriously misunderstood if this carefully crafted relationship between the individual and universal is thought of as an opposition or as the resolution of this opposition, for one of the essential paradoxes of romantic ideology is its simultaneous movement toward the individual and the universal. Those who would similarly oppose classic and romantic would be hard put to explain Schlegel's statement that through a broadened romantic perspective "die Aussicht auf eine granzenlos wachsende Klassizität eröffnet wird"; that is, that classicism, which is nothing if not the creation of boundaries, is not dispensed with but made infinite.

The latter image is expressed most vividly in a metaphor Schlegel fashions in the same fragment just mentioned:

> Und doch giebt es noch keine Form, die so dazu gemacht wäre, den Geist des Autors voll ständig auszudrücken: so dass manche Kunstler, die nur auch einen Roman schreiben wollten, von ungefähr sich selbst dargestellt haben. Nur sie kann gleich dem Epos ein Spiegel der ganzen umgebenden Welt, ein Bild des Zeitalters werden. Und doch kann auch sie am meisten zwischen dem Dargestellten und dem Darstellenden, frei von allem realen und idealen Interesse auf den Flügeln der poetischen Reflexion immer wieder potenzieren und wie in einer endlosen Reihe von Spiegeln vervielfachen. `
> [And yet no form has thus far arisen appropriate to expressing the author's mind perfectly, so that artists who just wanted to write a novel have by coincidence described themselves. Romantic poetry alone can, like the epic, become a mirror of the entire surrounding world, a picture of its age. And yet, it too can soar, free from all real and ideal interests, on the wings of poetic reflection, midway between the work and the artist. It can even exponentiate this reflection and multiply it as in an endless series of mirrors.][17]

Romantic poetry is "suspended on the wings of poetic reflection" between two mirrors, one representing the poet's subjectivity ("der Geist des Autors," "dem Darstellenden"), the other representing the world outside ("die ganze umgebende Welt," "dem Dargestellten"). Because poetry is both poles but also neither, an infinite regress or *mise-en-abyme* occurs. The world is reflected in the poet who is reflected in the world which is reflected in the poet, ad infinitum, "in einer endlosen Reihe von Spiegeln vervielfachen." The sense of "grenzenloss Wachsende" potency results from hanging suspended or soaring (the German *schweben* allows both translations, and perhaps requires both) "in der Mitte." As in the chiastic interplay just discussed, the boundary between the poet's representation of himself and the world is not dissolved, for each component is enhanced because of its reflection in the other.

Schlegel's imagery refers to the structure of romantic poetry as well as to its comparative essence as "eine progressive Universalpoesie." The comparatist realizes that the borderlines which separate and join the artist and his work, the individual work and the rest of the artist's oeuvre, that oeuvre from those of contemporaries and *their* contemporaries in neighboring countries, and the so-called contemporary age from other so-called periods, are all figurative, the essence of figuration being the transgression of borderlines or definitions to predicate a native term with one that is foreign. Comparativism in this sense redefines definitions, keeping in mind that such a process is ultimately paradoxical. But what are borderlines if not figures that are drawn? The study of *foreign* literatures should be modeled on what Aristotle and others have seen as the essential doubling of metaphor: its uncanny quality of being both foreign and native, of both disrupting and maintaining the logic of the literal.[18]

Because of the figurative status of literary—versus literal—boundaries, all the individual components of literary studies just mentioned, starting with the individual text and including the individual national literature, maintain their validity. This is true despite the fact that such "individual" approaches usually involve borrowings from some discipline or other foreign to literature (for example, linguistics, socio-anthropology, history, philosophy). Within the comparative, figurative schema outlined above, we are only expanding the boundaries of the individual text and its national context "in einer endlosen Reihe von Spiegeln," we are never transcending them. In this respect Wellek was right in saying that all professors of literature are comparatists, and all comparatists are or should be designated simply professors of literature.

*

Curious, that the age which is so closely identified with a rise in national consciousness should also be an age that gave birth to ideal or universal history, where the individual nation takes its place within the larger drama of the world. Why did the romantics stress the individuality of nations replete with cultural differences and, at the same time, the need for going outside the borders of one's particular culture? Despite the two opposing directions of these concerns, there is really no contradiction here. In

nineteenth-century linguistics, the discovery of a common language underlying the different Indo-European tongues was often combined, as in the
case of the brothers Grimm, with an ever-deepening awareness of a nation's individual *Volksgeist*. For the romantics, the part is the whole, the
universal and the particular are synonymous. Ideally, a nation takes its
place with the great chain of universal history, not by forfeiting its most
distinct characteristics, but by discovering those characteristics within a
broader system of meaning than its own. The Hegelian method, which was
adopted by many comparative studies of literature such as Posnett's, is concerned only with the empirical study of historical facts insofar as it reveals
theoretical interrelations. Wellek holds these idealists up as his own ideal
when he says, "Whatever the difficulties into which a conception of universal literary history may run, it is important to think of literature as a
totality and to trace the growth and development of literature without regard to linguistic distinctions. . . . This ideal was envisaged and, within
their limited means, fulfilled, by the founders of literary history in the early
nineteenth century: such men as the Schlegels." [19]

If comparative literature and comparative linguistics owe their existence to the same romantic quest for an original teleological unity, it is not
surprising to find in the earliest statements urging a comparative approach
to literature notions to the effect that the "foreign" literature is in a sense
native, or somehow our own:

> "The Chinese novel?" I asked. "That must appear very foreign and
> strange."
> "Not as much as one might think," replied Goethe. "The characters
> think, act, and feel much as we do, and one feels very much their equal,
> except that, with them, everything is clearer, purer and more refined.
> With them everything is more reasonable and customary, without any
> great suffering and poetic striving. The Chinese novel has a lot in com-
> mon with my own 'Hermann und Dorothea,' and with the novels of the
> Englishman Richardson." [20]

Goethe's famous disdain, in his later years, for most things romantic
might cause us to suspect this embrace of the classical serenity of the Chinese novel as a rhetorical ploy. We turn, then, to a work written twenty
years earlier, Mme de Staël's *De l'Allemagne*, as equally insistent on this
doubling of the native and the foreign implied in finding our homeland
outside the strict borders of our own native terrain.

As is often the case for epoch-making treatises, Mme de Staël's revo-
lutionary work *De l'Allemagne* (1821) was prompted by a revelation:
"Lorsque j'ai commencé l'étude de l'allemand, il m'a semblé que j'entrais
dans une sphère nouvelle où se manifestaient les lumières les plus frap-

pantes sur tout ce que je savais auparavant [As soon as I began studying German it seemed as if I had entered a different world, one where the most penetrating light struck everything I had previously known]."[21] In *Corinne* Mme de Staël wrote in a similar vein: "La littérature de chaque pays découvre à qui sait la connaîtra une nouvelle sphère d'idées" (bk. 7); numerous other statements similarly voice the spirit of discovery with which Mme de Staël approached the study of a foreign literature. For what would be the justification for beginning the arduous process of studying a foreign literature if it did not promise the acquisition of something we do not possess already, something our own literature, our own thought (Mme de Staël was equally interested in German philosophy) does not already provide?

This process of "comparison," which is strict in its rejection of any common middle ground, or comparison as such, is paradoxical. We would not study a foreign literature if it were not, at least in certain respects, essentially different from our own, but we would also not study a foreign language or literature if it did not communicate—translate—its difference for our own native understanding. In a chapter entitled "Pourquoi les Français ne rendent-ils pas justice à la littérature allemande?" Mme de Staël insists that the truly foreign literatures that are the objects of her study are precisely those that do not translate:

> Très peu de personnes en France savent l'allemand, et que les beautés de cette langue, surtout en poésie, ne peuvent être traduites en français. Les langues teutoniques se traduisent facilement entre elles; il en est de même des langues latines: mais celles-ci ne sauraient rendre la poésie des peuples germaniques. Une musique composée pour un instrument n'est point exécutée avec succès sur un instrument d'un autre genre.
> [Very few people in France know German; moreover, the beauty of that language, especially its poetry, cannot be translated into French. The Germanic languages translate easily enough among themselves; likewise the Romance languages; but the latter could not begin to render the poetry of the German peoples. Music composed for one instrument is hardly transposable to an instrument of a different kind.] (*De l'Allemagne*, 159)

The process of comparative literature is relatable to this paradox of trans-lation or trans-position (both are, again, related to meta-phor): the possibility of poetic translation is conditioned by its impossibility.[22] The translation of foreign literary works is necessitated both because the work cannot be kept within the boundaries of its native terrain and because it is not really possible to remove it from those boundaries and translate a foreign work of literature. If the primary impetus for Mme de Staël's comparative treatise is that French and German are essentially different (the two cultures exhibit "différences prononcées qui existent entre la manière de voir et de sentir"), this very impossibility creates the possibility of discovering "une nouvelle sphère d'idées," a "new manner of thinking and seeing." Metaphors, translations, and comparisons are all transgressions (another word for metaphor) in that they sneak across borders that continue to maintain their authority.

For Mme de Staël, the way to relate the two opposing terms of French and German culture that do not relate is by means of the many binary oppositions that structure her work:

> Des écrivains et des lecteurs allemands et français rappelle[nt] cette fable de La Fontaine où la cigogne ne peut manger dans le plat, ni le renard dans la bouteille. Le contraste le plus parfait se fait voir entre les esprits développés dans la solitude et ceux formés par la société. Les impressions du dehors et le recueillement de l'âme, la connaissance des hommes et l'étude des idées abstraites, l'action et la théorie donnent des résultats tout à fait opposés. La littérature, les arts, la philosophie, la religion des deux peuples attestent cette différence; et l'éternelle barrière du Rhin sépare deux regions intellectuelles qui, non moins que les deux contrées, sont étrangères l'une à l'autre.
> [German and French writers remind one of La Fontaine's fable concerning the stork that cannot eat out of a plate, and the fox that cannot eat out of a bottle. The most perfect contrast can be seen between minds cultivated in solitude and those formed by society. Outside impressions and the soul's retreat, the acquaintances of society and the study of abstract ideas, action, and theory all produce opposite results. The literature, art, philosophy, and religion of the two peoples attest to this difference, and the eternal barrier of the Rhine separates two intellectual spheres which, no less than the two regions, are strangers to one another.] (163)

Few pages in Mme de Staël's work are not stamped by such opposing terms, oppositions that might be said to generate her entire text. Because the two countries, like the stork and the fox, are so essentially different, each having solved its problems in ways suitable to its own needs, Mme de Staël sees value in translating these differences for the benefit of each. It is as though Mme de Staël wished, staying within the context of her fable, that the fox acquired some of the stork's attributes and vice versa, except that, true to her romantic ideology, she also desires that they maintain their individual integrity. To all the oppositions mentioned in this quote one can add some of the many others which appear elsewhere in *De l'Allemagne*: *antique/ancien*, concrete/abstract, civil/barbaric, real/ideal, exterior/interior, witty/serious, conversation/reading, and, of course, classic/romantic:

"Il n'y a dans l'europe littéraire que deux grands divisions très marquées.
. . . On pourrait dire avec raison que les Français et les Allemands sont aux
deux extrémités de la chaine morale, puisque les uns considèrent les objects
extérieurs comme le mobile de toutes les idées, et les autres, les idées
comme le mobile de toutes les impressions [In literary Europe there are only
two major divisions. . . . One could say with good reason that the French
and the Germans are at two opposing moral poles, since the former consider external objects as the motivation for all their ideas, whereas the latter
consider ideas as the motivation for all impressions]" (46).

Since all of Mme de Staël's terms are analogous (a:b::c:d::e:f:: . . .) to
the point where one can predict, at any point in the text, which attribute
is predicated upon which country and what its opposing term is, any of the
terms may be examined as symptomatic of all the others. The classic/ro-
mantic dichotomy is the most important for our purposes, but because the
oppositions are so analogous we do not always find out everything one
needs to know under the terms in question.

Mme de Staël chooses to oppose "l'esprit de conversation," not to silence (although she will have much to say about silence as well), but to
literature: "Les Allemands ont le tort de mettre souvent dans la conversation ce qui ne convient qu'aux livres; les Français ont quelquefois aussi
celui de mettre dans les livres ce qui ne convient qu'à la conversation [Ger-
mans are wrong to put into their conversations what properly belongs in
books, whereas the French often err by putting into their books what belongs only in conversations]" (47). As Mme de Staël's argument—or is it
a conversation?—develops, it seems to the reader that it is meant to ridicule
the vanity, or *amour-propre*, of the French:

> En Orient, quand on n'a rien à se dire, on fume du tabac de rose ensem-
> ble, et de temps en temps on se salue les bras croisés sur la poitrine pour
> se donner un temoignage d'amitié; mais dans l'Occident on a voulu se
> parler tout le jour, et le foyer de l'âme s'est souvent dissipé dans ces en-
> tretiens où l'amour-propre est sans cesse en mouvement pour faire effet
> tout de suite et selon le goût du moment et du cercle où l'on se
> trouve. . . .
> Le genre de bien-être que fait éprouver une conversation animée ne
> consiste pas *précisément* dans le sujet de cette conversation; les idées ni
> les connaissances qu'on peut y développer n'en sont pas le principal in-
> térêt; c'est une certaine manière d'agir les uns sur les autres.
> [In the Orient, when one has nothing to say, one smokes rose tobacco
> together and, from time to time, motions by crossing one's arms across
> one's breast in order to give a sign of friendship; but in the West we
> prefer to speak all day long, and the soul's hearth is often dissipated in

those engagements in which the ego is ceaselessly in motion in order to make an immediate effect according to the flavor of the moment and the circle of which one is a part. . . .

The kind of well-being that an animated conversation produces does not consist *precisely* of the subject in question; neither the ideas nor the knowledge one gleans there are the principal interest; rather, it is a certain manner of interacting upon one another.] (101–2; italics mine)

There is much here that is meant to create a certain disdain for the French, for their discourse is a false one at many different levels. First, the content or subject matter, *what* is being said, is insignificant; what is foremost is the effect of what is said on the hearer. But even that is false, for the desire to create an effect on the hearer, which at one point is described as intersubjective ("to relieve some of their excess vivacity, and awaken the others from their painful apathy"), is fundamentally *amour-propre*, the desire to create an effect on oneself. The conversationalist merely manipulates the reactions of the audience so that their pleasure will reflect on him ("There is no arena where vanity shows itself in more forms than in conversation"). The Frenchman's or -woman's ego is contingent on society's esteem and hence external, while the German evaluates the truth according to itself: "They are as gay as they are honest for the satisfaction of their own conscience, and they will have laughed at what they have said a long time before even thinking of amusing someone else" (109). The individual is thus placed in opposition to society as serious literature is opposed to conversations and truth is opposed to rhetoric: that is, as that which is true according to itself is opposed to that which is true for society: "Les Français pensent et vivent dans les autres. . . . Les écrivains français sont toujours en société" (160).

In the chapter on "The Spirit of Conversation" Mme de Staël had said, "The course of ideas for the last hundred years has been solely directed by conversations. One thought only in order to speak, one spoke only in order to be applauded, and whatever could not be spoken seemed to be so much excess mental baggage" (102). Lyric poetry, as one might predict, is viewed as the antithesis of this conversational wit associated with the French:

Ce qui est vraiment divin dans le coeur de l'homme ne peut être défini; s'il y a des mots pour quelques traits, il n'y en a point pour exprimer l'ensemble, et surtout le mystère de la véritable beauté dans tous les genres. . . . les hommes les plus vulgaires se servent, à leur insu, d'images et de métaphores; ils appellent à leur secours la nature extérieure pour exprimer ce qui se passe en eux d'inexprimable.
[That which is truly divine in the human heart cannot be defined; even

if there are some words for certain features, there is none for the whole, and, above all, for the mystery of true beauty in all its forms. . . . The most common people make use, unbeknownst to themselves, of images and metaphors; they rely on external nature in order to express the inexpressible which is happening inside of them.] (205–6)

The section "De la poésie," probably the most famous of *De l'Allemagne*, is referred to by the text's editor as a "romantic manifesto," and one does not have to look far to find examples of the opposition between symbolic and literal language that Wellek and numerous other critics were to focus on as essential to romanticism. But it remains to be seen whether the "images" and "metaphors" that the German must use "to express the inexpressible" are really different from the kinds of rhetorical figures the conversationalist would use to "cheer up the phlegmatic and calm down the enervated" (a similar version of this figure is attributed by Aristotle to the sophist/rhetor Gorgias, where one ought to "treat wit with seriousness and seriousness with wit").[23]

As one might expect, the rhetoric of the French and the metaphors and images of the German are not essentially different. For example, the *amour-propre* of the conversationalist's rhetoric of effect is not really different from the solitary romantic's equally meaningless (from the standpoint of human understanding) poetry to God, for the symbolist who must "rely on external nature in order to express what happens in him that is inexpressible" is not to be opposed to the conversationalist who must rely on outside persons to determine one's "inner truth." I am not claiming that Mme de Staël's conversationalist who uses rhetoric and her romantic who uses lyric poetry are the same, only that they are not "at two opposite poles," for both rhetoric and poetics rely on figurative displacements of the literal. The ultimate confluence of these two poles is nowhere more apparent than in Mme de Staël's use of a decidedly French "conversational" style, one teeming with the kinds of *bons mots* she often derides, to describe an opposition between the French and Germans that is, as an opposition, a witty turn of phrase that substitutes effect for truth.[24] For example: "En Allemagne, un diplome vous y faisait entrer; en France, une faute de goût vous en faisait sortir [In Germany, a diploma will always get you in the door, whereas in France a single *faux pas* will always get you thrown out]." Or: "Un Français s'ennuierait d'être seul de son avis comme d'être seul dans sa chambre [A Frenchman left alone with his own opinion would be as bored as if he were left alone in his bedroom]" (106).

This demonstration of the comparative essence of doubling, where the opposing attributes of each country merge in the very process of defining their individual integrity, is most apparent in Mme de Staël's eminently rhetorical comparison between French and German literature. For if symbolic language, here equated with the romantic Germans, is closer to the language of God because it says more than is suited for mere human understanding, it is not difficult to imagine God as something of a conversationalist if he can produce the kind of "electrical sparks" Mme de Staël attributes to the best French wit:

> C'est une certaine manière d'agir les uns sur les autres, de se faire plaisir réciproquement et avec rapidité, de parler aussitôt qu'on pense, de jouir à l'instant de soi-même, d'être applaudi sans travail, de manifester son esprit dans toutes les nuances par l'accent, le geste, le regard, enfin de produire à volonté comme une sorte d'électricité qui fait jaillir des étincelles, soulage les uns de l'excès même de leur vivacité, et réveille les autres d'une apathie pénible.
> [It is a certain way of interacting with one another, of causing reciprocal pleasure rapidly, of speaking as soon as one thinks, of enjoying oneself instantaneously, of being applauded without having labored, of manifesting spirit in all its nuances by accent, gesture, look, and, finally, of producing at will a sort of electricity that makes sparks fly and assuages some of their excess vivacity, and awakens others from their painful apathy.] (102)

One can easily cite other examples of the rhetoric of Mme de Staël's opposition between rhetoric and truth, conversation and literature, classic and romantic, and so on. In the section on "the spirit of conversation," Mme de Staël wavers in her condemnation of the Frenchman's insincerity just long enough to recognize the virtues of a good wit:

> Coquetterie n'appartient pas exclusivement aux femmes, il y en a dans toutes les manières qui servent à témoigner plus d'affection qu'on n'en éprouve réellement. La loyauté des Allemands ne leur permet rien de semblable; ils prennent la grâce au pied de la lettre, ils considèrent le charme de l'expression comme un engagement pour la conduite, et de là vient leur susceptibilité; car ils n'entendent pas un mot sans en tirer une conséquence, et ne conçoivent pas qu'on puisse traiter la parole en art libéral, qui n'a ni but ni résultat que le plaisir qu'on y trouve.
> [Coquetry is not the special province of women, it is found in all behavior that tries to demonstrate more affection than is really there. The Germans' sense of loyalty does not permit them anything of the sort; kindness is taken literally, and they view a charming expression as an invitation to action, which explains their susceptibility. For they fail to understand words without consequences, and they never conceive of treating speech as an art that has no other end or result beyond the pleasure it provides.]
> (103)

The borderline between France and Germany in *De l'Allemagne* is thus, like all borders, a doubling that joins and separates at one and the same time; that is, it joins where it separates and separates where it joins. We have already shown how this schema of figurative truth served Friedrich von Schlegel's purposes of uniting poetry with philosophy to produce a philosophic poetry and poetic philosophy; Mme de Staël's similar goal is to make the French German and the German French without disfiguring the integrity of each.

The romantic repugnance for reified boundaries and definitions is the essential doubling—boundary or definition, if you will—of comparative literature. The texts of Schlegel and Mme de Staël are important not only because they address the so-called origins of comparative literature, but because they illustrate the figurative nature of all comparative boundaries, *where lines are drawn only to be denied.* The much-maligned and misunderstood name "comparative literature" can and should be retained, for it refers us to the lack of reference, of reification, of all literary boundaries, *as well as* to the discovery of their possibility. This is nowhere more apparent than in the alliance that has been struck between de-con-structionism and departments of comparative literature since the former's reception in this country during the early 1970s. For where else should a movement reside which takes as its goal the impossibility of literal literary boundaries than in that "department of departments" that preserves but eschews all structure?

My goal throughout this chapter has been to argue for the validity of *comparative* literature as a necessary function of the figurative doubling of all literary boundaries. For figurative borderlines (and, again, what are borderlines if not figures which are drawn?) assert their meaning in their transgression; both the original borderline, as well as its transgression, are equally true. As we saw in the opening chapters on metaphoric and rhetorical doubling, this is precisely the structure of metaphor's predication of a "true" term with a "false" one, and of rhetoric's fundamental, Protagorean notion of meaning which denies itself as such. In terms of "comparative literature" per se, the double, synecdochal structure of the romantic universal/particular relationship compels us to study literature as one, but, at the same time, to acknowledge that the part (for example, the individual text) that is reflected in the whole also is the whole. The texts by Friedrich Schlegel and Mme de Staël were chosen to illustrate this pattern because they call into question not only boundaries, but also their transgressions of those boundaries—thus challenging the boundaries of their own transgressions.

Notes

Righting an Introduction

1. "For whatever it may be suitable to state about philosophy in a preface . . . , this cannot be accepted as the form and manner in which to expound philosophical truth." Georg Wilhelm Friedrich Hegel, *The Phenomenology of Mind*, trans. J. B. Baillie (New York: Harper, 1967).

2. "Le solemnisation des débuts et des fins . . . est un problème qui dépasse le rhétorique (rites, protocoles, liturgie)." Roland Barthes, "L'ancienne rhétorique," *Communications* 16 (1970): 172–229.

3. Jacques Derrida, *La vérité en peinture* (Paris: Flammarion, 1978), 322–23.

4. H. Diels, *Die Fragmente der Vorsokratiker* (Berlin: Werdman, 1903). The doctrine of the *dissoi logoi* or "double meanings" is found in fragments A1 and A20.

5. Martin Heidegger, *Der Ursprung des Kunstwerkes* (Stuttgart: Reclam, 1960); "The Origin of the Work of Art," in *Poetry, Language, Thought*, trans. Albert Hofstadter (New York: Harper and Row, 1975), hereafter cited in text as "Origin"; Meyer Schapiro, "The Still Life as a Personal Object," in *The Reach of Mind: Essays in Memory of Kurt Goldstein*, ed. Marianne Simmel (New York: Springer, 1968); Derrida, *La vérité en peinture* (English translation [unless otherwise noted]: *The Truth in Painting*, trans. Geoff Bennington and Ian McLeod [Chicago: University of Chicago Press, 1987]).

6. "Until the second half of the past century a single wooden cast in a given size served to shape either right or left shoe." T. R. Wilcox, *The Mode in Footwear* (New York: Scribners, 1948), 140.

7. "*Autonomasia est dictio per accidens proprium significans.* Statt eines Eigennamens ein ihn kennzeichnendes Epitheton." Friedrich Nietzsche, *Friedrich Nietzsche on Rhetoric and Language*, ed. Sander Gilman (New York: Oxford University Press, 1989), 58–59.

8. Derrida, *The Truth in Painting*, 260.

9. Schapiro, "Still Life," 205.

10. This definition of doubling stems from an offhand comment made by Paul de Man in one of his lectures on Hegel at Yale (1980).

11. The term is Henry James's and is discussed in chapter 6.

12. Franz Kafka, *Parables and Paradoxes* (New York: Schocken, 1961), 93.

13. Derrida, *La vérité en peinture*, 360ff. (see especially 367).

14. This biblical quote, which may well stand as a motto for exegesis in general, is discussed in chapter 3.

15. "But each time I've seen the celebrated passage on 'a famous picture by Van Gogh' as a moment of pathetic collapse, derisory, and symptomatic" (Derrida, *The Truth in Painting*, 262).

16. Diels, *Die Fragmente der Vorsokratiker*, fragments A1 and A20.

17. This notion, which is crucial to the entire enterprise of this book, is discussed at length in chapter 1.

18. For example: "Deconstruction, it seems, is dead in literature departments today. While plenty of discourse is still produced concerning deconstruction, its heyday has apparently passed" (Jeffrey Nealon, "The Discipline of Deconstruction," *PMLA* 16 [1992]: 1266).

19. In his commentary on the so-called Gadamer-Derrida debate, David Krell refers to Derrida as "the most impressive interpreter of our time . . . the supreme *hermeneutician* of the twentieth century." He then refers to Gadamer as "the most romantic and adventurous of readers and most flexible of conceptual thinkers . . . in short, the most French of contemporary thinkers" ("Ashes, Ashes, We All Fall," in *Dialogue and Deconstruction: The Gadamer-Derrida Encounter*, ed. Diane P. Michelfelder and Richard E. Palmer [Albany: State University of New York Press, 1989]), 232. Concerning the supposed conflict of their respective methodologies, I would refer to Gadamer's own objection that his supposed "stress on the unity of and in meaning" (*Dialogue and Deconstruction*, ed. Michelfelder and Palmer) is a misunderstanding of his position and the wrong way to differentiate hermeneutics from deconstruction.

20. Hans-Georg Gadamer, *Wahrheit und Methode* (Tübingen: Mohr, 1972), 1–96; *Truth and Method*, trans. Garrett Barden and John Cumming (New York: Crossroad, 1975), 1–73. Hereafter, *Truth and Method* is cited parenthetically in the text.

21. Jacques Derrida, *Psyché: Inventions de l'autre* (Paris: Galilée, 1987), 535–95. The English version of Derrida's recent essay is found in *Languages of the Unsayable: The Play of Negativity in Literature and Literary Theory* (New York: Columbia University Press, 1989), 4–70; hereafter the English translation ("How to Avoid Speaking") is cited parenthetically in the text.

22. "Derrida, all denials notwithstanding, remains close to Jewish mysticism." Jürgen Habermas, *The Philosophical Discourse of Modernity* (Cambridge, Mass.: MIT Press, 1990), 182.

23. Walter Benjamin, "Die Aufgabe des Übersetzers," in *Illuminationen* (Frankfurt: Suhrkamp, 1961).

1. The Metaphoric Double

1. I. A. Richards, *The Philosophy of Rhetoric* (Oxford: Oxford University Press, 1936), 93; italics mine.

2. Freud explicitly relates the *Doppelgänger* motif to the uncanny, as well as implicitly relating metaphor to the uncanny through his use of some of Aristotle's key terms of metaphoricity (*xenos*, "foreign," and *oikeios*, "of the house"). Sig-

mund Freud, "On the Uncanny," in *Complete Psychological Works*, vol. 27 (London: Hogarth Press, 1973).

3. This remark was made by Paul de Man in one of his lectures on Hegel at Yale in 1980. I later asked him if he would allow me to quote his statement, to which he agreed in his usual diffident manner.

4. "Cet espacement est la production, à la fois active et passive (le *a* de la *différance* indique cette indécision par rapport à l'activité et à la passivité, ce qui ne se laisse pas encore commander et distribuer par cette opposition), des intervalles sans lesquels les termes 'pleins' ne signifieraient pas, ne fonctionneraient pas." Jacques Derrida, *Positions* (Paris: Minuit, 1972), 38–39.

5. Diels, *Die Fragmente der Vorsokratiker*, A20.

6. "Your supposed 'agreement' . . . can only be kindness, for if you object to what I say about metaphor, you must, as it should be, object to everything." From a letter written by de Man to Derrida, quoted by the latter in *Mémoires* (New York: Columbia University Press, 1986), 129. When, elsewhere, de Man cautions that "the rhetorically self-conscious reading puts into question the authority of metaphor as a paradigm of poetic language" ("Genesis and Genealogy," in *Allegories of Reading* [New Haven, Conn.: Yale University Press, 1979], 98), this, I believe, should be read as a valid warning against pretending to understand "metaphor."

7. Aristotle, *The Art of Rhetoric*, trans. John Henry Freese (Cambridge, Mass.: Harvard University Press, 1975), 3.2.12, 3.11.6.

8. Aristotle, *Poetics*, trans. W. Hamilton Fyfe (Cambridge, Mass.: Harvard University Press, 1973), 22.3.

9. Jacques Derrida, "La mythologie blanche," in *Marges—de la philosophie* (Paris: Minuit, 1972), 249–324; "Le retrait de la métaphore," *Analecta Husserliana* 14 (1983): 273–300. (All translations from these two essays are my own.)

10. Paul Ricoeur, *La métaphore vive* (Paris: Seuil, 1975), 25.

11. Such a clear subordination of metaphor is evident in this statement from John Locke's *An Essay Concerning Human Understanding* (bk. 3, chap. 10): "But yet, if we would speak of things as they are, we must allow that all the art of rhetoric, besides order and clearness, all the artificial and figurative application of words eloquence hath invented, are for nothing else but to insinuate wrong ideas, move the passions, and thereby mislead the judgment . . . they are certainly wholly to be avoided."

12. Barthes, "L'ancienne rhetorique," 221.

13. Derrida, "La mythologie blanche," in *Marges—de la philosophie*, 291.

14. This uncanny relationship between the same substance as both salutary and poisonous is explored in Derrida's discussion of the *pharmakon* in "La pharmacie du Platon" (in *Marges—de la philosophie*, 69–197) and in J. Hillis Miller's discussion of the "parasite" in "The Critic as Host" (in *Deconstruction and Criticism* [New York: Seabury Press, 1979], 217–53).

15. I could not disagree more with Else's statement that "they [chaps. 20–22 of the *Poetics*, including the analysis of metaphor] have very little—astonishingly little—connection with any other part of Aristotle's theory of poetry." *Aristotle's Poetics: The Argument* (Cambridge, Mass.: Harvard University Press, 1957), 567.

16. Richards, for example, opposes his own theory to those of other individu-

als and "whole schools of rhetoric and criticism" which have "gone astray" (*The Philosophy of Rhetoric*, 98). The same pattern is also apparent in more recent works; especially Paul Ricoeur's *La métaphore vive* and articles collected in the volume of *Critical Inquiry* (Autumn 1978) devoted to metaphor.

17. Richards, *The Philosophy of Rhetoric*, 89–138.

18. Max Black, *Models and Metaphors* (Ithaca, N.Y.: Cornell University Press, 1962).

19. Monroe Beardsley, *Aesthetics* (New York: Harcourt Brace and World, 1958).

20. Sarah Kofman, *Nietzsche et la métaphore* (Paris: Galilée, 1983).

21. Derrida, "La mythologie blanche," in *Marges—de la philosophie*, 247–324. Paul de Man, "Rhetoric of Tropes" in *Allegories of Reading*, 103–18; J. Hillis Miller, "Dismembering and Disremembering in Nietzsche's 'On Truth and Lies in a Normal Sense,'" *Boundary* 9, no. 3 and 10, no. 1 (Spring and Fall 1981): 41–54.

22. de Man, *Allegories of Reading*, 110. The *Philosophenbuch* (ca. 1872) contains many remarkable pieces, including "Die Philosophie im tragischen Zeitalter der Griechen" and "Über Wahrheit und Lüge"—all originally intended as one book.

23. "Verstellung: 1. . . . *to shift, remove, displace* (an falsche Stelle)" (*Wildhagen German-English Dictionary* [Wiesbaden: Brandstetter, 1954]).

24. Aristotle, *Poetics* 21.7.

25. E.g., "Der Intellekt, jener Meister der Verstellung, ist so lange frei, und seinem sonstigen Sklavendienste enthoben, als er täuschen kann." *Nietzsche Werke*, Friedrich Nietzsche, vol. 2, ed. Giorgio Colli and Mazzino Montinari (Berlin: de Gruyter, 1973), 3: 382. All translations of Nietzsche's essay are from *Philosophy and Truth*, trans. Daniel Breazeale (Atlantic Highlands, N.J.: Humanities Press, 1979).

26. Nietzsche actually refers to Protagoras's "man as measure" when he states: "Similar to the way in which astrologers considered the stars to be in man's service and connected with his happiness and sorrow, such an investigator considers the entire universe in connection with man. . . . His method is to treat man as the measure of all things [*Maass an alle Dinge*], but in doing so he again proceeds from the error of believing that he has these things (which he intends to measure) immediately before him as mere objects. He forgets that the original perceptual metaphors are metaphors and takes them to be the things themselves" (*Philosophy and Truth*, 86).

Protagoras's statement is discussed in some detail in chapter 2 of this work.

27. E.g., chapter 3 of Rousseau's *Essai sur l'origine des langues* (1817; rpt. Paris: Bibliothèque du Graphe, n.d.). This section is also the object of a significant difference of opinion between Derrida and de Man (see the latter's "The Rhetoric of Blindness," in *Blindness and Insight*, ed. Wlad Godzich [Minneapolis: University of Minnesota Press, 1983], 102–41).

28. Two of the most obvious examples of this important romantic inversion are such statements by Goethe's Faust as "What we don't know is exactly what we need / And what we know fulfills no need at all" (lines 191–92) and "When we

have reached what in this world is good / That which is better is labelled a fraud, a blind" (lines 286–87; Johann Wolfgang von Goethe, *Faust: Parts I and II*, trans. Louis Macneice [New York: Norton, 1961]), and Wordsworth's "Ode: Intimations of Immortality from Recollections of Early Childhood": "Our birth is but a sleeping and forgetting" (line 59).

29. Friedrich Schlegel, "Fragment #668," in *Philosophische Lehrjahre*, ed. Ernst Behler (Paderborn: Schöningh, 1962). Schlegel's ironical reference to "eine permanente Parekbase" is discussed by Paul de Man in "The Rhetoric of Temporality," in *Blindness and Insight*, 218.

30. As Breazeale explains (*Philosophy and Truth*, 89, n. 31), "Actually, Pascal says that the workman would be 'almost as happy' as the king in this case!"

31. There are important references to temporality throughout this essay, as when Nietzsche begins by stating that the beginning of knowledge "was the most arrogant and mendacious minute of 'world history,' but nevertheless it was only a minute" ("Truth and Lies," 79). "Momentariness" is of course critical to Nietzsche's concept of the "Eternal Return." See "Vom Gesicht und Rätsel," in *Also Sprach Zarathustra* (Munich: Goldmann, 1970).

32. Richards, "Metaphor," in *The Philosophy of Rhetoric*, 89–115.

2. The Rhetorical Double

1. Diels, *Die Fragmente der Vorsokratiker*, A1, A20.

2. Ibid., A1; R. K. Sprague, ed., *The Older Sophists* (Columbia: University of South Carolina Press, 1972), 4.

3. In its usual fifth-century meaning, *Aisthēsis* "ne doit pas être traduit uniquement par *sensation*, c'est *perception* qu'il signifie dans ce débat, et non pas seulement *perception* sensible, mais *aperception* en général, le fait de saisir, de constater l'objet, sensible ou non-sensible." Eugène Dupréel, *Les Sophistes* (Neuchatel: Griffon, 1945), 22.

4. Plato, *Theaetetus*, in *The Dialogues of Plato*, trans. Benjamin Jowett, 3d ed. (London: Oxford University Press, 1924), 4:161.

5. Diels, *Die Fragmente der Vorsokratiker*, A14; Sprague, *The Older Sophists*, 11.

6. See the discussion of this in Vlastos's edition of the *Protagoras* (Indianapolis: Bobbs-Merrill, 1956), xiii.

7. See *Theaetetus* 185c; also G. S. Kirk and J. E. Raven, *The Presocratic Philosophers* (Cambridge: Cambridge University Press, 1975), 297.

8. "Speech," "account," "thought" are all present in Protagoras's typically fifth-century definition of *logos*.

9. *The Dialogues of Plato*, trans. Jowett, vol. 4. Unless otherwise noted, all English translations of the *Theaetetus* are Jowett's.

10. Nietzsche, *Werke*, vol. 2.3.

11. Cf. *Theaetetus* 152e: "I am about to speak of a high argument, in which all things are said to be relative; you cannot rightly call anything by any name, such as great or small, heavy or light, for the great thing will be small and the heavy

light—there is no single thing or quality, but out of motion and change and admixture all things are becoming relatively to one another, which "becoming" is by us incorrectly called being, but is really becoming, for nothing ever is, but all things are becoming."

12. The three places where Plato discusses Protagoras extensively are *Cratylus* 385ff.; *Theaetetus* 152aff., 166cff.; *Euthydemus* 285eff.

13. See *Protagoras*, ed. Vlastos, xii.

14. On the validity of Protagoras's so-called defense, see Heinrich Gomperz, *Sophistik und Rhetorik* (1912; rpt. Darmstadt: Wissenschaftliche Buchgesellschaft, 1965); Dupréel, *Les Sophistes*, 20.

15. Gadamer's analysis of this notion of "taste" is discussed in the introduction to this work.

16. Aristotle, *The Art of Rhetoric* 1355a.

17. "He [Protagoras] was also the first to distinguish the tenses of a verb. . . . He first divided speech into four modes: entreaty, question, answer, and command" (Diels, *Die Fragmente der Vorsokratiker*, A1; Sprague, *The Older Sophists*, 5).

18. Plato's *Gorgias* contains a detailed description of the intrinsic relationship of sophistic to rhetoric.

19. Diels, *Die Fragmente der Vorsokratiker*, B1; Sprague, *The Older Sophists*, 18.

20. Georg Wilhelm Friedrich Hegel, *Lectures on the History of Philosophy* (London: Routledge and Kegan Paul, 1963), 1:375.

21. *Theaetetus* 161.

22. *Protagoras*, ed. Vlastos, xii.

23. Cited in Gomperz, *Sophistik und Rhetorik*, 202.

24. Diels, *Die Fragmente der Vorsokratiker*, A14; Sprague, *The Older Sophists*, 10–11. Euenos, for example, also translates *chremata* as *pragmata* (Bergk, fragment 8, cited in Gomperz, *Sophistik und Rhetorik*, 202).

25. Sprague, *The Older Sophists*, 22.

26. Dupréel, *Les Sophistes*, 52.

27. Ibid.

28. Diels, *Die Fragmente der Vorsokratiker*, B4; Sprague, *The Older Sophists*, 20.

29. *Theaetetus* 161c.

30. Dupréel, *Les Sophistes*, 52.

31. Diels, *Die Fragmente der Vorsokratiker*, B4.

32. W. K. C. Guthrie, *A History of Greek Philosophy* (Cambridge: Cambridge University Press, 1962), 371.

33. Diels, *Die Fragmente der Vorsakratiker*, A20.

34. There are seven references by five different authors (ibid., A19–21).

35. *Protagoras*, ed. Vlastos, xii.

36. Diels, *Die Fragmente der Vorsokratiker*, A1; Sprague, *The Older Sophists*, 4.

37. Diels, *Die Fragmente der Vorsokratiker*, A20; Sprague, *The Older Sophists*, 13.

38. Plato's "peritrope," or refutation of Protagoras, is found in *Theaetetus* 171a.

39. Theodor Gomperz, *Greek Thinkers* (New York: Humanities Press, 1955), 462.

3. The Parabolic Double

1. Mark 4:3–9 (*The New English Bible* [Oxford: Oxford University Press, 1976]).

2. 2 Sam., chap. 12; 1 Kings, chaps. 20, 39.

3. Aristotle, *The Art of Rhetoric*, II.xx.4.

4. J. Jeremias, *Rediscovering the Parables* (New York: Scribners, 1966), 10.

5. T. W. Manson, *The Teaching of Jesus* (Cambridge: Cambridge University Press, 1963), 81.

6. Discussion of parable as a legitimate literary genre is found in the initial volume of *Semeia* (1974).

7. W. S. Kissinger's survey (*The Parables of Jesus: A History of Interpretation and Bibliography* [Metuchen, N.J.: Scarecrow Press, 1979]) provides a very useful summary and bibliography of writings on parable.

8. Charles E. Carlston, *The Parables of the Triple Tradition* (Philadelphia: Fortress Press, 1975). Adolf Jülicher, *Die Gleichnisrede Jesu* (Tübingen: Mohr, 1910), 118–48.

9. "The disciples have demonstrated their inability to cope unaided with the statements of their master." Leigh Hafrey, "Parabola: The Interpolated Tale as Parable" (Ph.D. dissertation, Yale University, 1978), 7.

10. Frank Kermode explains his preference for the "hardening theory" in much the same was as I do here, but he does not try to show how this "intolerable" notion is exemplified in the Sower itself. Frank Kermode, *The Genesis of Secrecy* (Cambridge, Mass.: Harvard University Press, 1979), 23–47.

11. Jülicher, *Die Gleichnisrede Jesu*, 129.

12. Jeremias, *Rediscovering the Parables*, 9.

13. As J. D. Crossan also notes (*In Parables* [New York: Harper and Row, 1973]), Thomas 82:3–13 does not include this allegorical interpretation.

14. Peter Beicken's useful if necessarily abbreviated annotated bibliography of Kafka criticism (*Franz Kafka: Eine kritische Einführung in die Forschung* [Munich: Athenaion, 1974]) clearly reveals the gap in critical appreciation of the parables, as well as offering valuable insights into the general trends of Kafka criticism, such as the important correlation between the staggered appearance of Kafka's works both in the German-speaking world and abroad and between certain popular conceptions of his work. The *Hochzeitsvorbereitungen auf dem Lande* collection, for example, first appeared only in 1953, thus signaling a shift away from a more exclusive focus on the longer works. Politzer, however, appears to have been the first (1939) to have used the term *parable* in a general way to refer to Kafka's works.

15. Of the texts published in Kafka's lifetime, there are precious few that have come to be recognized as parables per se. It is noteworthy that both "Die

Baüme" and "Vor dem Gesetz" survive in the published works as parabolic fragments from larger unpublished narratives.

16. It is fair to say that the above-mentioned "masters" of Kafka criticism neglect the parables because of approaches that are more thematic than linguistic; e.g., the following passage from Wilhelm Emrich's book *Franz Kafka* (New York: Ungar, 1968): "Kafka in his own detached explanations of, say, the parable 'Before the Law' nowhere states or hints at what its individual characters or events really signify, what its more profound spiritual allegorical, or parabolic 'meaning' consists of. . . . Allegory and parable are possible only against the background of a firmly defined religion, philosophy, or world-view. The background of Kafka's 'parables,' however, is a void" (82–83).

More recent trends have been to decry such tendencies as doing no less violence to Kafka's texts than the text itself does in "In the Penal Colony." Perhaps as a result of Gunther Anders's remarkable work *Kafka: Pro und Contra* (Munich: Beck, 1951), certainly as a result of general trends in criticism (Karst, Corngold, Hillmann, Kraft, Kreis, et al.), as much attention has been paid recently to the medium as to Kafka's supposed message.

17. Max Brod's readings of Kafka (e.g., *Franz Kafka* [New York: Schocken, 1963]) laid great emphasis on Kafka's Judaism and religious beliefs. More recently, a less biased reading of Kafka's religiosity, particularly with regard to the important aphorisms in the *Hochzeitsvorbereitungen* volume, is contained in Werner Hoffmann's *Kafkas Aphorismen* (Berne: Francke, 1975).

18. "Sicher is mein Widerwille gegen Antithesen" (Franz Kafka, *Tagebücher*, [Frankfurt: Fischer, 1951], November 1911).

19. Erwin Steinberg ("Kafka's *Before the Law*," *Cithara* 18, no. 1 [November 1978]: 27–45) argues that "the parable ["Before the Law"] reflects Kafka's temptation by Christianity." I disagree, however, that the law in "Vor dem Gesetz" is not specifically Judaic, although the man from the country's position vis à vis this law is itself ambiguous. Kafka's affinity for a Christian outlook could easily be demonstrated from such important tales as "Ein Hungerkünstler," "Die Verwandlung," and "In der Strafkolonie."

20. Kafka, *Oeuvres complètes*, ed. Claude David (Paris: Gallimard, 1980), 2:20.

21. Beda Allemann ("Kafka: Von den Gleichnissen," *Zeitschrift für deutsche Philologie* 83 [1964]) raises the valid objection that if *Gleichnisse* are the "words of wise men" then they cannot have been uttered by the persistently self-denigrating Kafka.

22. Hartmut Binder, *Kafka-Kommentar* (Munich: Winkler, 1975), 297–99.

23. Franz Kafka, "Von den Gleichnissen," in *Sämtliche Erzählungen* (Frankfurt: Fischer, 1979); "On Parables," in *Parables and Paradoxes*, 11).

24. Kafka, *Tagebücher*, 1921, 550–51.

25. Helmut Arntzen, "Franz Kafka: Von den Gleichnissen," *Zeitschrift für deutsche Philologie* 38 (1964): 106–12.

26. Richards, *The Philosophy of Rhetoric*, 94.

27. "La notion de métaphore n'est elle-même qu'une métaphore" (Kofman, *Nietzsche et la métaphore*, 65).

28. Franz Kafka, "Betrachtungen," in *Hochzeitsvorbereitungen auf dem Lande* (Frankfurt: Fischer, 1983), no. 57.

29. Maurice Blanchot, *De Kafka à Kafka* (Paris: Gallimard, 1981), 132 (translation mine).

30. I. A. Richards, *Practical Criticism* (New York: Harvest, 1929), 239.

31. "*Hina* des Mc und Lc ist hier durch *hoti* ersetzt; was dort Absicht heisst, heisst hier Ursache" (Jülicher, *Die Gleichnisrede Jesu*, 129).

32. Walter Benjamin, "The Task of the Translator," in *Illuminations*, trans. Harry Zohn (New York: Schocken, 1969), 82.

4. The Tragic Double

1. Gerald Else, *The Origin and Early Form of Greek Tragedy* (New York: Norton, 1972); Brian Vickers, *Towards Greek Tragedy* (London: Longman, 1973).

2. E. R. Dodds, ed., *Euripides' "Bacchae"* (Oxford: Oxford University Press, 1977); Charles Segal, "The Menace of Dionysus: Sex Roles and Reversals in Euripides' *Bacchae*," *Arethusa* 11 (1978): 185–202; and *Dionysiac Poetics and Euripides' "Bacchae"* (Princeton, N.J.: Princeton University Press, 1982); R. P. Winnington-Ingram, *Euripides and Dionysus: An Interpretation of the "Bacchae"* (London: Cambridge University Press, 1948).

3. Winnington-Ingram, *Euripides and Dionysus*, 149, 7, 160.

4. Segal, *Dionysiac Poetics*, 217.

5. Ibid., 10.

6. George Steiner, *The Death of Tragedy* (New York: Knopf, 1961).

7. Vickers, *Towards Greek Tragedy*, 17, 48 n. 35.

8. From the Suda, quoted in Else, *Origin of Greek Tragedy*, 106.

9. Ibid., 4, 8, 31.

10. For example, Else ignores choral odes in Sophocles' *Oedipus Rex*, lines 1090ff., and *Antigone*, lines 1118ff., to name but two of Sophocles' plays. Helene Foley, *Ritual Irony: Poetry and Sacrifice in Euripides* (Ithaca, N.Y.: Cornell University Press, 1985), 206; G. M. A. Grube, *The Drama of Euripides* (London: Methuen, 1941); J. E. Sandys, *The Bacchae of Euripides* (Cambridge: Cambridge University Press, 1900). "Yet tragedy does not seem the right word nor Pentheus to be of the stature of tragic heroes; and any attempt to make such a hero of him is bound in one way or another to distort the character as revealed by the text of the play" (Winnington-Ingram, *Euripides and Dionysus*, 160).

11. "Anger be now your song, immortal one" (*The Iliad*, trans. Robert Fitzgerald [New York: Doubleday, 1974]). First lines are not Fitzgerald's strong point, for his *Odyssey* begins with a similar problem: "Sing (*ennepe!*) in me Muse . . . "

12. *Euripides*, vol. 5: *Electra, The Phoenician Women, The Bacchae*, ed. Daniel Grene and Richmond Lattimore (Chicago: University of Chicago Press, 1968).

13. Walter F. Otto, *Dionysus: Myth and Cult* (Bloomington: Indiana University Press, 1965), 73.

14. Freud, "On the Uncanny," in *Complete Psychological Works*, vol. 17. Freud's essay is discussed in chapter 5.

15. Vickers, *Towards Greek Tragedy*, 316.

16. Dodds, *Euripides' "Bacchae,"* xvii.

17. Ibid., xviii.

18. Ibid., xvi.

19. Winnington-Ingram, *Euripides and Dionysus*, 156.

20. Albert Henrichs, "Greek and Roman Glimpses of Dionysus," in *Dionysus and His Circle* (Cambridge: Cambridge University Press, 1979).

21. Friedrich Hölderlin, "Anmerkungen zum Odipus," in *Sämtliche Werke*, vol. 6 (Stuttgart: Beissner, n.d.).

22. Winnington-Ingram, *Euripides and Dionysus*, 160.

23. Vickers, *Towards Greek Tragedy*, 39.

24. The myth of Pentheus's suffering is one of many that recounts the opposition to the spread of Dionysianism; compare the myths of Lycurgos, Proetus of Tiryns and Minyas of Orchomenos. Dionsysianism, one can argue, does not exist without Pentheanism; the "primary" forces of nature are "always already" in conflict with the "secondary" repressive forces of culture.

25. To be sure, attempts to apply psychoanalysis to Pentheus's desire for the repressed are not unknown, even among classicists. See William Sale, "The Psychoanalysis of Pentheus in the *Bacchae* of Euripides," *Yale Classical Studies* 22 (1972): 63–82.

26. Vickers, *Towards Greek Tragedy*, 317; A. R. Bellinger, "The *Bacchae* and the *Hippolytus*," *Yale Classical Studies* 1 (1939): 15–27; Winnington-Ingram, *Euripides and Dionysus*, 20. The figure of the chiasmus as a particular form of doubling is discussed in chapter 6.

27. J.-P. Guépin, in *The Tragic Paradox* (Amsterdam: Hakkert, 1968), identifies this particular paradox but explains it in ritual terms as the result of ambivalence toward the sacrificial victim.

28. See Freud's "The Development of the Libido," in *Introductory Lectures on Psychoanalysis*, trans. James Strachey, vol. 21 (New York: Norton, 1977).

29. Segal, *Dionysiac Poetics*, 247–54; Normand Berlin, *The Secret Cause: A Discussion of Tragedy* (Amherst: University of Massachusetts Press, 1981), 14.

30. See Sarah Pomeroy's "Selected Bibliography on Women in Antiquity," *Arethusa* 6 (1973): 140–43.

31. Segal, "The Menace of Dionysus," 187.

32. Sheila McNally, "The Maenad in Early Greek Art," in *Women in the Ancient World: The Arethusa Papers*, ed. John Peradotto and J. C. Sullivan (State University of New York Press, 1984), 137; Marylin B. Arthur, "The Origins of the Western Attitude Toward Women," *Arethusa* 6, no. 1 (1973): 7–58.

33. Sophocles, *Sophocles I*, ed. David Grene and Richmond Lattimore (Chicago: University of Chicago Press, 1954).

34. In *Tragedy: Modern Essays in Criticism*, ed. Laurence Michel and Richard Sewell (Englewood Cliffs, N.J.: Prentice-Hall, 1963), 172.

35. This is also the gist of Nietzsche's reading of Oedipus. (Friedrich Nietzsche, *The Birth of Tragedy*, trans. Francis Golffing [Garden City, N.Y.: Doubleday, 1956], ix).

36. In *Tragedy*, ed. Michel and Sewell, 80.

37. Euripides, *Hippolytus*, in *Euripides I*, trans. David Grene (Chicago: University of Chicago Press, 1955), lines 106–12.

5. The Psychoanalytic Double

1. This applies to all the writers mentioned in this essay (Kofman, Rey, Laplanche, et al.). Lacan does mention the essay in "Intervention sur le transfert" (in *Ecrits* [Paris: Seuil, 1966], 219) where he briefly alludes to a disagreement with Benveniste's dismissal of Abel/Freud.

2. As recently as 1988 David Macey wrote, "They [Freud/Abel's linguistic examples] are demolished with both elegance and eloquence by Benveniste" (*Lacan in Contexts* [London: Verso, 1988], 141).

3. Sarah Kofman, *L'enfance de l'art: Une interprétation de l'esthétique freudienne* (Paris: Galilée, 1985), 113.

4. Ibid., 53.

5. Sigmund Freud, "On the Antithetical Sense of Primary Words," in *Creativity and the Unconscious* (New York: Harper, 1958) 55; italics mine.

6. Freud, "The Moses of Michelangelo," in *Creativity and the Unconscious*, 11.

7. Freud, "The Relation of the Poet to Daydreaming," in *Creativity and the Unconscious*, 51.

8. Ricoeur discusses "the linguistic aspects of the unconscious" and, specifically, Lacan's famous notion that "the unconscious is structured like a language," in book 3 of his monumental essay on Freud in *Freud and Philosophy* (New Haven, Conn.: Yale University Press, 1970).

9. Although Julia Kristeva, herself a student of Benveniste's, takes great pains to rescue "le moment capital de l'étude du rapport entre le sujet et son langage [qui] a sans doute été marqué . . . par l'oeuvre magistrale de Freud" (*Le langage, cet inconnu* [Paris: Seuil, 1981], 263) from its unavoidable conflict with the science of linguistics, she does not discuss Freud's essay "On the Antithetical Sense of Primary Words." (However, like Ricoeur, she does quote from Benveniste's essay on the same.)

10. William McGuire, ed., *Freud/Jung Letters*, trans. Ralph Manheim and R. F. C. Hulle (Princeton, N.J.: Princeton University Press, 1974), 219.

11. John Forrester, *Language and the Origins of Psychoanalysis* (New York: Columbia University Press, 1980), 97.

12. Emile Benveniste, "Language in Freudian Theory," *Problems in General Linguistics*, trans. Mary Elizabeth Meek (Miami: University of Miami Press, 1971), 65–75.

13. Ibid., 70.

14. Ibid., 71; italics mine.

15. Charles R. Peters, "On the Possible Contribution of Ambiguity of Expression to the Development of Proto-Linguistic Performance," in *Language Origins*, ed. Roger Wescott (Silver Springs, Md.: Linstock Press, 1974). Although Peters sees the gradual evolution of language as a process of correcting its inherent ambigui-

ties, it is nonetheless possible to use Peters's findings to support the view that a certain class of words, like *sacer*, resists this evolutionary process of clarification because the antithetical meanings, as in art, are experienced as essential.

16. Benveniste, "Language in Freudian Theory," 72.

17. Ibid.

18. Even a phenomenologist like Ricoeur adopts Benveniste's treatment of Freud's essay: "It is impossible to make the absence of logic in dreams, their ignorance of 'No,' accord with a state of real language. Freud once tried to do this, without success, in his essay on 'The Antithetical Meaning of Primal Words.' It is impossible, however, to make the archaism of the processes of distortion and pictorial representation coincide with a primitive form of language or in general with any chronological reality whatsoever; as Benveniste aptly states, the Freudian archaic 'is such only in relation to that which deforms or represses it'" (*Freud and Philosophy*, 397).

19. Freud, "Antithetical Sense," 62.

20. Benveniste, "Language in Freudian Theory," 74.

21. Ibid., 75; italics mine.

22. Aristotle, *Poetics*, 21.7; Diels, *Die Fragmente der Vorsokratiker*, A1, A20.

23. Rainer Warning, "Reading Irony in Flaubert," *Style* 19 (1985): 304.

24. Jean Laplanche, *Life and Death in Psychoanalysis* (Baltimore: Johns Hopkins University Press, 1976), 16, 12.

25. Ibid., 17, 20 (italics Laplanche's).

26. Ibid., 20, 19. "The whole of sexuality, or at least the whole of infantile sexuality, ends up by becoming perversion" (23). Like Freud, Laplanche sees "sensual sucking" (*Lutschen*) as exemplary in its importance for "the whole of sexuality"; see "The Order of Life," in *Life and Death*.

27. Sigmund Freud, "Libidinal Types," in *Collected Papers* (New York: Basic Books, 1959), 5:251; italics mine. See also "Analysis Terminable and Interminable," in *Collected Papers*, 5:316–57.

28. Freud, "Hysterical Fantasies and Their Relation to Bisexuality," in *Collected Papers*, 2:57.

29. Ibid., 56–57.

30. Ibid., 57; "Some Psychological Consequences of the Anatomical Distinction Between the Sexes," in *Collected Papers*, 5:186–97.

31. Sigmund Freud, *Standard Edition* (London: Hogarth Press, 1953–74), 6:396; italics mine.

32. Jean-Michel Rey, *Parcours de Freud* (Paris: Galilée, 1974), 19.

33. Freud, *Standard Edition*, 6:359.

34. Rey, *Parcours de Freud*, 21.

35. Sigmund Freud, "Femininity," in *New Introductory Lectures* (New York: Norton, 1965), 117.

36. Freud, "Medusa's Head," in *Collected Papers*, 5:105; and "Fetishism," in *Collected Papers*, 5:198–204.

37. Neil Hertz, *The End of the Line* (New York: Columbia University Press), 1985.

38. Freud, "Medusa's Head," in *Collected Papers*, 5:165.

39. Freud, "'A Child Is Being Beaten': A Contribution to the Study of the Origin of Sexual Perversions," in *Collected Papers*, 2:172–201.

40. Jean Starobinski, *La relation critique* (Paris: Gallimard, 1970), 270.

41. Freud, "On the Uncanny," in *Creativity and the Unconscious*, 122–61.

42. Freud, "The Taboo of Virginity," in *Creativity and the Unconscious*, 187–205.

43. Mary Jacobus, "Judith, Holofernes, and the Phallic Woman," in *Reading Woman* (New York: Columbia University Press, 1985).

44. Juliet Mitchell's *Psychoanalysis and Feminism* (London: Lane, 1974) is one of a number of feminist works that argue against the notion that Freud's writings are "prescriptively" antifeminist.

45. "The ontogenetic structure supposedly refers to a phylogenetic event. But this grounding rests on a myth, the myth of the primal horde. . . . The Oedipal structure is a construction of science, an *anhypothetical hypothesis*" (Sarah Kofman, *The Childhood of Art*, trans. Winifred Woodhull [New York: Columbia University Press, 1988], 100; italics mine).

46. Freud, "Femininity," 196.

47. Sarah Kofman, *Quatre romans analytiques* (Paris: Galilée, 1973), 87, 84.

48. Kofman, "Freud's Method of Reading," in *The Childhood of Art*, 100–101.

49. Freud, "The Theme of the Three Caskets," in *Creativity and the Unconscious*, 63–75.

50. Sigmund Freud, *Beyond the Pleasure Principle* (1920; rpt. New York: Norton, 1961).

51. Ibid., 52.

6. The Critical Double

1. This discussion of James's title is indebted to Jacques Derrida's discussion of Kafka's "Vor dem Gesetz" ("Devant la loi,") in *Kafka and the Contemporary Critical Performance*, ed. Alan Udott [Bloomington: Indiana University Press, 1987], 128–49). There Derrida plays upon the doubling inherent in the position of the reader who finds himself before the text—*before* "Before the Law"—thus mirroring the predicament of Kafka's protagonist.

2. Wolfgang Iser, *The Act of Reading* (Baltimore: Johns Hopkins University Press, 1978).

3. Gide's comment is reported in Jean Perrot's *Une écriture énigmatique* (Paris: Aubier, 1982).

4. Henry James, *Eight Tales from the Major Phase* (New York: Norton, 1969).

5. J. Hillis Miller, "The Figure in the Carpet," *Poetics Today* 1, no.3 (Spring 1980): 107–18. As indicated in the sentence quoted, Miller relates the figure to the paradox of a metaphysical ground that can only be a figure of itself: "All these figures reinforce or restate the traditional metaphysical paradox of the creative

logos, as well as its always present subversive anaglyph, the 'idea' that there is no idea, the idea that the figure behind the surface is a phantasm generated by the play of superficial and visible figurative elements. Neither of these ideas is possible without the other. Each generates the other in a regular rhythm of unreadability, figure and ground reversing constantly" (114).

6. Todorov's related reading of James's story contained in *The Poetics of Prose* (Paris: Seuil, 1971) nonetheless differs from mine. Although there is indeed a "cause absolue et absente" generating James's tales, such as the figure in "The Figure in the Carpet," Todorov never finds this absent figure within the figurative patterns of meaning inherent in James's text itself. Instead, he agrees with other critics (Blackmur, Blanchot, Sollers)—although with a decidedly structuralist twist —that the search for the secret is the secret; this does not go far enough in explaining the text as secret, although it certainly points the reader in the right direction.

7. Cicero, quoted in the *Oxford English Dictionary*, s.v. "chiasmus."

8. Herbert Weir Smythe, *Greek Grammar*, ed. Gordon Messing (Cambridge, Mass.: Harvard University Press, 1976), 677.

9. de Man, "The Rhetoric of Tropes," in *Allegories of Reading*, 113.

10. Ibid., 107–8.

11. Ibid., 168.

12. Ibid., 109.

13. Miller, "The Figure in the Carpet," 113.

14. "He had showed me Gwendolen's photograph with the remark that she wasn't pretty but was awfully interesting; she had published at the age of nineteen a novel in three volumes . . . about which, in *The Middle*, he had been really splendid" ("The Figure in the Carpet," 135).

15. Henry James, "The Altar of the Dead," in *The Turn of the Screw and Other Short Novels* (New York: New American Library, 1962), 253.

16. This particular doubling is discussed further in chapter 5.

17. "Max Brod rapporte que Kafka lui avait dit un jour, explicitant le contenu sexuel de l'interdit paternal, 'Sais-tu ce que signifie la phrase finale? J'ai pensé en l'écrivant à une forte éjaculation.'" Kafka, *Oeuvres complètes*, 2:883.

18. The narrator's relation to Corvick, Vereker, and Gwendolen continues the relation of James's other "positivists" to art, beginning with Rowland Mallet in James's first novel, *Roderick Hudson*.

19. In addition to stories like "The Beast in the Jungle," "The Altar of the Dead," and "The Jolly Corner," where women act as spiritual guides for their more obtuse male counterparts, compare especially Fleda Vetch's interest in Mrs. Gereth's son Owen in *The Spoils of Poynton*.

20. "If the function of interpretation is to extract the hidden meaning from a literary text, this involves certain rather peculiar presuppositions. . . . Vereker denounces both the archeological ('digging for meaning') approach, and the assumption that meaning is a thing which—as is made explicit in the text—embodies a treasure that can be excavated through interpretation" (Iser, *The Act of Reading*, 4–5).

21. "Master of his own fiction insofar as he, precisely, is its dupe . . . *James'*

very mastery consists in the denial and in the deconstruction of his own mastery" (italics mine). Shoshana Felman, "Turning the Screw of Interpretation," *Yale French Studies* 55/56 (1977): 205.

22. In his discussion of "The Jolly Corner," the story that most explicitly presents a confrontation with one's personal double, Helmut Kretzschmar (*Die Begriff "Consciousness" bei Henry James* [Düsseldorf: Zentral Verlag für Dissertationen, 1967]) calls attention to the psychology of repression needed to understand the hero's relation to his alter ego, but he does not develop this notion in James's other tales.

23. This particularly Jamesian term is more explicitly operative (although no more important) in another novella of the preceding year (1895), "The Altar of the Dead."

7. The Deconstructive Double

1. Paul de Man, *The Rhetoric of Romanticism* (New York: Columbia University Press, 1984), viii. This statement is not included in Deborah Esch's comments on this introduction, which she sees as supporting her views on the "failure" of de Man's "corpus to coalesce" ("A Defense of Rhetoric," in *Reading de Man Reading*, ed. Lindsay Waters and Wlad Godzich [Minneapolis: University of Minnesota Press, 1989], 72). But de Man's reference to such a failure is specifically directed against "dialectical progression or, ultimately, . . . historical totalization" (*The Rhetoric of Romanticism*, viii), which does not mean that certain unifying patterns such as the one discussed here and which themselves admit of a certain lack of "totalization" should be precluded—that in itself would be one of the most totalizing of gestures.

2. Although de Man never refers to this pairing as explicitly as the others cited, numerous statements, such as the following, made *en passant* make it clear that Jakobson's polar opposition between metaphor and metonymy must be added to this list: "By passing from a paradigmatic structure based on substitution, such as metaphor, to a syntagmatic structure based on contingent association such as metonymy, the mechanical, repetitive aspect of grammatical forms is shown to be operative in a passage that seemed at first sight to celebrate the self-willed and autonomous inventiveness of a subject" ("Semiology and Rhetoric," in *Allegories of Reading*, 15–16).

Werner Hamacher also notes this connection when he writes that "de Man's rhetorical analysis remains largely determined by Jakobson's distinction between the paradigmatic and syntagmatic levels of language, despite important additions, radicalizations, and hints at a fundamental critique" ("*Lectio*: de Man's *Imperative*," in *Reading de Man Reading*, ed. Waters and Godzich, 178–79). There are countless references in de Man's writings to the "re-valorization" of metonymy over metaphor, such as the humorous description of metaphor as a "blind metonymy" at the end of "Genesis and Genealogy" (in *Allegories of Reading*, 102). Cf. also "Rhetoric of Temporality," in *Blindness and Insight*, 195, "Reading (Proust)" (in *Allegories of Reading*, 57–78), and "Semiology and Rhetoric" (in *Allegories of*

Reading, 14) for similar statements. It is also relevant to recall in this regard that de Man was a student and teacher at Harvard in the late 1950s and early 1960s, and that one of his closest colleagues, Reuben Brower, was an associate of Jakobson's.

3. This is not to say that de Man's best critics, like J. Hillis Miller, have not focused on some aspect of the opposition between these two types of figures: "In allegory anything can stand for anything. No ground whatever, subjective, divine, transcendent, nor even that of social convention, supports the relationship. It just happens, by a linguistic or narrative necessity. Just go on talking or writing and you will be sure to narrate allegorically the impossibility of reading your prior narration" ("'Reading' Part of a Paragraph," in *Reading de Man Reading*, ed. Waters and Godzich, 163).

Christopher Norris's important writings on de Man come closest to an explicit recognition that one of de Man's two main theses "has to do with the delusory character of any such appeal to *organic* or *naturalizing* metaphors when dealing with questions of poetry, language, or representation" (*Paul de Man: Deconstruction and the Critique of Aesthetic Ideology* [London: Routledge, 1988], xii; Norris's italics). Although Norris is more concerned with what he sees as the second of de Man's main theses, the notion of ineluctable critical blindness, I have made every effort to incorporate his scattered but penetrating comments on the first thesis into this chapter. My own analysis can be considered a kind of "microscopic" analysis of the same issue Norris identifies as one of the the central ones in all de Man's writings after 1960 (*Paul de Man*, 49). However, there are ways Norris's interpretation is not only "un–de Manian" in its frequent recourse to generalities, but misrepresentative of de Man's thought. For example, to detect an "existential pathos" running through all de Man's writings (basically, a nostalgia for man in a language-based world) rather than de Man's very consistent tone of self-mockery is to risk returning to a kind of reading de Man did everything he could to avoid (*Paul de Man*, xvi–xx).

4. Paul de Man, "Sign and Symbol in Hegel's *Aesthetics*," *Critical Inquiry* 8, no. 4 (1982): 761–75. Hereafter, "Image and Emblem," "Sign and Symbol," and "Rhetoric of Tropes" are cited parenthetically in the text.

5. Jonathan Culler, "Paul de Man's War and Aesthetic Ideology," *Critical Inquiry* 15, no. 4 (Summer 1989): 777–83; and Christopher Norris, "The Critique of Romantic Ideology," in his *Paul de Man*, 28–64.

6. Paul de Man, *The Resistance to Theory* (Minneapolis: University of Minnesota Press, 1986), 25.

7. Aristotle, *Poetics*, xxii.17; Jean-Jacques Rousseau, "Que le premier langage dut être figuré," chap. 3 of *Essai sur l'origine des langues* (1817; rpt. Paris: Bibliothèque du Graphe, n.d.).

8. Gaston Bachelard, *La poétique de l'espace* (Paris: PUF, 1957); Ricoeur, *La métaphore vive*; Gadamer, *Truth and Method*, 63ff.

9. William Butler Yeats, *Ideas of Good and Evil* (London: Bullen, 1903), 227ff.

10. This tendency and the quotation from Hölderlin are discussed more fully in de Man's "The Intentional Structure of the Romantic Image," in *The Rhetoric of Romanticism*, 1–18.

11. "De Man's thought is resolutely secular, or more precisely, sufficiently freed of the transcendental to be called finite" (de Man, *Blindness and Insight*, ed. Godzich, xxx). Geoffrey Hartmann, in glossing a statement of de Man's that language "is as such not made by us as historical beings, it is perhaps not even made by humans at all. Benjamin says, from the beginning, that it is not at all certain that language is in any sense human"; he insists that "by 'not human' de Man . . . certainly does not mean divine, as if language were instituted by God" ("Looking Back on Paul de Man," in *Reading de Man Reading*, ed. Waters and Godzich, 20–21).

12. See, for example, the discussion of Rilke's "purely auditive rhetoric" in de Man's "Tropes: Rilke" (in *Allegories of Reading*, 20–56). Two strikingly similar statements found in two different essays also shed light on the muteness of language. Compare the passage from "Reading (Proust)" where "reading" is said to "bar access, once and forever, to a meaning that yet can never cease to call out for its understanding" (ibid., 77) to this very similar statement concerning "Among School Children": "The grammatical structure is fully obscured by the duplicity of a figure that cries out for the differentiation that it conceals" (ibid., 12).

13. de Man, "Autobiography as De-Facement," in *The Rhetoric of Romanticism*, 81.

14. Although Geoffrey Bennington's article "Aberrations: de Man (and) the Machine" (in *Reading de Man Reading*, ed. Waters and Godzich) is less a reading of de Man than an application of his Derridean notion of the machine to Pascal, de Man, and others, Bennington does note the "displaced importance of the mechanical" (215) in de Man's later writings. The passage he quotes from *Allegories of Reading* ("Rousseau: *Excuses*," 298–99) is of capital importance in this regard: "The text as body, with all its implications of substitutive tropes ultimately always retraceable to metaphor, is replaced by the text as machine and, in the process, it suffers the loss of the illusion of meaning. The deconstruction of the figural dimension is a process that takes places independently of any desire; as such it is not unconscious but mechanical, systematic in its performance but arbitrary in its principle, like a grammar. . . . the entire construction of drives, substitutions, repressions, and representations is the aberrant, metaphorical correlative of the absolute randomness of language, prior to any figuration or meaning."

15. de Man, "Semiology and Rhetoric," in *Allegories of Reading*, 15–16, italics mine; hereafter cited parenthetically in the text.

16. de Man, "Reading (Proust)," in *Allegories of Reading*, 59–67.

17. Since Nietzsche's essay "On Truth and Lies in an Extra-Moral Sense" was de Man's fundamental reference point in his own theory of figuration, one can safely assume that Nietzsche's notion in that essay of a masquerade in which the Greek gods necessarily appear as something other than themselves is relevant here (see my discussion of this passage in chap. 1).

18. de Man, "Genesis and Genealogy (Nietzsche)," in *Allegories of Reading*, 102.

19. de Man, "Rhetoric of Temporality," in *Blindness and Insight*, 213.

20. "The Fall, in the literal as well as the theological sense, reminds [man] of the purely instrumental, reified character of his relationship to nature" (ibid., 214).

In other words, fallen humanity is reminded of its arrogance in assuming more than a subordinate role vis à vis Nature.

21. Another source is the opening essay of *Allegories of Reading*, "Semiology and Rhetoric," 11–12. This is the reading Jonathan Culler discusses in *On Deconstruction: Theory and Criticism After Structuralism* ([Ithaca, N.Y.: Cornell University Press, 1982], 246–47), an analysis which is not lacking its own interpretive brilliance.

22. "The various birds that appear throughout the work are among Yeats's prevailing emblem of the soul's longing for the divine, and the eternal manifestation of the divine will in this world is often represented by the infallible knowledge with which birds build their nests" (de Man, "Image and Emblem in Yeats," in *The Rhetoric of Romanticism*, 191).

23. Even though de Man disdained escapes from temporality as part of symbolism's synthesis of humanity and nature, the temporal awareness of allegory, for example, is an awareness of the "mystification" of past and future ("Rhetoric of Temporality," in *Blindness and Insight*, 222) and so compatible with Yeats's identification of emblems with divine timelessness.

24. As Jonathan Culler adds, the usual reading of "Among School Children" is contradictory insofar as the lack of separation between world and word requires that one eliminate the "literal reading": "The claim that the poem has been interpreted as making—the affirmation of fusion or continuity—is subverted by the discontinuity that must be assumed in order to infer that claim" (*On Deconstruction*, 247). Norris's interpretation of this interpretation (*Paul de Man*, 83–85) acknowledges that de Man's alternative reading denies the "natural" union between *signifiant* (the dancer) and *signifié* (the dance), but does not connect this with what de Man sees as Yeats's linguistic, or emblematic, consciousness, as I have tried to do here.

25. de Man, "Sign and Symbol," 769.

26. Ibid.

27. In a rather mean-spirited attack on de Man's supposed lack of philosophical rigor ("In-difference to Philosophy," in *Reading de Man Reading*, ed. Waters and Godzich, 268), Rudolph Gasché accuses de Man of, of all things, failing to read Hegel's *Aesthetics* in even the most basic way and thus failing to notice the obvious fact that Hegel uses "symbolic art" to refer to but one of three distinct stages in the history of art (symbolic, classic, and romantic). Gasché's surprise must have been even greater when he read Christopher Norris's statement that "for Hegel, the symbolic is the highest form of art" (*Paul de Man*, 29). Neither de Man nor Norris is unaware that Hegel uses the term in both a generic and specific sense; if the former is stressed, it is simply because the latter is so obvious. Even more bizarre is the fact that while Gasché is maintaining that Hegel uses the term "specifically," he keeps quoting passages which demonstrate the other, generic meaning.

28. The quotations are from de Man, "Sign and Symbol," 772–73.

29. Ibid., 773; italics mine.

30. Ibid. W. J. T. Mitchell's notion of "iconophobia" (*Iconology: Image, Text, Ideology* [Chicago: University of Chicago Press, 1986]), or the repression of the visual, ought to be compared with this notion of "iconophilia." Such a comparison

would show how Mitchell's "phobia" is compatible with the supposed "philia" asserted by de Man.

31. de Man, like Derrida, argues almost exclusively *against* the seductive powers of metaphor. It is important to add, however, that those two writers are as aware as any that the supposed return of meaning to itself of metaphor is only one ideological way of viewing meta-phor's trans-gressive nature. For example, see the end of "La mythologie blanche" (*Marges—de la philosophie*, 323–24) where Derrida talks about "another metaphor."

32. de Man, "Sign and Symbol," 773.

33. Christopher Norris's contention (*Paul de Man*, xix).

34. de Man, "Genesis and Genealogy," in *Allegories of Reading*, 81.

35. Some interesting but relatively untheoretical attempts to understand this relationship have been made by Otto Bohlmann (*Yeats and Nietzsche* [Totowa, N.J.: Barnes and Noble, 1982]); Keith May (*Nietzsche and Modern Literature* [New York: St. Martin's Press, 1988]); and Eitel Timm (*Yeats und Nietzsche* [Wurzburg: Konigshausen and Neumann, 1980]).

36. This statement is not meant to underestimate the importance of Benjamin, to whom de Man devoted one of his final lectures ("Walter Benjamin's 'The Task of the Translator,'" in *The Lesson of Paul de Man*), a piece which is certainly as much about a signic, versus symbolic, view of language as any of those discussed here.

37. Glossing Nietzsche's notion that "'truth kills' insofar as it realizes its own foundation in error," de Man states, "Philosophy turns out to be an endless reflection on its own destruction at the hands of literature" ("Rhetoric of Tropes," in *Allegories of Reading*, 115).

38. Werner Hamacher has formulated an ingenious response to this state of suspended reality, for he sees the very lack of referentiality as making the movement outside the text necessary, although that too must result in a suspended state of imperative contingency: "The law to which the imperative is subject—the law of the law—makes the imperative a linguistic event susceptible of occurring in the world of figures oriented toward synthetic totality and rational necessity only as contingent force: as chance, as a meaningless mechanical repetition, as groundless positing, as the failure and the disruption of the intentions of a will that wills itself" ("Lectio: de Man's Imperative," in *Reading de Man Reading*, ed. Waters and Godzich, 179).

On the other hand, David Simpson tries to dismiss de Man's failure to breathe the fresh air of referentiality, which for Simpson means rejecting de Man's "pseudophilosophy" and relating texts to the real world. The facile opposition between a healthy Simpson who is trying to lead the reader "out into the world of referentiality" and a sickly de Man who sees "only a light burning late in the study," as well as Simpson's own cursory treatment of de Man, is itself proof of the danger inherent in rejecting textual complexity as merely "seeking to defend the integrity of inertia and corporate disbelief" ("Literary Criticism and the Return to 'History,'" *Critical Inquiry* 14 [Summer 1988]: 726). For a passionate and, at the same time, brilliant defense of the ethics of deconstruction, see J. Hillis Miller's recent work *The Ethics of Reading* (New York: Columbia University Press, 1987).

8. The Comparative Double

1. René Wellek wrote a series of articles on comparative literature, beginning with the chapter "General, Comparative and National Literature" (1949) in *Theory of Literature* (New York: Harcourt Brace, 1962). The other principal articles, carried out over almost twenty years, are "The Concept of Comparative Literature," *Yearbook of Comparative and General Literature* 2, (1953); "The Crisis of Comparative Literature," reprinted in *Concepts of Criticism* (New Haven, Conn.: Yale University Press, 1963); and "Comparative Literature Today," *Comparative Literature* 17 (1965): 325–37.

2. The debate about comparative literature centers around a definition of what the discipline is supposed to study as well as how it is to proceed. In addition to Wellek's articles mentioned above, see Henry Remak's "Comparative Literature: Its Definition and Function," in *Comparative Literature*, ed. Newton P. Stallknecht and Horst Frenz (Carbondale: Southern Illinois University Press, 1971).

3. Victor Lange, "Stand und Aufgaben der vergleichenden Literaturgeschichte in den USA," in *Forschungsprobleme der vergleichenden Literaturgeschichte*, ed. Kurt Wais (Tubingen: Niemeyer, 1951).

4. The romantic origins of comparative literature are generally viewed as resulting in the first explicit call for an international or universal approach to literature. This romantic etiology is also at work in the other nineteenth-century comparative disciplines. For a discussion of the romantic forerunners of comparative literature, see Arno Kappler's *Die literarische Vergleich* (Frankfurt: Lang, 1976).

5. Paul Van Tieghem, *La littérature comparée* (Paris: Libraire Armand Colin, 1931); translation and italics mine. This is the essential text from which to form an opinion either pro or contra the "French school," for, as Werner Friedrich says, "French criticism stands on Van Tieghem's *La Littérature comparée*" (*The Challenge of Comparative Literature* [Chapel Hill: University of North Carolina Press, 1970]).

6. Van Tieghem, *La littérature comparée*, 12–13; italics Van Tieghem's.

7. Wellek, *Theory of Literature*, 46.

8. Ibid., 52.

9. For example, "The great argument for comparative literature is the obvious falsity of the idea of a self-enclosed national literature" (Wellek, "The Concept of Comparative Literature," 5). Compare similar statements in *Concepts of Criticism* (282) and *Theory of Literature* (49).

10. Auerbach exemplifies this in his famous comparison of Homer and the Old Testament: "By this example of the contrary, we see the significance of the descriptive adjectives and digressions of the Homeric poems; with their indications of the earlier and as it were absolute existence of the persons described, they prevent the reader from concentrating exclusively on a present crisis" (*Mimesis*, trans. Willard Trask [Princeton, N.J.: Princeton University Press, 1968], 11).

11. For the importance of the romantic recognition of the symbolic function of language, see Wellek, "The Concept of Romanticism in Literary History," in *Concepts of Criticism*, 129–98.

12. Goethe's conversation with Eckermann of January 31, 1827.

13. Friedrich Schlegel, *Gespräch über die Poesie* (Stuttgart: J. B. Metzler, 1968), 286; *Dialogue on Poetry and Literary Aphorisms*, trans. Ernst Behler and Roman Struc (University Park: Pennsylvania State University Press, 1968), 55.

14. Schlegel, *Gespräch über die Poesie*, 10–11; *Dialogue*, 140.

15. Arthur Lovejoy has argued against reading Schlegel's "Fragment" as "in praise of" the novel, particularly Goethe's *Wilhelm Meister* ("Romantic in Early German Romanticism," in *Essays in the History of Ideas* [Baltimore: Johns Hopkins University Press, 1948]). Although for different reasons, I would also interpret Schlegel's remarks as directed to romanticism in general and not *Wilhelm Meister* in particular.

16. Schlegel, *Gespräch über die Poesie*, 11; *Dialogue*, 140.

17. Schlegel, *Gespräch über die Poesie*, 11; *Dialogue*, 140.

18. This notion is elaborated in chapter 1 of this work.

19. Wellek, *Theory of Literature*, 49.

20. Goethe's conversation with Eckermann of January 31, 1827.

21. Anne-Louise-Germaine de Staël [Mme de Staël], *De l'Allemagne* (Paris: Garnier Flammarion, 1968), 18–19, all translations mine; hereafter cited parenthetically in text.

22. This is also the main point of Walter Benjamin's influential essay "Die Aufgabe des Übersetzers."

23. Aristotle, *Rhetoric* 3.18.7.

24. In their study of early German romanticism, particularly of the *Athenaeum*, Philippe Lacoue-Labarthe and Jean-Luc Nancy, the authors of *L'absolu litteraire* (Paris: Seuil, 1978), discuss the importance of *Witz* as a recurrent motif in Schlegel's writings and as an essential aspect of the particular genre of the "Fragment." This seems to run counter to Mme de Staël's claim that wit is to be associated with the French in opposition to the German, but Mme de Staël's own witty and romantic style makes apparent that the romantic, in contrast to both the French and German, is capable of a more synthetic "serious wit." Lacoue-Labarthe and Nancy also note that Schlegel himself argues for the more synthetic and against the more exclusively "French" form of wit: "L'écriture du fragment constitue donc en somme l'*Aufhebung* dialectique de l'antinomie interne du *Witz*" (77).

Bibliography

Allemann, Beda. "Kafka: Von den Gleichnissen." *Zeitschrift für deutsche Philologie* 83 (1964): 97–106.

Anders, Gunther. *Kafka: Pro und Contra*. Munich: Beck, 1951.

Aristotle. *The Art of Rhetoric*. Translated by John Henry Freese. Cambridge, Mass.: Harvard University Press, 1985.

———. *Poetics*. Translated by W. Hamilton Fyfe. Cambridge, Mass.: Harvard University Press, 1973.

Arntzen, Helmut. "Franz Kafka: Von den Gleichnissen." *Zeitschrift für deutsche Philologie* 38 (1964): 106–12.

Artaud, Antonin. "Theatre and Culture" (1936?). In *Collected Works*, by Antonin Artaud. Translated by Victor Corti. London: Calder and Boyars, 1974.

Arthur, Marylin B. "The Origins of the Western Attitude Toward Women." *Arethusa* 6, no. 1 (1973): 7–58.

Auerbach, Erich. *Mimesis*. Translated by Willard Trask. Princeton, N.J.: Princeton University Press, 1968.

Bachelard, Gaston. *La poétique de l'espace*. Paris: PUF, 1957.

Barthes, Roland. "L'ancienne rhétorique: Aide-memoire." *Communications* 16 (1970): 172–229.

Bataille, Georges. *Erotisme*. Paris: Minuit, 1957.

Beardsley, Monroe. *Aesthetics*. New York: Harcourt, Brace and World, 1958.

Beicken, Peter. *Franz Kafka: Eine kritische Einführung in die Forschung*. Munich: Athenaion, 1974.

Bellinger, A. R. "The *Bacchae* and the *Hippolytus*." *Yale Classical Studies* 1 (1939): 15–27.

Benjamin, Walter. "Die Aufgabe des Übersetzers." In *Illuminationen*. Frankfurt: Suhrkamp, 1961.

———. *The Origins of German Tragic Drama*. Translated by John Osborne. London: New Left Books, 1977.

———. "The Task of the Translator." In *Illuminations*, translated by Harry Zohn. New York: Schocken, 1969.

Benveniste, Emile. "Language in Freudian Theory." In *Problems in General Linguistics*, translated by Mary Elizabeth Meek. Miami: University of Miami Press, 1971.

Berlin, Normand. *The Secret Cause: A Discussion of Tragedy*. Amherst: University of Massachusetts Press, 1981.

Binder, Hartmut. *Kafka-Kommentar*. Munich: Winkler, 1975.

Black, Max. *Models and Metaphors*. Ithaca, N.Y.: Cornell University Press, 1962.

Blanchot, Maurice. *De Kafka à Kafka*. Paris: Gallimard, 1981.

Bohlmann, Otto. *Yeats and Nietzsche*. Totowa, N.J.: Barnes and Noble, 1982.

Brereton, Geoffrey. *Principles of Tragedy*. London: Routledge and Kegan Paul, 1968.

Brod, Max. *Franz Kafka*. New York: Schocken, 1963.

Butcher, S. H. *Aristotle's Theory of Poetry and Fine Art*. New York: Dover, 1951.

Bywater, Ingram. *Aristotle on the Art of Poetry*. London: Oxford University Press, 1909.

Carlston, Charles E. *The Parables of the Triple Tradition*. Philadelphia: Fortress Press, 1975.

Conacher, D. J. *Euripidean Drama: Myth, Theme, and Structure*. Toronto: University of Toronto Press, 1966.

Cooper, Lane. *Aristotle on the Art of Poetry*. Ithaca, N.Y.: Cornell University Press, 1922.

Corngold, Stanley. "Kafka's Double Helix." *Literary Review* 26 (1983): 521–36.

Crossan, J. D. "A Basic Bibliography for Parables Research." *Semeia* 1 (1974): 236–74.

———. *In Parables*. New York: Harper and Row, 1973.

Culler, Jonathan. *On Deconstruction: Theory and Criticism After Structuralism*. Ithaca, N.Y.: Cornell University Press, 1982.

———. "Paul de Man's War and Aesthetic Ideology." *Critical Inquiry* 15, no. 4 (Summer 1989): 777–83.

de Man, Paul. *Allegories of Reading*. New Haven, Conn.: Yale University Press, 1979.

———. *Blindness and Insight*. Edited by Wlad Godzich. Minneapolis: University of Minnesota Press, 1983.

———. "The Epistemology of Metaphor." *Critical Inquiry* 5 (Autumn 1978): 13–30.

———. *The Lesson of Paul de Man*, ed. Peter Brooks, Shoshana Felman, and J. Hillis Miller. Yale French Studies, no. 69. New Haven, Conn.: Yale University Press, 1985.

———. *The Resistance to Theory*. Minneapolis: University of Minnesota Press, 1986.

———. *The Rhetoric of Romanticism*. New York: Columbia University Press, 1984.

———. "Sign and Symbol in Hegel's *Aesthetics*." *Critical Inquiry* 8, no. 4 (1982): 761–75.

Derrida, Jacques. "Denials: How to Avoid Speaking." *Languages of the Unsayable: The Play of Negativity in Literature and Literary Theory*, edited by Sanford Burdick and Wolfgang Iser. New York: Columbia University Press, 1989.

———. *La Dissemination*. Paris: Seuil, 1972.

———. *Mémoires*. New York: Columbia University Press, 1986.

———. "La mythologie blanche." In *Marges—de la philosophie*. Paris: Minuit, 1972.

———. *Positions*. Paris: Minuit, 1972.

————. *Psyché: Inventions de l'autre*. Paris: Galilée, 1987.

————. "Le retrait de la métaphore." *Analecta Husserliana* 14 (1983): 273–300.

————. *The Truth in Painting*. Translated by Geoff Bennington and Ian McLeod. Chicago: University of Chicago Press, 1987.

————. *La vérité en peinture*. Paris: Flammarion, 1978.

————. "Vor dem Gesetz." In *Kafka and the Contemporary Critical Performance*, edited by Alan Udott. Bloomington: Indiana University Press, 1987.

Diels, H. *Die Fragmente der Vorsokratiker*. Berlin: Werdman, 1903.

Dodds, E. R., ed. *Euripides' "Bacchae."* Oxford: Oxford University Press, 1977.

Dupont-Roc, Roselyne, and Jean Lallot. *Aristote: La "Poétique."* Paris: Seuil, 1980.

Dupréel, Eugene. *Les Sophistes*. Neuchatel: Griffon, 1945.

Else, Gerald F. *Aristotle: Poetics*. Ann Arbor: University of Michigan Press, 1967.

————. *Aristotle's Poetics: The Argument*. Cambridge, Mass.: Harvard University Press, 1957.

————. *The Origin and Early Form of Greek Tragedy*. New York: Norton, 1972.

Emrich, Wilhelm. *Franz Kafka*. New York: Ungar, 1968.

Euripides. *Euripides*. Vols. 1 and 5. Edited by David Grene and Richmond Lattimore. Chicago: University of Chicago Press, 1955, 1968.

Felman, Shoshana. "Turning the Screw of Interpretation." *Yale French Studies* 55/56 (1977): 94–207.

Foley, Helene. *Ritual Irony: Poetry and Sacrifice in Euripides*. Ithaca, N.Y.: Cornell University Press, 1985.

Forrester, John. *Language and the Origins of Psychoanalysis*. New York: Columbia University Press, 1980.

Freud, Sigmund. *Beyond the Pleasure Principle*. 1920. Reprint. New York: Norton, 1961.

————. *Collected Papers*. Edited by Ernst Jones. New York: Basic Books, 1959.

————. *Complete Psychological Works*. Standard Edition. Edited by James Strachey. London: Hogarth Press, 1953–74.

————. *Creativity and the Unconscious*. New York: Harper, 1958.

————. "Femininity." In *New Introductory Lectures*, translated by W. J. H. Serott. (1933). Reprint. New York: Norton, 1965.

————. *Introductory Lectures on Psychoanalysis*. Translated by James Strachey. New York: Norton, 1977.

————. *Three Essays*. 1910. Reprint. New York: Basic Books, 1975.

Friedrich, Werner. *The Challenge of Comparative Literature*. Chapel Hill: University of North Carolina Press, 1970.

Funk, Robert W. "The Parable as Metaphor." In *Language, Hermeneutics, and the Word of God*. New York: Harper and Row, 1966.

Fyfe, W. H. *Aristotle: The Poetics*. Cambridge, Mass.: Harvard University Press, 1953.

Gadamer, Hans-Georg. *Truth and Method*. Translated by Garrett Barden and John Cumming. New York: Crossroad, 1975.

————. *Wahrheit und Methode*. Tübingen: Mohr, 1972.

Goethe, Johann Wolfgang von. *Faust*. Translated by Louis MacNeice. New York: Norton, 1961.

Golden, Leon, and O. B. Hardison. *Aristotle's Poetics*. Englewood Cliffs, N.J.: Prentice-Hall, 1968.

Gomperz, Heinrich. *Sophistik und Rhetorik*. 1912. Reprint. Darmstadt: Wissenschaftliche Buchgesellschaft, 1965.

Gomperz, Theodor. *Greek Thinkers*. New York: Humanities Press, 1955.

Grube, G. M. A. *The Drama of Euripides*. London: Methuen, 1941.

Guthrie, W. K. C. *A History of Greek Philosophy*. Cambridge: Cambridge University Press, 1962.

Guépin, J.-P. *The Tragic Paradox*. Amsterdam: Hakkert, 1968.

Habermas, Jürgen. *The Philosophical Discourse of Modernity*. Cambridge, Mass.: MIT Press, 1990.

Hafrey, Leigh. "Parabola: The Interpolated Tale as Parable." Ph.D. dissertation, Yale University, 1978.

Hardy, Joseph. *Aristote: Poétique*. Paris: Collection des Universités de France, 1952.

Harrison, Jane Ellen. *Ancient Art and Ritual*. New York: Holt, 1913.

Hegel, Georg Wilhelm Friedrich. *Lectures on the History of Philosophy*. Vol. 1. Translated by E. S. Haldane and Frances Simson. London: Routledge and Kegan Paul, 1963.

———. *On Tragedy*. Translated by Henry Paolucci. New York: Harper and Row, 1975.

———. *The Phenomenology of Mind*. Translated by J. B. Baillie. New York: Harper, 1967.

———. *Vorlesungen über die Aesthetik*. Frankfurt: Suhrkamp, 1979.

Heidegger, Martin. *Poetry, Language, Thought*. Translated by Albert Hofstadter. New York: Harper, 1975.

———. *Der Satz vom Grund*. Pfullingen, Germany: Neske, 1957.

———. *Der Ursprung des Kunstwerkes*. Stuttgart: Reclam, 1960.

Henrichs, Albert. "Greek and Roman Glimpses of Dionysus." In *Dionysus and His Circle*. Cambridge: Cambridge University Press, 1979.

Hertz, Neil. *The End of the Line*. New York: Columbia University Press, 1985.

Hillmann, Heinz. *Franz Kafka: Dichtungstheorie und Dichtungsgestalt*. Bonn: Bouvier, 1973.

Hoffmann, E. T. A. "The Sandman." 1816. Reprinted in *Stories*, ed. Victor Lange. New York: Continuum, 1982.

Hoffmann, Werner. *Kafkas Aphorismen*. Berne: Francke, 1975.

Hölderlin. "Anmerkungen zum Odipus." In *Sämtliche Werke*, vol. 6. Stuttgart: Beissner, n.d.

Homer. *The Iliad*. Translated by Robert Fitzgerald. New York: Doubleday, 1974.

Iser, Wolfgang. *The Act of Reading*. Baltimore: Johns Hopkins University Press, 1978.

Jacobus, Mary. "Judith, Holofernes, and the Phallic Woman." In *Reading Woman*. New York: Columbia University Press, 1985.

James, Henry. "The Altar of the Dead." In *The Turn of the Screw and Other Short Novels*. New York: New American Library, 1962.
———. *Eight Tales from the Major Phase*. New York: Norton, 1969.
Jeremias, Joachim. *Rediscovering the Parables*. New York: Scribners, 1966.
Jülicher, Adolf. *Die Gleichnisrede Jesu*. Tübingen: Mohr, 1910.
Kafka, Franz. "Betrachtungen." In *Hochzeitsvorbereitungen auf dem Lande*. Frankfurt: Fischer, 1983.
———. *Hochzeitsvorbereitungen auf dem Lande*. Frankfurt: Fischer, 1983.
———. *Oeuvres complètes*. Edited by Claude David. Paris: Gallimard, 1980.
———. *Parables and Paradoxes*. New York: Schocken, 1961.
———. *Sämtliche Erzählungen*. Frankfurt: Fischer, 1979.
———. *Tagebücher*. Frankfurt: Fischer, 1951.
Kappler, Arno. *Die literarische Vergleich*. Frankfurt: Lang, 1976.
Karst, Roman. "Kafka und die Metaphor." *Literatur und Kritik* 179/80 (1983): 472.
Kermode, Frank. *The Genesis of Secrecy*. Cambridge, Mass.: Harvard University Press, 1979.
Kirk, G. S., and J. E. Raven, eds. *The Presocratic Philosophers*. Cambridge: Cambridge University Press, 1975.
Kissinger, W. S. *The Parables of Jesus: A History of Interpretation and Bibliography*. Metuchen, N.J.: Scarecrow Press, 1979.
Kofman, Sarah. *The Childhood of Art*. Translated by Winifred Woodhull. New York: Columbia University Press, 1988.
———. *L'enfance de l'art: Une interprétation de l'esthétique freudienne*. Paris: Galilée, 1985.
———. *Nietzsche et la métaphore*. Paris: Galilée, 1983.
———. *Quatre romans analytiques*. Paris: Galilée, 1973.
Kraft, Herbert. *Kafka: Wirklichkeit und Perspektive*. Bebenhausen: Rotsch, 1972.
Kreis, Rudolf. *Die doppelte Rede des Franz Kafka*. Paderborn: Schöningh, 1976.
Kretzschmar, Helmut. *Die Begriff "Consciousness" bei Henry James*. Düsseldorf: Zentral Verlag für Dissertationen, 1967.
Kristeva, Julia. *Le langage, cet inconnu*. Paris: Seuil, 1981.
Lacan, Jacques. *Ecrits*. Paris: Seuil, 1966.
Lacoue-Labarthe, Philippe, and Jean-Luc Nancy. *L'absolu litteraire*. Paris: Seuil, 1978.
Lange, Victor. "Stand und Aufgaben der vergleichenden Literaturgeschichte in den USA." In *Forschungsprobleme der vergleichenden Literaturgeschichte*, edited by Kurt Wais. Tübingen: Niemeyer, 1951.
Laplanche, Jean. *Life and Death in Psychoanalysis*. Baltimore: Johns Hopkins University Press, 1976.
Locke, John. *An Essay Concerning Human Understanding*. Oxford: Clarendon Press, 1975.
Lovejoy, Arthur. "Romantic in Early German Romanticism." In *Essays in the History of Ideas*. Baltimore: Johns Hopkins University Press, 1948.
Lucas, D. W. *Aristotle: Poetics*. Oxford: Clarendon Press, 1968.

Macey, David. *Lacan in Contexts*. London: Verso, 1988.

McGuire, William, ed. *Freud/Jung Letters*. Translated by Ralph Mannheim and R. F. C. Hulle. Princeton, N.J.: Princeton University Press, 1974.

McNally, Sheila. "The Maenad in Early Greek Art." In *Women in the Ancient World: The Arethusa Papers*, edited by John Peradotto and J. P. Sullivan. Albany: State University of New York Press, 1984.

Manson, T. W. *The Teaching of Jesus*. Cambridge: Cambridge University Press, 1963.

May, Keith. *Nietzsche and Modern Literature*. New York: St. Martin's Press, 1988.

Michel, Laurence, and Richard Sewell, eds. *Tragedy: Modern Essays in Criticism*. Englewood Cliffs, N.J.: Prentice-Hall, 1963.

Michelfelder, Diane P., and Richard E. Palmer, eds. *Dialogue and Deconstruction: The Gadamer-Derrida Encounter*. Albany: State University of New York Press, 1989.

Miller, J. Hillis. "The Critic as Host." In *Deconstruction and Criticism*, edited by Harold Bloom. Seabury Press, 1979.

———. "Dismembering and Disremembering in Nietzsche's 'On Truth and Lies in a Normal Sense.'" *Boundary* 9, no. 3 and 10, no. 1 (Spring/Fall 1981): 41–54.

———. *The Ethics of Reading*. New York: Columbia University Press, 1987.

———. "The Figure in the Carpet." *Poetics Today* 1, no. 3 (Spring 1980): 107–18.

Mitchell, Juliet. *Psychoanalysis and Feminism*. London: Lane, 1974.

Mitchell, W. J. T. *Iconology: Image, Text, Ideology*. Chicago: University of Chicago Press, 1986.

Murray, Gilbert. *Aeschylus, the Creator of Tragedy*. Oxford: Clarendon Press, 1940.

Nealon, Jeffrey. "The Discipline of Deconstruction." *PMLA* 16 (1992): 1266–78.

Nestle, Wilhelm. *Euripides*. Stuttgart: Kohlhammer, 1901.

The New English Bible. Oxford: Oxford University Press, 1976.

Nietzsche, Friedrich. *Also Sprach Zarathustra*. Munich: Goldmann, 1970.

———. *The Birth of Tragedy*. Translated by Francis Golffing. Garden City, N.Y.: Doubleday, 1956.

———. *Friedrich Nietzsche on Rhetoric and Language*. Edited by Sander Gilman. New York: Oxford University Press, 1989.

———. *Die Geburt der Tragödie*. In *Werke*, vol. 1. Edited by K. Schlechta. Frankfurt: Ullstein, 1984.

———. *Nietzsche Werke*. Edited by Giorgio Colli and Mazzino Montinari. Vol. 2, pt. 3. Berlin: de Gruyter, 1973.

———. *Philosophy and Truth*. Translated by Daniel Breazeale. Atlantic Highlands, N.J.: Humanities Press, 1979.

Norris, Christopher. *Paul de Man: Deconstruction and the Critique of Aesthetic Ideology*. London: Routledge, 1988.

Otto, Walter F. *Dionysus: Myth and Cult*. Bloomington: Indiana University Press, 1965.

Perrin, Norman. "Historical Criticism, Literary Criticism, and Hermeneutics." *Journal of Religion* 52 (1972): 361–75.

Perrot, Jean. *Une écriture énigmatique*. Paris: Aubier, 1982.

Peters, Charles. "On the Possible Contribution of Ambiguity of Expression to the Development of Proto-Linguistic Performance." In *Language Origins*, edited by Roger Wescott. Silver Springs, Md.: Linstock Press, 1974.

Plato. *The Dialogues of Plato*. Translated by Benjamin Jowett. 3d ed. London: Oxford University Press, 1924.

———. *Protagoras*. Edited by Gregory Vlastos. Indianapolis: Bobbs-Merrill, 1956.

Politzer, Heinz. *Parable and Paradox*. Ithaca, N.Y.: Cornell University Press, 1962.

Pomeroy, Sarah. "Selected Bibliography on Women in Antiquity." *Arethusa* 6 (1973): 125–57.

Propp, Vladimir. *Morphologie du conte*. Translated by Tzuetan Todorov. Paris: Seuil, 1970.

The Random House Dictionary of the English Language. New York: Random House, 1967.

Remak, Henry. "Comparative Literature: Its Definition and Function." In *Comparative Literature*, edited by Newton P. Stallknecht and Horst Frenz. Carbondale: Southern Illinois University Press, 1971.

Rey, Jean-Michel. *Parcours de Freud*. Paris: Galilée, 1974.

Richards, I. A. *The Philosophy of Rhetoric*. Oxford: Oxford University Press, 1936.

———. *Practical Criticism*. New York: Harvest, 1929.

Ricoeur, Paul. *La métaphore vive*. Paris: Seuil, 1975.

———. *Freud and Philosophy*. New Haven, Conn.: Yale University Press, 1970.

Rousseau, Jean-Jacques. *Essai sur l'origine des langues*. 1817. Reprint. Paris: Bibliothèque du Graphe, n.d.

Sale, William. "The Psychoanalysis of Pentheus in the *Bacchae* of Euripides." *Yale Classical Studies* 22 (1972): 63–82.

Sandys, J. E. *The "Bacchae" of Euripides*. Cambridge: Cambridge University Press, 1900.

Schapiro, Meyer. "The Still Life as a Personal Object." In *The Reach of Mind: Essays in Memory of Kurt Goldstein*, edited by Marianne Simmel. New York: Springer, 1968.

Schlegel, Friedrich von. "Fragment #668." In *Philosophische Lehrjahre*, edited by Ernst Behler. Paderborn: Schöningh, 1962.

Schlegel, Friedrich. *Dialogue on Poetry and Literary Aphorisms*. Translated by Ernst Behler and Roman Struc. University Park: Pennsylvania State University Press, 1968.

———. *Gespräch über die Poesie*. Stuttgart: J. B. Metzler, 1968.

Segal, Charles. *Dionysiac Poetics and Euripides' "Bacchae."* Princeton, N.J.: Princeton University Press, 1982.

———. "The Menace of Dionysus: Sex Roles and Reversals in Euripides' *Bacchae*." *Arethusa* 11 (1978): 185–202.

Semeia. Vol. 1 (1974).

Seuss, Dr. [Theodor Seuss Geisel]. *The Foot Book.* New York: Random House, 1968.

Simpson, David. "Literary Criticism and the Return to 'History.'" *Critical Inquiry* 14 (Summer 1988): 721–47.

Smythe, Herbert Weir. *Greek Grammar.* Edited by Gordon Messing. Cambridge, Mass.: Harvard University Press, 1976.

Sophocles. *Sophocles I.* Edited by David Grene and Richmond Lattimore. Chicago: University of Chicago Press, 1954.

Sprague, R. K., ed. *The Older Sophists.* Columbia: University of South Carolina Press, 1972.

Staël, Anne-Louise-Germaine de [Mme de Staël]. *De l'Allemagne.* Paris: Garnier Flammarion, 1968.

Starobinski, Jean. *La relation critique.* Paris: Gallimard, 1970.

Steinberg, Erwin. "Kafka's *Before the Law.*" *Cithara* 18, no. 1 (November 1978): 27–45.

Steiner, George. *The Death of Tragedy.* New York: Knopf, 1961.

Szondi, Peter. *Versuch über das Tragische.* Frankfurt: Insel, 1961.

Timm, Eitel. *Yeats and Nietzsche.* Wurzburg: Konigshausen and Neumann, 1980.

Todorov, Tzvetan. *The Poetics of Prose.* Paris: Seuil, 1971.

Van Tieghem, Paul. *La littérature comparée.* Paris: Libraire Armand Colin, 1931.

Vickers, Brian. *Towards Greek Tragedy.* London: Longman, 1973.

Warning, Rainer. "Reading Irony in Flaubert." *Style* 19, no. 3 (1985): 304–16.

Waters, Lindsay, and Wlad Godzich, eds. *Reading de Man Reading.* Minneapolis: University of Minnesota Press, 1989.

Wellek, René. "Comparative Literature Today." *Comparative Literature* 17 (1965): 325–37.

———. "The Concept of Comparative Literature." *Yearbook of Comparative and General Literature* 2 (1953).

———. *Concepts of Criticism.* New Haven, Conn.: Yale University Press, 1963.

———. "General, Comparative and National Literature." In *Theory of Literature.* New York: Harcourt Brace, 1962.

Wilcox, T. R. *The Mode in Footwear.* New York: Scribners, 1948.

Winnington-Ingram, R. P. *Euripides and Dionysus: An Interpretation of the "Bacchae."* Cambridge: Cambridge University Press, 1948.

Yeats, William Butler. *The Collected Poems.* New York: Macmillan, 1964.

———. *Ideas of Good and Evil.* London: Bullen, 1903.

Index

Adler, Alfred, 83–84
ainigma ("riddle"), 21
allegory, 4, 114–16
Antigone, 69–71
Aristotle: on metaphor, 20–26, 78, 113
audibility (of language), 115–16
Auerbach, Erich, 164 (n. 10)
autonomosis, 2

Bacchae, 64–68
Bachelard, Gaston, 113
Baldensperger, F., 128
Barthes, Roland, 24, 145 (n. 2)
Baudelaire, Charles Pierre, 118–19
Beardsley, Monroe, 31–33
Benjamin, Walter, 163 (n. 36), 165 (n. 22)
Bennington, Geoffrey, 161 (n. 14)
Benveniste, Emile, 74–79, 156 (n. 18)
Bildung, 13–14
bisexuality, 80
Black, Max, 29–31
Blanchot, Maurice: on Kafka, 59
Breton, André, 78

catachresis, 95
chiasmus, 67, 98–101, 133, 154 (n. 26)
comparative literature, 128–43, 164 (nn. 1, 2, 4, 9)
Culler, Jonathan, 113, 160 (n. 5), 162 (nn. 21, 24)

David, Claude, 56–57
deconstruction, 12–13, 146 (n. 18)
de Man, Paul, 112–27, 145 (n. 10), 147 (n. 3), 159 (nn. 1, 2), 160 (nn. 2, 3, 10), 161 (nn. 11, 14, 17), 162 (nn. 22, 23, 24, 27), 163 (nn. 30, 31, 36, 38)
Derrida, Jacques, 1, 157 (n. 1), 163 (n. 31);

Truth in Painting, 16–18; *How to Avoid Speaking*, 22–23, 146 (nn. 15, 19, 22)
Dionysus: and tragedy, 62, 154 (n. 24)
disciples: and parable, 151 (n. 9)
dissimulation: in Nietzsche, 33–35
Dodds, E. R., 65
Doppelgänger, 12, 146 (n. 2)

Else, Gerald F., 63, 153 (n. 10)
emblem, 114–16
Esch, Deborah, 159 (n. 1)

Felman, Shoshana, 158–59 (n. 21)
Fitzgerald, Robert, 64
Fliess, W., 83–84
forgetfulness: in Nietzsche, 35–36
Freud, Sigmund, 72–92; *Beyond the Pleasure Principle*, 92; "A Child Is Being Beaten," 83; "Theme of the Three Caskets," 90, 92; "On 'the Uncanny,'" 84–85; "The Taboo of Virginity," 85–90

Gadamer, Hans-Georg, 13–16, 146 (n. 19)
Gasché, Rudolph, 162 (n. 27)
Gedächtnis: vs. *Erinnerung*, 122–23
Goethe, Johann Wolfgang von, 129, 132, 136, 148–49 (n. 28), 165 (n. 15)
Gorgias of Leontini, 43, 141
Greek temple: Heidegger on, 5–7
Guépin, J.-P., 154 (n. 27)

Hamacher, Werner, 159 (n. 2), 163 (n. 38)
Hartmann, Geoffrey, 161 (n. 11)
Hegel, George Wilhelm Friedrich, 121–24, 145 (n. 1)
Heidegger, Martin, 2; "On the Origin of the Work of Art," 3–11
hermeneutic circle, 4
Hertz, Neil, 82

Hippolytus, 71–72
Hoffmann, E. T. A., 84–85
Homer, 22

Iser, Wolfgang, 93, 110, 158 (n. 20)

Jacob: and the Angel, v, 5
Jacobus, Mary, 86–90
Jakobson, Roman, 159 (n. 2)
James, Henry: "The Altar of the Dead," 105, 158 (n. 19), 159 (n. 23); "The Beast in the Jungle," 102, 103, 109; "The Figure in the Carpet," 93–112, 158 (nn. 6, 14); "The Jolly Corner," 159 (n. 21); *Roderick Hudson*, 158 (n. 18); *The Spoils of Poynton*, 158 (n. 19)
Judith, 86–90
jumble, 93, 108

Kafka, Franz, 5, 151 (n. 14); "Von den Gleichnissen," 56–61; "Metamorphosis," 58, 59, 158 (n. 17); on death, 59; and Christianity, 152 (n. 19); *Ein Hungerkunstler*, 61; "parables," 152 (n. 16); religiosity, 152 (n. 17)
Kant, Immanuel, 14–15
Kofman, Sarah, 51, 74–79, 89–90, 157 (n. 45)
Kristeva, Julia, 155 (n. 9)

Lacan, Jacques, 155 (nn. 1, 8)
Lacoue-Labarthes, Philippe, and Jean-Luc Nancy, 165 (n. 24)
Lange, Victor, 128
Laplanche, Jean, 79–80
Lovejoy, Arthur, 165 (n. 15)
Lutschen ("sensual sucking"), 156 (n. 26)

Magritte, René, 93
mashal ("parable"), 52
mechanicity: in de Man, 116–18
Medusa, 82
mēnis ("wrath of humiliation"), 64, 153 (n. 11)
metaphor, 19–37, 137–38, 147 (nn. 6, 11, 15), 148 (nn. 16, 26)
Miller, J. Hillis, 147 (n. 14), 157–58 (n. 5), 160 (n. 3), 163 (n. 38)
Mitchell, Juliet, 157 (n. 44)
Mitchell, W. J. T., 162–63 (n. 30)

Nietzsche, Friedrich, 63, 65, 124–27, 148 (n. 26), 161 (n. 17); on metaphor, 33–37
Norris, Christopher, 112, 113, 160 (n. 3)

Oedipus, 71, 73

parable, 51–61; The Sower, 51–56; Kafka's "Von den Gleichnissen," 56–61
"parables of parable," 51
penis envy, 82
Peters, Charles R., 155–56 (n. 15)
Protagoras, 1, 11, 12, 38–50, 148 (n. 26); *aesthēsis*, 38–43; *dissoi logoi*, 38, 41, 47–50; *homo-mensura*, 43–47
Proust, Marcel, 117–18, 161 (n. 12)

Rey, Jean-Michel, 81
Richards, I. A., 27–29, 60, 108
Ricoeur, Paul, 19, 113, 156 (n. 18)
Rilke, Rainer Maria, 161 (n. 12)
Rousseau, Jean Jacques, 113

Schapiro, Meyer, 2–11
Schlegel, Friedrich von, 126, 132–36
Segal, Charles, 65
Semele, 65
Seuss, Dr., 1
Simmel, Georg, 15
Simpson, David, 163 (n. 38)
sparagmos, 67
Staël, Mme de, 132, 136–43, 165 (n. 24)
Steiner, George, 63

tenor/vehicle distinction, 27–29, 32, 108
titles: of fiction, 93–94
Todorov, Tzvetan, 158 (n. 6)
tragedy, 62–73; in Aristotle, 21–22
tyrannos: in tragedy, 68–69

uncanny (*das Unheimliche*), 22

Van Gogh, Vincent, 2–11, 146 (n. 15)
Van Tieghem, Paul, 128–30, 164 (n. 5)
Vermeer, Jan, 5

Wellek, René, 128, 130, 164 (n. 1)
Women: and tragedy, 69–71

Yeats, William Butler, 33, 114–16, 162 (nn. 22, 24), 163 (n. 35); "Among School Children," 120–21

ABOUT THE AUTHOR

PAUL GORDON is Associate Professor of Humanities, University of Colorado at Boulder. He received his B.A. in Classics from State University of New York at Buffalo and his Ph.D. in Comparative Literature from Yale University.